Journey to GLORY

Contending for the Faith

by Gary Garner

Come, Holy Spirit

...Fan into flame the gift of God, which is in you...
For the Spirit God gave us does not make us timid,
but gives us power, love and self-discipline.
—2 Timothy 1:6-7 (NIV)

You and I were each on the journey of a lifetime long before we ever gave it a thought. We were likely just going about, living our lives, scarcely conscious that we were moving along a particular path. But unexpected events can awaken us to the seriousness of the journey, where we are headed, and where exactly we are in our travels.

Many people may be surprised to learn that God wants to give us not only salvation and eternal life, but also an abundant life in the Holy Spirit *here and now*, as we interact with His call and mission. This "here and now" life can be awesome beyond description!

I pray that the events in this book and the revelation knowledge gleaned from them will help set you on an unwavering course toward the ultimate destination of Glory, and may stir the grace within you so that you will passionately contend for the faith and for the call that the Lord has on your life.

No matter where we have been or where we are now, the Lord meets us right there, and He has more for each one of us.

To Him who is able to keep you from stumbling and to present you
before His glorious presence without fault and with great joy—to the
only God our Savior be glory, majesty, power and authority, through
Jesus Christ our Lord, before all ages, now and forevermore! Amen.
—Jude 1:24-25 (NIV)

MARY
MANY THANKS AGAIN FOR YOUR
HELP WITH OUR BOOK AND FOR YOUR
ENDORSEMENT. MAY YOUR JOURNEY
AHEAD BE FILLED WITH BLESSINGS.
IN HIS NAME
GARY AND NANCY GARNER

Dedication

This book is dedicated to all who have made the hard choices to put the Lord first, have lived out those choices and have completed the journey to Glory, and to each of you pressing on with your whole being for your glorious arrival and recompense.

You have chosen the narrow road, the highest road, life's greatest fulfillment, while accepting whatever costs or dangers may be incurred. You have said "Yes" to the Lord's call and His will without knowing nearly all of what that "Yes" might require. You have repeatedly said "No" to your own self-will and all that the world tries to offer and all its temptations.

You are the courageous and the faithful who have taken on the journey, and not just the journey, but also the higher good of the travelers placed along your way. The reward prepared for each of you will surely be indescribable joy and contentment. Your exemplary lives call the rest of us on. We pray for the perseverance and endurance to live out our calls and arrive in Glory.

PRAISED BE JESUS CHRIST, NOW AND FOREVER!

"And then the sign of the Son of Man will appear in the sky, and then all the tribes of the earth will mourn, and they will see the SON OF MAN COMING ON THE CLOUDS OF THE SKY with power and great Glory.

"And He will send forth His angels with A GREAT TRUMPET BLAST and THEY WILL GATHER TOGETHER His elect from the four winds, from one end of the sky to the other."
—Matthew 24:30-31 (NASB)

Acknowledgments

First, I am so grateful to the Father, Son and Holy Spirit for the opportunity to speak about the awesome life of faith I've gotten to experience through their grace, which has made both the content and the writing of this book possible.

Many thanks to the members of the Alleluia Community for your strong, constant witness of living your lives around your faith in the Lord. You are the most authentic and best-intentioned group of people I have seen or known and are an ever-present support to me.

I am grateful to Bob Garrett, elder in Alleluia, for his belief in me and in my writing talents and his encouragement to me to use them, and for the thousands of priceless early morning prayers and sharing times with Bob and his group and the ongoing transformation that has occurred through them.

Thank you to the many prayer warriors who have provided invaluable prayer support and stormed heaven on my behalf for the Lord's anointing on my writing and on the readers' reception of it—you are doing the priceless work of evangelization.

I am grateful to Fr. Brett Brannen for writing the foreword, for his approach to lay people as being on a level playing field with the clergy, and for his understanding of how to work together in the Spirit to build the Kingdom.

To each of the very fine people who have given of their time and have read and written an endorsement, and those who have read parts of the book and given input: I certainly appreciate your heart for the Lord's work and your courage and participation.

My thanks to Damian Comparetta for his careful listening and for the effort and skill needed to search out and capture a cover photo that seemed appropriate for the book and its challenging journey to Glory subject matter.

I thank Barbara Harshman for her heart to use her computer skills and creativity for the book cover and for her patience in dealing with my specific requests.

I am grateful to Dora Lockhart for her endless editing efforts over nine long years (plus four years on our first book)—it was a true evangelistic labor of love and service to us and to the Lord. Many thanks to Dora's husband Doug for sharing her and giving her the time and space needed to edit this book. Dora's consistent call to bring forth a well-written book while not changing my voice or my "impact" words and phrases was quite a challenge, but our intent was always to be one hundred percent truthful and real.

And my deepest thanks to Nancy, who has typed every word, many times over, from the beginning to the last edits, and has been the middle person in handling all the versions that go back and forth to Dora. Nancy's is always the "first look"; she is the de facto content editor, my toughest critic and strongest support. This book has been a challenging workload for her in the midst of her other responsibilities, but as always, she is up to the call and gets it all done, and very well. Without her, there would be no book!

And of course, many thanks to my woodwork clients, who have been patient with the completion and delivery of their projects so I could work on this book along with their wood. Inspiration and creativity have their own timing, and it is wise to always respect that.

It takes a tremendous amount of work to write, edit and produce a book that can touch and change people's lives. You were each a valuable part of making this happen. May your care and your efforts have deposited some treasures in your own account in Heaven.

Contents

Following his crystal-clear exposition of awakening to the Christian faith in *Swept Up by the Spirit*, Gary Garner's new book *Journey to Glory* moves us beyond the discovery of a new life in the Spirit to lay out how to make this journey—as walking by faith rather than by natural sight in response to our own Call.

I was amazed reading Gary's first book, because I already thought I knew him as an ordinary good guy. But as he told his stories, the depth of his faith life came alive to me—like a miraculous spring flowing out of an apparent rock. He just went on and on giving personal witness to his conversion, dedication and discipleship through a series of vignettes of one miracle after another in his life story. Now, in his second book, Gary has continued this masterful and compelling exposition of gospel living in a new and fresh way, taking the long view.

As a theologian, a believer seeking understanding, it amazes me how clear and understandable Gary's simple exposition of the core truths of our faith walk become as we almost run through the pages, encountering one key point after another. His unassuming but clear conversational style leads, or almost compels, you to continue reading page after page as he unfolds more and more of the intrinsic beauty of the gospel life that continually transforms the ordinary into the extraordinary.

When we finish this "race," we find ourselves with an undeniable choice of believing and responding or allowing this message to drift out of consciousness and be lost in the clutter of life's daily challenges. But the book's clarity, persistence and wisdom make the latter far less likely. We are brought to the point of embracing even what we already knew with a new power, and what we did not already know with wonder at God's plan and message for our lives.

This book is a clearly presented invitation to "sell all" and follow the Lord as His disciple, an invitation that requires a total *metanoia*, a total surrender, a total willingness to be and do all that God calls us to be and do. The most powerful gift that the book gives is Gary's witness to it really being possible, when done within a community of like-minded brethren living out the gospel together in our world today.

Gary concludes with a summary of today's atheistic culture and a challenge to actualize the "IF… THEN" of 2 Chronicles 7:14. The closing list of key scripture quotes places the whole book into its Biblical perspective, a sprinkling of pearls from the Word of God, passages that penetrate our hearts and minds, revealing our treasure in heaven, pearls of great price, and keys to God's Kingdom, all of which clearly inspire us to join Gary on his *Journey to Glory*.

—David A. Peterman, PhD
Founding Coordinator God's Delight Covenant Community,
Dallas, TX

Foreword

When Gary Garner asked me to write the foreword for his new book, *Journey to Glory: Contending for the Faith*, my mind immediately went to the famous axiom of St. Junipero Serra. Fr. Serra was the Franciscan priest who hiked up and down the California coast bringing Jesus Christ and the Catholic faith to the native peoples who lived there. His maxim was, "Siempre adelante, nunca atras." It means, "Always forward, never back!"

I first met Gary and his wife Nancy when I was sent to be the pastor of The Church of the Most Holy Trinity in Augusta, Georgia, in 2004. They were faithful and devoted parishioners, always praying for me and supporting me in every way. But when I first met Gary, I thought to myself, "This man might be a little crazy!" He was on fire for Jesus Christ and a true missionary for the Lord and his ecumenical faith, through the inspiration of the Holy Spirit. He was prayerful, he served others generously, he was passionately pro-life and active in praying in front of the abortion clinic, and he truly and unapologetically desired to bring the whole world to Jesus! Because of his exuberance, my recent arrival, and the learning curve that's part of life in a new parish, I did not quite know what to think of him. Then the Holy Spirit reminded me of that famous theological expression: "There is a fine line between sanctity and insanity." Gary Garner was crazy for Jesus, and as I got to know him, I became inspired by his fire!

Journey to Glory is a book containing many wonderful stories and slices of life showing how the Holy Spirit pursues us and orchestrates our lives. It describes Gary's walk with the Lord and how Jesus transformed his mind, heart, soul and body into those of a fully committed apostle. Gary insightfully shares how he came to know that we are in a spiritual battle between God and Satan, a battle for our souls. We live on the battlefield, and to fail to even

3

realize that there is a battle raging around us is to default to the enemy. We will become "spiritual casualties."

In imitation of the Master, our Lord Jesus, when He was tempted by the devil, Gary offers many spiritual arrows from the sacred Scriptures that can be pulled out of one's quiver and shot when the battle begins. *"Resist the devil and he will take flight. Draw close to God and He will draw close to you." (James 4:7-8)* In so many words, and through his accounts of sin, goodness, repentance and conversion, and many miracles besides, Gary reminds the reader never to bring a knife to a gun fight!

We are put on this earth to learn to love like they love in Heaven. We are here to learn how to love like God loves. As St. Augustine explains, God wants to give us so many gifts, but when He tries, our hearts are too small. They must be stretched. I like to say that there are only two things that will stretch the human heart: mental prayer and suffering. This is the life-long process God uses to accomplish our magnanimity (magnus-animus), our "greatness of soul." You will read many stories in this book that illustrate this process, always accomplished through prayer and suffering. As St. Augustine also tells us, God is so good that not only does He permit evil and bring good from it, but He brings about a greater good than would have been.

Jesus reminds us: *"Enter through the narrow gate; for the gate is wide and the road broad that leads to destruction, and those who enter through it are many. How narrow the gate and constricted the road that leads to life. And those who find it are few." (Matthew 7:13-14)*

The narrow gate through which we all must walk, if we choose to go to Heaven, is the gate of Calvary. It is the way of love, truth and suffering. We must follow our crucified Jesus, the Way, the Truth and the Life, and be obedient to His teachings and to His will for our respective lives. I both smiled and ached as I read through the stories of people who tried to walk down that broad road that leads to destruction. These people (just like me) needed a Nathan for King David, an Ananias for St. Paul, a Simon of Cyrene for Jesus, and a Mary Magdalene for the Apostles at the Resurrection.

Sadly, the road to destruction has become wider in recent years as our U. S. culture becomes more and more post-Christian. This means that the very basics of Christianity—that Jesus is Lord and that He died and rose from the dead, that there is a real Heaven and Hell, the Ten Commandments—these things are no longer the primary underlying assumptions in most people's lives. Evil comes at us through the world, the flesh and the devil, or a combination thereof, and this evil is being exacerbated by the lessening of awareness that we are even on a battlefield. Never has there been a time when we more desperately needed all Christian hands on deck, at their battle stations and with their weapons ready!

And yet, these weapons are the same "primitive" weapons they have always been, truth and love. As Christians we have to be willing "to be bothered" enough to go out and serve others humbly in the name of Jesus, to love them by serving them. These acts of love will open people's hearts to the Truth that will follow. As the expression goes: Love is a bridge over which truth can pass, but it must be strong enough to support that truth. Love always wins!

"Jesus Christ is the answer to the question posed by every human life," said St. John Paul II. Again, Jesus is the Way, the Truth and the Life! **And this Jesus wants us to be there for one another.** To pray for one another, to grow together in our knowledge of the Lord, to walk together to Calvary and finally to live together with our God in Heaven. This life is our journey to glory!

I am so happy that God sent Gary and Nancy Garner into my life to walk with me towards glory. We have a funny expression that we use in priestly formation: "When the shepherd is on fire, the sheep feel the heat." Gary has been a good shepherd for so many people in their Christian lives. And he is on fire. So, in the words that St. Augustine heard (from the Holy Spirit) just before his profound conversion: *Tolle et lege.* Take and read!

Always forward, never back, until we hear the words that our hearts so desire to hear: "Well done, good and faithful servant. Enter now into your Master's glory."

Fr. Brett Brannen
Spiritual Director
The Pontifical College Josephinum
Author of *To Save a Thousand Souls*

Introduction

In our everyday lives, we live among multitudes of people who are like *sheep without a shepherd*, living their lives without meaningful purpose or direction. They are guessing at the choices or decisions they make, squandering years or decades chasing the wind and the world's empty promises, and by their futile example, causing their kids and others to do the same, or worse. No one should be limited to this hollow, false and deceptive life that the world offers. God wants each person to discover and live in the fullness and blessing of His world through the leading and power of the Holy Spirit. This is the good news and it deserves to be said clearly so that people can make sensible, life-giving choices. This good news needs to be shouted from the rooftops!

The multitudes of lost people rushing headlong or just dragging themselves along are not bad people. Each is made in God's likeness and image. They are just lost, on a dead-end road, and they need to find the Savior who can redeem *any* life and give *anyone* a great future. To be drawn along by the ways of the world may look for a while like glamour and success, but without exception leads to disappointment, despair and destruction—and no one has to settle for such. The Lord has put before every person the opportunity to *choose life or choose death*. To choose the Lord and His ways leads to abundant, everlasting life. To choose the world or self leads to death and eternal darkness. *The Lord would have that none be lost*.

I bought into that worldly merry-go-round for forty years and also subjected my family to it. Except for the Lord's sovereign intervention, my life could have ended at age thirty-three and I would have deserved to go straight to hell, but God had His plan for my life. I surely didn't know or even suspect that such was possible. No one had ever explained to me the real presence of God among us here and now. I didn't know anyone who could. If there was such interaction with the living God here on earth, I knew no one who had experienced it.

Well, I came to know (did I ever!) that there *is* such a life, and what a life it is! I came to know that I have a best friend in the Lord and have ready access to the triune God at any time. That amazing access is available for anyone to discover and receive.

So this is *why* I had to write this book, to give my personal account of the Lord's mercy, greatness and love, and (it is my hope) to point some people toward Him. Through the Lord's incredible mercy, my eyes were opened! I was blind and now I see; I was dead and now I live. The Lord did it, and at 11:59! I have cause to be excited! You would be, too!

When I meet Jesus face to face, I don't want to feel guilty for not writing this book or have Him ask, "Why did you not?" After receiving the incredible second life that Jesus has given me, I must share with as many travelers as I can the directions for the journey to Glory.

"If you return, then I will restore you—before Me you will stand;
and if you extract the precious from the worthless,
You will become My spokesman."
—*Jeremiah 15:19 (NASB)*

Journey to Glory: Contending for the Faith is about life and death, contrasting the most important subject there is—the freedom of the abundant life through the Holy Spirit and the many facets of living it—with Satan's efforts to block us from that fulfilling life and pull us into endless captivity and darkness. It is my hope that reading this will help you with the battle that is in progress, endlessly, for each and every soul, every day. Please join me on the journey that awaits between these covers. We ask the Holy Spirit to be our guide. All are welcome as we delve into the extraordinary workings of God among us and sow more seeds of expectant faith.

If this overview sounds outside your usual interests or a stretch for you, I understand that all too well. This would have been outside my own area of interest for far too long—for decades. So, I encourage you to stay with me and keep reading, even if you do so just for the opportunity to write off what you are reading about. That is fine. I have seen dramatic change in the lives of people with that same intent. Let us never give Satan the victory by forfeit; he will defeat us in any way we allow him.

I was led to the material within the covers of this book through my own life experience. I am by no means a scholar, a theologian or an academic, but I have lived for many years in the trenches, meeting life as it happens, and learning that only faith in the Lord enables us to move forward and take hold of real life itself. I am one of the redeemed, another prodigal son who came home. The Lord wants redemption for everyone.

All of us also lived among them at one time, gratifying the cravings of our flesh and following its desires and thoughts. Like the rest, we were by nature deserving of wrath. But because of His great love for us, God, who is rich in mercy, made us alive with Christ even when we were dead in transgressions—it is by grace you have been saved. And God raised us up with Christ and seated us with Him in the heavenly realms in Christ Jesus...

—Ephesians 2:3-6 (NIV)

Brothers and sisters, think of what you were when you were called.
Not many of you were wise by human standards; not many were influential;
not many were of noble birth.
But God chose the foolish things of the world to shame the wise;
God chose the weak things of the world to shame the strong.

—1 Corinthians 1:26-27 (NIV)

All the stories recorded here are completely true, told as they happened, along with the dialogue as it was spoken. Some of the events I describe may seem almost simplistic at first, but on closer inspection, profound. Some happenings I still find almost unbelievable, even having witnessed them firsthand. Many are priceless to me. The intervention of the Holy Spirit can bring about spontaneous responses and results like nothing else. They can happen anytime and without notice. That is the way of the Holy Spirit. He is the giver of life, alive and well and very active here among us on earth. He has no limitations, can meet every need, and can be reached at any time, any place. The best work of fiction can't compare to the real-life adventure of walking in the Holy Spirit, yet Scripture tells us that most people never experience it.

As you invest time and effort into reading this book, I fully believe that you will be rewarded with blessings far greater than you could expect or imagine. We cannot outgive God, so as we give of our time, He returns more to us in exchange. He may even take us to a whole new level of faith that we have never yet experienced! We dare to ask for that!

I pray you will feel present to the stories, able to imagine yourself as an eyewitness or participant, standing alongside as each event unfolds, caught up in the setting and the mood of the moment. Preposterous-seeming events become quite normal when we move into the Holy Spirit's world.

> *For we did not follow cleverly devised stories when we told you about the coming of our Lord Jesus Christ in power, but we were eyewitnesses of His majesty.*
> —*2 Peter 1:16 (NIV)*

The Spirit showed me that in writing this book, I was to be as a scribe, recording the events, and in so doing, I would be opening a treasure chest to the reader.

> *And Jesus said to them, "Therefore every scribe who has become a disciple of the kingdom of heaven is like a head of a household, who brings out of his treasure things new and old."*
> —*Matthew 13:52 (NASB)*

The stories together are like a Whitman's sampler of life experiences. They touch on a broad range of spontaneous events (only a few among many) that have happened throughout my Christian walk. Since the Lord moves freely through time and space to accomplish His mission, the stories do not appear in strict chronological order but are placed in groups according to the nature of their content, to better illustrate the ways the Holy Spirit interacts with mankind in ordinary settings to accomplish His work among us.

At times, this book may seem like a jigsaw puzzle, with seemingly random pieces and no picture on the box cover to follow. Life in the Spirit is often like that. If we handle each puzzle piece with care and patience, then at the proper time, the Lord will show us where and how they fit, and every one will fit somewhere. Some may fit together with pieces we have had for quite a while, pieces that had looked like misfits or seemed as though they would never be used. The Spirit may connect some pieces to complete a previously unfinished picture or to deepen our understanding, and it might be just what is needed to move us forward.

The reflections that appear in various parts of the book are all recently written. They share much of what I have learned and gleaned over four decades of intentional life in the power of the Holy Spirit. They will serve as road markers for our journey.

I hope that as you read, you will receive any revelation He has for you personally, as well as more awareness of His plan for your life. We are all on this journey, traveling life's road together, and we each need more direction from the Spirit to lead and guide us. The Spirit has unlimited ways to open our eyes to the "more" personally. Pray that He may do that for you, as only He can, and you will be given a new freedom or a special moment of peace and joy. (Thank you, Lord!)

As we take this journey, I encourage you to go the distance. We will be covering a marathon—a marathon to Glory. Just prepare yourself for what's ahead. There are beautiful things here—some challenging, eye-opening, heartwarming, simplistic, spectacular—the things that life is made up of, as seen through the eyes of men and women on a journey with the Holy Spirit to Glory.

The Journey

Our journey is through a world that is dangerous, tempting and perverse, probably more so now than at any other time in history. It is a world under siege by secular humanism, temptations to unlimited pleasures and comforts, incredibly blinding deceptions, and mind-boggling distractions, all multiplied in an era of all-consuming technology. In the midst of it all, Satan lurks, seeking victims to lure and take captive. He employs denial, deception and unbelief as some of his major snares for humanity, and these can divert us from the imminent danger.

> *Be alert and of sober mind. Your enemy the devil prowls around like a roaring lion looking for someone to devour.*
> *—1 Peter 5:8 (NIV)*

Scripture reminds us that the intent of demonic forces is to steal, kill and destroy all who venture into their grasp. Since Glory is reached only through the narrow gate, we must be ever mindful of where we walk. Our path is a virtual minefield for destruction, and the mines it contains are rarely visible to the natural eye. To arrive alive and well, we must be led by the Holy Spirit, who will get us home in mint condition if we walk with Him.

No doubt the journey is perilous, but every person is taking it, whether they know it or not. Along the way we may traverse some personal misfortune or calamities, but with God, we can walk through anything. If we make the journey as it is planned for us, it becomes more glorious, fulfilling and rewarding than we could have hoped.

It has always been the Lord's desire to capture the hearts of all living individuals, pour out His grace over them, shower them with His favor and love, direct their steps and ways, engage them in His work, draw them close to help build His Kingdom here on earth and develop an unbreakable bond with them that will last through eternity.

Let us always remember we are aliens in this foreign land, passing through on the way to Glory that awaits us. As great as this present life may seem to some of us, let us hold it loosely; we will take nothing with us, and that which awaits us is infinitely better. No matter how challenging the events of this temporal world may get, the Beautiful City will be there when we arrive, and we will experience it in a glorified body, with everything working perfectly. We only need to hold true to our faith all the way to the finish line and trust the Lord with everything. Then our future is assured! The Lord has a great plan waiting for each soul. It is His desire that none stay lost—and as long as we still have breath, it is not too late to change course. What a disappointment and shame it would be to overlook the blessed life and arrive at the end of the line far from the destination, or with the gates locked and no passport to enter Glory.

No one who has come into this world had any control over how they entered. However we may have started life, however much trouble we may have had, the Lord wants each of us to finish well.

> *Taste and see that the Lord is good:*
> *blessed is the one who takes refuge in Him.*
>
> —*Psalm 34:8 (NIV)*

> *Blessed is the one who does not walk in step with the wicked*
> *or stand in the way that sinners take or sit in the company of mockers,*
> *but whose delight is in the law of the Lord, and who meditates on His*
> *law day and night.*
> *That person is like a tree planted by streams of water,*
> *which yields its fruit in season and whose leaf does not wither—*
> *whatever they do prospers.*
> *Not so the wicked! They are like chaff that the wind blows away.*
> *Therefore, the wicked will not stand in the judgment,*
> *nor sinners in the assembly of the righteous.*

For the Lord watches over the way of the righteous,
but the way of the wicked leads to destruction.

—*Psalm 1:1-6 (NIV)*

The stories in the next two chapters reveal some of the struggles I had with myself, the world and Satan to land on the right road and take it, lock in on the destination with real certainty and never look back. Our present besieged world needs the absolute answer more than ever before—and there is one. *The Answer awaits.*

Chapter 1

What Is Most Important?

Like most people, for years I had known the obvious answer to the question of what is most important. Many areas of life are important, but what is most important on this earth is the final destination, and living a life worthy of the right destination. If we get this right, a good life just goes with it, and we will ultimately be welcomed home. If we miss it, we miss it all, forever. I grew up hearing this truth countless times, and as a young person, never doubted it. I had even been deeply moved in my spirit at fourteen years old and had responded to an altar call and accepted it as truth.

So now, as an adult, why was I not living a life that reflected this truth? Why did I not want to think about it or hear about it, or be around people who did? Did I actually believe I had outgrown God? Did I seriously want to be separated from Him for all eternity and be banished to Hell? To know the right answer and not live it is far worse than not knowing it at all. When I chose to not live out what I had come to know in my youth, I opened myself to major deception, and step by step, I had been led astray under the pretext of trying to find a "better way." As I followed this route, choosing to pay no attention to the direction it was taking me, I stumbled into the alluring way of the world, with its various temptations, and then even into Satan's world of entrapment (he plays for keeps), all the while ignoring The Way.

Surely, making the most costly mistake of all must bring about the worst of outcomes. No responsible person would knowingly rush forward headlong, leading his family toward imminent disaster. I am in no way proud of it, but I have to confess that I blindly did just that for over twenty years, putting my wife and four children at risk.

Like countless others, during my teen years I tired of using my time to attend what I considered a lifeless church and decided I had no more need of God or His ways or restrictions. After all, I was growing up. I may have rationalized this decision by telling myself that His creation work and any part He had in my life were completed as planned and I was on my own. I didn't see this step as a falling out with God. I just decided that I could move beyond my need or further dependence on Him. Maybe this was my idea of maturity—growing into new freedom. I would take life from here and manage just fine. So I walked away from the church and faith and closed the door behind me. I was driven on by my pride, ambition and confidence. I would depend on those and the dreams they supported. I would just make things happen and push through. To be honest, my plans were based far more on wishful thinking and dreaming than on any reality.

I chose to use my free will to turn away, rather than listen to my once reliable conscience, which had protected me so well all through my early life. I would later learn that for *anyone* to disregard his conscience and reject the Lord's counsel is a very dangerous decision. I made the major mistake of relegating God to religion and church only, instead of seeing Him as the central figure around which all life revolves. I remember being bolstered along by the "world's hymns," listening over and over to Frank Sinatra's mega-hit song, "I Did It My Way." Wow! And his other self-booster, "New York, New York." I heard no mention of God or His help in either of those songs, and I was quite impressed with how well Frank seemed to be doing. He had the world by the tail, and maybe it would happen for me, too.

The stories I had learned growing up in church had become to my mind almost fables, disconnected from my adult "real world" and my pursuit of success. I had hung onto the stories when I was young; they were encouraging and talked of the promise of eternal life, but as a grown man, I was dealing with now, not then. Had anyone ever returned to earth and verified Heaven's glory and grandeur? I certainly had not known anyone who lived out a faith in (or even talked of the possibility of) "Thy kingdom come, Thy will be done, on earth as it is in Heaven." Great rhetoric, but to me, this had become just part of a nice prayer used in church, and that was it!

Any acceptance of or belief in the idea that Satan lives in our age, actually impacts life, and has demons to do works of evil became to me something to smile at, like a myth intended to scare, and those who actually believed such a notion deserved ridicule. I didn't know one person who had encountered Satan or confessed to torment by any of his demons. I had no idea that Satan was leading me to believe these denials. I was choosing what I wanted to believe rather than seeking the truth. I was filled with far too much of myself to be open to God and his adjustments.

For over twenty years, I wandered further out into this vast no man's land, sometimes willfully, other times without knowing. It seemed an infinite space that had only suggested guidelines and flexible boundaries—no rules, just right—where I could live my life unquestioned, doing my own thing. I saw it as stepping into a greater future, one for which I had worked hard. After all, I was not chasing the wind or the wild life. What bad could come of it? I was only pursuing worldly success to attain the good life. That would be enough, and all my family and friends would certainly benefit. Even the world might benefit from my increased knowledge, capabilities and resources.

Amazingly, with all this rationalizing, I still couldn't talk myself out of feeling uneasy and out of place. My conscience kept trying to turn me around, but with little result. The fact was that, while not noticing it, I had come to be a misled, materialistic, self-consumed, workaholic unbeliever. It was the route I was most likely to have strayed onto with my attraction to excellence in work and to beautiful, expensive things, and my diminishing regard for humanity and the Creator of all.

> *"Today, if you hear His voice, do not harden your heart as you did in the rebellion."*
> —*Hebrews 3:15 (NIV)*

> *"Enter through the narrow gate. For wide is the gate and broad is the road that leads to destruction, and many enter through it. But small is the gate and narrow the road that leads to life, and only a few find it."*
> —*Matthew 7:13-14 (NIV)*

Crossing the Line

Our family returned to Atlanta so I could take a better job with a manufacturer of molding and framed pictures. This opportunity afforded us a new house, a new subdivision, many social opportunities, and tempted us to add more "show" to go with it. Since I had held a subscription to Playboy magazine for a couple of years (a gift from Nancy), one of our early lifestyle embellishments was a membership to the Atlanta Playboy club. This was probably our attempt to actualize our improved status in life and "broaden our horizons." Nancy and I went to dinner there a couple of times. They had plenty of centerfolds on their walls, plus the live Playboy Bunnies right next to you serving. The food was good and it was a posh and energized environment. But somehow it felt uncomfortable and wrong to be there. We didn't really belong—even though our membership card said that we did. Without understanding quite what we had consented to, we were being drawn into a dangerous lifestyle, one that we had never known much about before. The "Playboy" world was a high-risk enticement, and held no respect for virtue or the virtuous but was intended to allure and captivate the unaware and vulnerable.

My new employer had hired me to head up design and product development. The company was over forty years old and had recently been bought by an old friend of mine. Restructuring the company was an uphill battle from the outset. My friend, the new owner, was a self-made high roller, very progressive and pro-change, but he was surrounded by an old company, old employees, old ways and resistance to change. None of us who were part of the "new regime" knew the business, but we frequently acted on impulse, often too aggressively, in our efforts to establish a new order.

I had been brought in as a vice president and head of design. My first and main task was to revamp the framed picture line that was sold across the country, mostly to small furniture stores. Without any research on the company's most popular items or regard for sales figures, I began to rebuild the line based on my personal taste, attempting to update the offerings to make them more sleek, contemporary, artistic and appealing. I added some graceful nude prints to the line, definitely a first for the old-school company. The nudes undoubtedly scandalized some of the established customers (some probably pitched their new catalogs after their first glance). I even brought home a framed print of a nude young woman and hung it on my office wall. Nancy thought it was artistic, but our young daughter was embarrassed and didn't like coming into the room with it hanging there. I thought she might come to accept it over time, but instead she avoided my office.

My next area of focus was the supply of religious prints, which the company carried in abundance. To me, these seemed the most outdated and old fashioned. One by one, they came under my scrutiny, and none survived the cut. Not the boy and girl on the bridge with the angel watching over them ("Angel on the Footbridge"). Not even Jesus on His knees, praying in the Garden. They all had to go. It was time to make way for the new look. The plaintive cry that arose from the mom-and-pop stores across the country was horrific. They couldn't believe we had dropped everyone's favorites, their best-sellers, and even Jesus. Some thought it was sacrilegious, virtual blasphemy, and others expected the business to be struck by lightning. I thought our veteran vice president, a staunch Christian, might have a heart attack. None of that meant anything to me. At that point I had no spiritual understanding, nor did I have concern for others or for the prosperity of the businesses that bought goods from us. I was just interested in a better look for the line and in using the authority I had been given. Within a few months, the company was also gone—bankrupt. My big job with its impressive title was a memory.

I share these details to illustrate a pattern that the Lord later enabled me to see with clarity. This is just an excerpt from the story of the battle between good and evil that was going on in my life at the time, a subtle battle to which I paid no attention. I had courted friendship with the "world," and my choices and decisions reflected that, as did the results.

As I look back on my removal of the Christian art from the company's framed picture line, it seems unbelievable, as though I must be talking about the actions of someone else. I can hardly believe that I did that. The memory of it chills me, but at the time I saw it as something I had a right to do. Each turn down the wrong road was bringing me to new depths—a little further from God and from truth—but that was meaningless to me then.

By that time, with no devotion to God and a budding new friendship with the world, I had slipped from the lifelong moorings of conscience and morals. I had crossed the line. With no awareness or thought of doing so, I had become a virtual mocker of God. I had been on this dead-end road for only about five years. Decades later, I would come to realize that it wasn't the art in those prints that had bothered me, it was their message of faith, which was challenging my spirit. God was trying to call me back to Himself, but the world and Satan were pulling me further away. And the world and Satan had my attention.

Over the next five years, with my lack of active faith, increasing temptations and poor choices would almost completely erode the belief of my early years. I came to a point of not knowing what, if anything, I believed. I had essentially become an agnostic. It was then that Satan would seize the opportunity to make his move and aggressively pursue my downfall. I would come to learn that Satan can be very patient and cunning as he works to position us for destruction. He may even help us along with a few "victories" and feed our pride in order to set us up—and then bait us into crushing defeat.

Do not love the world or anything in the world. If anyone loves the world, love for the Father is not in them. For everything in the world—the lust of the flesh, the lust of the eyes, and the pride of life—comes not from the Father but from the world. The world and its desires pass away, but whoever does the will of God lives forever.

—1 John 2:15-17 (NASB)

Foreboding

It was a winter day, and I stood on a wooded hillside high above Riverchase Parkway, which curves past prestigious homes near the Chattahoochee River in North Atlanta. I was an independent designer and builder of contract luxury homes, complex to build anywhere but especially so on challenging, inclined lots. I was building my first house in this very desirable neighborhood. The subdivision was nearly "built out" and had only a few remaining lots. Some of the residents had lived there for years, and probably considered the building of any new house to be a violation of their space.

The year was 1976. It was almost over now, and what a year it had been for us—the most difficult one yet, as the effects of the crippling recession (we knew it as a depression) of '74-'75 continued to mercilessly pummel building contractors, mortgage bankers and construction suppliers. One of my major building material suppliers had gone under, and even one of the banks that we often dealt with had stumbled badly. These were perilous times for anyone associated with the construction business who didn't have backup money. For well over two years, the recession had been exerting tremendous pressure on me as I tried to keep my business afloat. Nancy was unaware of our dire financial straits. I had intentionally kept her in the dark, not wanting to involve her in this tightrope situation. Of course, not sharing the problems with her just increased my own level of stress.

I was nearing completion on another contract house a few miles away and was ready to begin construction on this one. I had to get it going and keep it moving; to continue the cash flow was essential. The bank draws from the construction loan were our only source of income, and they were paid out only for progress made on the house. The weather had been colder than usual in Atlanta and very rainy, leaving the ground saturated. Within a few weeks the temperature would drop to ten degrees below zero, the coldest ever recorded for the area. Of course, that kind of extreme weather could bring outside construction to a virtual halt. I needed to get the house "dried in" before the weather got really bad so that work could continue inside.

The initial grading of the property revealed a shocking surprise: There was a massive rock present. Even a D-9 caterpillar (the size used for grading highways) could not vibrate the rock; it was a continuous, immovable vein. So after a nerve-racking delay, we made the decision to build on top of the vein of rock.

The house site was atop the hill, over fifty feet above the street. The foundation and wall crew would be pouring the foundation on this raw, bleak day. Williams Brothers Concrete Company had sent their field representative out the day before to take a look at the site, since I had advised them of the steep incline. Right away the rep told me that the only way their loaded mixers could get up to the house site would be for their company to send a seventy-five-ton winch truck to pull the concrete mixers by way of a cable to the top. I tried to act nonchalant, but was actually jolted by the idea that this would be the method used for embarking on this construction project. I had never even heard of anything like this.

The rep also said that all of the concrete to be poured later for the walls, slabs and driveway would have to be pumped by a pump truck positioned down on the street. Although I had built on several difficult lots before, none had needed to have the concrete pumped. Somehow though, I wasn't really surprised. Until then, I guess I hadn't wanted to acknowledge the extreme height and difficulty that this beautiful but barely buildable lot would present. It was quickly becoming obvious that the costs of the extra ground work and the concrete work would far exceed my estimate. I could only hope that those cost underestimations wouldn't be the case for the entire project—but I knew better than to believe that. I was already wondering if my clients, Joel and Carla, had financially overextended to undertake this sizable project so early in his medical career.

When the winch truck arrived that afternoon, I was astounded by its size. The driver slogged on foot up to the top of the hill, secured the cable around trees out back, and then used the winch to begin pulling the huge truck up the muddy driveway bed toward the backyard. Halfway up the hillside, the massive weight of the truck uprooted one of the trees and it crashed to the ground. The driver had to go back up and hook the cable around larger trees to pull the winch truck to the top. It would be a three-truck pour, each truck filled with concrete. That progressed as planned through the afternoon. After each mixer was pulled to the top and emptied, the driver would then hook the cable from the back of the winch truck to his now empty cement truck and be carefully lowered down, in the empty truck, to the street below. This process was repeated with each truck.

I had never witnessed anything like this before. There was such power and strength in the winch and the cable, handling the mega weight of the concrete trucks as though they were oversized Tonka trucks. I'm sure I would have enjoyed this power demonstration much more as a casual spectator, rather than as the builder responsible, not only for this house, but for respecting this subdivision. I knew that a top official of the Atlanta Falcons as well as the CEOs of Coca-Cola and Delta Airlines all lived down the street, and many more individuals of similar status. This was not the place to have construction problems or to unsettle the residents driving past. Already we were caking the street with orange mud tracks as the empty mixers came back down. Now darkness was upon us and the temperature was dropping as the final truck "poured it out." As he maneuvered his empty truck to the hook-up spot, the young driver seemed anxious to get down from the hill. He hooked the cable onto his truck, told us, "I'm gone," and climbed up into the seat. He released the brakes on the big truck, and we all experienced a sudden shock as we saw the hook fall out of its slot—he had put the hook in from underneath, and as the truck eased forward, the hook was jostled out and fell loose to the ground. Lurching forward, this huge truck with driver inside went careening down the hillside toward the street. We just stood there frozen in disbelief and fear for the driver and anyone below, expecting the worst— that an unsuspecting driver might appear in his path or that the truck might flip and roll into the creek across the street.

As the runaway truck bounced into the street, somehow still upright, the driver pumped the air brakes, the truck hopped a few times, and then its momentum was surprisingly snuffed out. It came to an abrupt stop; the big machine seemed to just loudly heave and settle into place. The driver jumped out wildly and somehow ran all the way to the top of the hill, where we were standing. As he ran, he was shouting over and over, "I'm alive! I'm alive!" We just stood there motionless, relieved and grateful that neither the driver nor anyone on the street had been killed or maimed. I was stunned, hardly believing what I had just witnessed. I had seen men hurt by industrial equipment, but this was way outside of my experience. Until the day before, I hadn't known the first thing about winch trucks.

The two drivers for Williams Brothers headed their trucks out for the long drive back to their plant. I slid into my El Camino to start for home a few miles away. It was then that I realized how bone tired I was—stress tired. There was no way I could have known what was in store for me and my family during the months ahead. But even then, I had a foreboding that things were about to get a lot worse. If I'd had any idea how much worse, I would have been completely overwhelmed.

Two years earlier, on just one house, we had used over 30 mixers of concrete. We had already completed many hillside pours on other houses. Each truck had come, poured out, and left without incident. Now, after pouring just the foundation for this new project, I was shaken. I felt so alone. Something was very wrong. Could my ambition and self-confidence have taken me out too far? But even then, it seemed like this was something more than a building challenge pressing in. I had dealt with building challenges much of my adult life. This time, it felt as though something else was working against me, and it seemed that it wasn't going to go away.

I sensed the impending storm looming ahead, but I had no idea what it was or how to respond. I knew of nowhere to turn to lessen the feeling of dread, and no way to better manage the reality I found myself in. Driving out of the subdivision, I couldn't even focus on the fact that we had dodged the bullet with the runaway mixer. Instead I was mindful of how dark everything had become. I had no reference point to recognize what was beginning, no way of suspecting that this increasing darkness would soon manifest as Satan himself, right behind me, speaking into my ear.

Some sat in darkness and in gloom, prisoners in misery and in irons, for they had rebelled against the words of God, and spurned the counsel of the Most High. Their hearts were bowed down with hard labor; they fell down, with no one to help.

—Psalm 107:10-12 (NSRV)

For the enemy has pursued my soul; he has crushed my life to the ground; he has made me sit in darkness like those long dead. Therefore my spirit faints within me...

—Psalm 143:3-4 (ESV)

Chapter 2

What Must We Do?

Until the three airliners crashed into the Twin Towers and the Pentagon on September 11, 2001, most Americans did not accept that we were at war with terrorism. The previous bombings in various parts of the world had not awakened us like 9/11 did.

The attitude of most people about the battle with Satan is far too similar. Even though Scripture tells us many times that our battle is against evil forces, even Christians pay little attention and don't expect to be affected personally. They are either unaware or fail to accept that this is actually the battle of their lifetime.

> *For our struggle is not against flesh and blood, but against the rulers,*
> *against the authorities, against the powers of this dark world and against*
> *the spiritual forces of evil in the heavenly realms.*
> *—Ephesians 6:12 (NIV)*

Satan would have much less opportunity to ravage the culture if humanity was knowledgeable and alert, with defenses working. Unfortunately, as a people, we have been lulled by the unseen enemy into unbelief, apathy, and complacency and lack a sense of responsibility, especially in more recent times. Can we not hear the serpent still asking, "Has God really said you cannot eat from that tree? Surely you will not die." Are the people of the present culture not again shouting, "Crucify Him! Crucify Him!"—if not with their voices, then certainly with their dishonor, disobedience and rebellion, and the very lives they are living?

Our culture is saddled with widespread godlessness, unimaginable perversion, willful extermination of millions of babies, endless pursuits of power, pleasure-seeking self-concern, and frequent acts of terror, ranging from individual acts to those on a massive scale, all part of the plan of Satan himself. The world is time and again shocked and grieved over the problem, while avoiding or denying the only answer. Few know and fewer accept who our battle is against, and the result is godless chaos manifest in the most horrific ways.

But God has given humanity a timeless way out of this disaster. Christianity powered by the Holy Spirit is the hope for peace and order to be restored in this world, for God to have His rightful place in people's lives, for civility to return, and for love and virtue to replace hatred and destructive self-interest. Humanity is targeted 24/7 by evil in countless ways, from quiet, unnoticed theft of our minds and spirits to the most violent, inhumane outbursts of terrorism. Can we not realize that this planned and persistent offensive cannot be overcome by a passive faith? Such faith cannot even stay in sight as the culture continues its spiraling descent deeper into hedonism. Could we have imagined how far we would drop in our lifetimes, on our watch? What can be done? What must we do?

Throughout my young life, as I regularly attended church, I don't recall hearing any personal sharing about Pentecost or the Holy Spirit, power from on high. We sang, "Come, Holy Ghost, Creator God," but I never felt Him come, or felt that anyone there knew He had come, ever. We just sang the song, and then we sang another song. Maybe that's the way God heard us, too, as people just singing songs, without belief.

Without a doubt, the Holy Spirit is the best-kept secret of all time, and Pentecost is the most overlooked special day on the calendar. It is quite likely that only a small percentage of regular church attendees could give any explanation of Pentecost, and why the Holy Spirit was sent, and even these regular churchgoers may not know anyone who is living in the Holy Spirit. Should there be any wonder at the lack of power or action in most churches today? Or the lack of interest in faith among vibrant young adults in desperate need of answers for their lives?

If the truth of Pentecost and the Holy Spirit were known, that knowledge would turn the world right side up like never before. Satan will do anything he can to block people's awakening to the power from on high, the power to do anything that is needed, including defeating Satan himself!

Let us quickly review the day of Pentecost, which happened over 2000 years ago. Jerusalem was getting set for the battle lines of good and evil to be drawn. Jesus was moving about the land, performing great signs, wonders, healings and miracles. Untold numbers of followers were being converted. Satan made his move to block this wave of faith by stirring men to deception, jealousy, anger, rage and impulsive evil acts to take Jesus out.

Jesus was arrested, "tried," and beaten nearly to death. His freedom was given for the life of the worst criminal. He was led through a mocking mob to Golgotha, stripped, humiliated beyond belief and then nailed to a cross. On that day of the crucifixion, Good Friday, Satan may well have celebrated and believed he had won the battle between good and evil. Jesus, the Son of the Father, hung dead on the cross. Then His bloody, lacerated body was removed from the cross and placed in a tomb, and a huge boulder was rolled in front to seal it.

But death couldn't hold Him! Jesus was resurrected and came out of the tomb two days later, on Easter Sunday. Over the next forty days, Jesus was seen alive and well by hundreds of people. One of the most breathtaking events in history was breaking forth right in front of their eyes. Even tombs of saints broke open and the dead came back to life.

And the tombs broke open. The bodies of many holy people who had died were raised to life. They came out of the tombs after Jesus' resurrection and went into the holy city and appeared to many people.
—Matthew 27:52-53 (NIV)

The scene was so astonishing that many came to believe as it was happening.

After being raised from the dead, Jesus quietly moved among the apostles teaching, instructing and preparing them to carry on the work He had been doing—fully living out the Gospel. He would soon ascend to Heaven to return to the Father, but He was going to send the Holy Spirit to be their Counselor, Instructor, ever-present help in time of need, who would dwell in them and never leave them.

He appeared to them over a period of forty days and spoke about the kingdom of God...

"Do not leave Jerusalem, but wait for the gift My Father promised, which you have heard Me speak about. For John baptized with water, but in a few days you will be baptized with the Holy Spirit... You will receive power when the Holy Spirit comes on you; and you will be My witnesses in Jerusalem, and in all Judea and Samaria, and to the ends of the earth."
—*Acts 1:3-5, 8 (NIV)*

Jesus then ascended, and the one hundred twenty believers, including Mary and the apostles, went to the upper room to fervently wait for the Holy Spirit to come with power. Nine days passed, and by then, this waiting period had created great interest, excitement, doubt, fear, jeering, hope and other responses throughout Jerusalem and farther.

Then it happened. Seven weeks after Jesus' resurrection, the Holy Spirit came to earth to dwell within and empower any believer who was ready to live for the Lord.

When the day of Pentecost came, they were all together in one place. Suddenly a sound like the blowing of a violent wind came from heaven and filled the whole house where they were sitting. They saw what seemed to be tongues of fire that separated and came to rest on each of them.

All of them were filled with the Holy Spirit and began to speak in other tongues as the Spirit enabled them... When they heard this sound, a crowd came together in bewilderment, because each one heard their own language being spoken... Amazed and perplexed, they asked one another, "What does this mean?"
—*Acts 2:1-4, 6, 12 (NIV)*

What a reward for the faith of the one hundred twenty who waited for the promise to become reality. The devout followers had heard Jesus foretell the Spirit's coming, what a difference He would make in their lives, how they would be transformed into new, fully capable, empowered, wise, caring, gentle, courageous people. When the tongues of fire descended on those waiting to receive, they felt the effect. Right then, they knew they were different. Those disciples felt boldness and courage to live life and faith like they never had before. Those who had run away in fear at the crucifixion could and would now live and spread their faith at all costs—even death. They would become martyrs for their faith, and feel honored to do so.

Since for the first time, the transforming power of the Spirit had come to reside on earth, the report of this event went out across the land, and tremendous tension broke out in Jerusalem. Some jeered and made fun, many were perplexed and refused to believe, others were quite fearful and distanced themselves as fast and far as they could. But those who hungered for God and for the true purpose and fulfillment of life were drawn close by the presence among them of the Holy Spirit from on high. What an arrival! And He has come to stay until the very end!

Peter responded to the crowd of bystanders who were jeering about the actions of the one hundred twenty people who had come stumbling down from the upper room, overshadowed and filled by the Spirit, and now ecstatic and overjoyed, nearly delirious. They had each been touched by the Life Giver. Peter stepped forward and delivered a succinct message of direction in response to their questions:

> *When the people heard this, they were cut to the heart and said to Peter and the other apostles, "Brothers, what shall we do?" Peter replied, "Repent and be baptized, every one of you, in the name of Jesus Christ for the forgiveness of your sins. And you will receive the gift of the Holy Spirit. The promise is for you and your children and for all who are far off— for all whom the Lord our God will call." With many other words he warned them; and he pleaded with them, "Save yourselves from this corrupt generation." Those who accepted his message were baptized, and about three thousand were added to their number that day. They devoted themselves to the apostles' teaching and to fellowship, to the breaking of bread and to prayer. Everyone was filled with awe at the many wonders and signs performed by the apostles.*
>
> *—Acts 2:37-43 (NIV) [My underlining]*

What an outpouring of the Holy Spirit—and through it, Christianity and the church were formed.

Through the centuries, the principal question has never changed: "What must we do?" The answer has never changed: "Repent and be baptized in the name of Jesus Christ." The Lord's response is always the same: "I will pour out My Spirit and power and My grace on anyone who will come after Me, take up his cross daily, be obedient to My leading, and build My kingdom here on earth." That person will be blessed with the abundant life beyond all imagining—a life abundant and overflowing. Like Peter, the once terrified person who acted in his flesh and denied Jesus at the crucifixion, but after receiving the Spirit was called to be the spokesperson of the Lord, so we too have the opportunity of the *redeemed*: to live an empowered life and be spokespersons for Him. Glory!

"What no eye has seen, what no ear has heard, and what no human mind has conceived"—the things God has prepared for those who love Him...
—1 Corinthians 2:9 (NIV)

Darkness to Light

The events dealt with in the story "Foreboding" ushered in the most danger-ous challenge to my mental and emotional state that I had ever experienced, as well as significant struggles related to my building projects. The feeling of "aloneness" prevailed for many weeks and was dominant whether others were present or not. I had no basis for understanding its source; as an adult I had never felt that kind of aloneness, nor been given to depression. Later I would come to believe that the undergirding of help from the Lord that I had always been given, but had never acknowledged, had been withdrawn from me for my chastising, due to my series of bad choices. I had chosen to turn my back on religion and church long before, and the Lord had finally turned away from me.

"Whoever acknowledges Me before others, I will also acknowledge before My Father in heaven. But whoever disowns Me before others, I will disown before My Father in heaven."
—Matthew 10:32-33 (NIV)

I didn't understand what was happening, but the withdrawal of His hand and help made everything in my life and work more difficult. Much more difficult. I felt chilled to the core. I was having trouble thinking things through and staying focused as financial conditions worsened. Decisions became tougher to make, and I felt more uncertain about them. I was trying to cope with Atlanta's worst-ever winter and get the house "dried in" so that work could continue. It was in that compromised condition that I wrestled with and then rushed into a poor and costly decision about the house I was building. I chose to put in a long, straight driveway up a steep incline rather than a longer, cut-back driveway, and the result was literally too steep for most cars to drive up! I made this decision without even consulting my clients, who would need to use the driveway regularly. The brush with calamity involving the runaway concrete mixer at the same location weeks earlier was now followed by this stark, daunting reality—this one actually set in concrete. A mounting fear of failure and a lifetime spirit of perfectionism, combined with this overwhelming situation, opened the door for Satan to assault me at my weakest point. My financial survival and survival as a builder were squarely on the line, and I felt no peace, at any time. Nancy and I had no backup funds nor backup plans. We were personally liable for all debts; even our home was at risk. I was as close as I had ever come to mental and emotional collapse. My mind was constantly filled with crippling questions, and no answers.

The very next day after the driveway was poured, I knew that it would have to be completely torn out and replaced by a longer, curved driveway. There was no doubt this would be a major challenge in every way. To me, the humiliation seemed the worst part, since the home was being built in the midst of an established subdivision of affluent owners. I became even more isolated and withdrawn, almost paranoid. Even taking tranquilizers, I was getting little more than an hour of fitful sleep per night, at the most. This continued for weeks. I looked and felt like a walking dead man. Sleeplessness can wreck anyone. I'm now sure that this sleep deprivation was due to a voice I was hearing (I referred to it later as the "imposter voice") that was encouraging me to commit suicide for the payout of insurance money to my family. The voice spoke to me in a monologue: "Cash it in, do something good for your family. You're worth more dead than alive. Cash it in." It sounded more reasonable each day, almost like a solution, an escape.

But there were times the voice would add to the monologue, "You're a loser and you always have been and always will be." I didn't believe that one line, and that may have prevented me from taking self-destructive action. Satan hammered me for weeks, but he may have overplayed his hand trying to intimidate me with those particular derogatory words.

At the age of forty, I had hit a wall that I never saw coming and was knocked flat. I had totally lost my course while wandering deeper and deeper into a deadly darkness, with perils abounding, with no paths or markers, going totally in the wrong direction. I had stumbled into Satan's territory and could almost sense him close behind me. I was more desperate by the hour, and I finally came to a place where I had to acknowledge that I was without a clue which way to turn. I had relied on no one other than myself. I had not once prayed and asked the Lord for help, and now my life was in shambles. Everything was falling apart, and suddenly the truth dawned on me. I had been taken in, lied to. I had abandoned the godly life and gambled everything on the world's empty promises. I had tried to do it my way, the world's way, and had lost. The great deception had gotten me, and I felt totally lost. There was no one else to blame. I alone was responsible for making it right. I would have to acknowledge my failure, ask for the Lord's mercy and for another chance, go back to where I had run off track, make the necessary changes and correct my mistake. I couldn't go any further down this deadly road. Time had run out. My life was on the line and depended on my making this right. My family and others were counting on me.

Even though I had practiced no faith for nearly a quarter of a century, the faith that led to my long ago "yes" to an altar call at age fourteen may have been the thread of faith that never broke. When I came to finally acknowledge my need for the help of the Savior and humbled myself enough to ask for His help, just so I could sleep, He was there waiting for me. With no conditions or promises from me, He stepped into all of my chaos and fear and took it all on Himself. Just like the words in the old hymn, "Amazing Grace." Wow! That simple request to Jesus, just to be able to sleep, changed my life completely, overnight! All of this came about through a series of unexpected visits to a prayer group, a group unknown to us just a few weeks earlier, and through the prayers and laying on of hands by people who hardly knew me. I awoke the next morning a new person. At the moment I asked Jesus to take over my life, I could feel the unbearable burden had been lifted, and hope flooded in! Immediately, the Holy Spirit came to my side to begin to walk me through the black tunnel and assist me in every way. I had no more sleepless nights after that, ever. And no need of tranquilizers, either! Not only that, but my new Spirit-filled friends told me I had been born again and baptized in the Holy Spirit, all at once! I know this sudden turnaround sounds extreme (amen to that!), but that's the way my conversion and Baptism in the Spirit happened.

And God can do it, for anyone! Your own conversion experience may be quite different; we each have our own personal opportunity with the Savior. I was long overdue in asking Jesus for help, but when I did ask, He came in like a tidal wave, washing away my unbelief, doubts and fears. Even then, I sensed a major change was beginning that would leave nothing in my life untouched. And that has proven to be true. Has it ever!

The driveway demolition and rebuild was my river to cross in order to move on. It had the potential to be the most devastating week of my life. I could hardly get my mind around something this overwhelming. After all, concrete driveways six inches thick are not poured to then be immediately broken up in slabs and hauled off to the dump, only to be poured again. I couldn't allow myself to even think about the cost of it all. I just had to make it right. This Goliath had to be confronted, the sooner the better. It was the challenge of my lifetime, but His grace was more than sufficient. Through the Holy Spirit's presence and empowering, I somehow felt I was ready for ANYTHING. I had been prayed for and prayed over, and I stayed in prayer. It was a week full of every possible emotion, but I hung in there with prayer and trust. The affluent subdivision residents who slowly drove past the site, craning their necks, were obviously shocked. Things like this never happened there. Sharing their upscale street with noisy, dirty dump trucks crammed to the top with jagged slabs of concrete must have seemed "other worldly" or even "third worldly." The sounds of the heavy equipment breaking up the driveway (nothing sounds quite like concrete groaning and giving way) and loading those trucks reverberated throughout the neighborhood. Surely my presence must have seemed like anything other than a welcome addition to their lives. The young builder of luxury homes was taking a licking. They likely feared what kind of houses their subdivision would be stuck with for years to come. But five days later, when the driveway rebuild was completed and the equipment had gone silent, my deadly fear of failure had been met head on, and what a deliverance that was! I came through the challenging rebuild with a new awareness of the Scripture, *"No, in all these things we are more than conquerors through Him who loved us." (Romans 8:37, NIV)*

My embarrassment was more than replaced by a new trust and peace. I gained even more freedom as I admitted my mistake to the neighborhood residents and proclaimed to them where my new help and peace had come from. I was very surprised to see how the Holy Spirit held their attention. Many had already come to know the house I was building as "the driveway house." Before the drive was rebuilt, young men took it on as a challenge, attempting to see if their cars could make it to the top. To me, it will always be my conversion house. That experience reshaped me even more than it reshaped the driveway. No doubt about it! Today I can readily say that the driveway experience was a blessing from the Lord. My pride and self-reliance needed to be crushed and removed like the concrete.

> *Consider it pure joy, my brothers and sisters, whenever you face trials of many kinds, because you know that the testing of your faith produces perseverance. Let perseverance finish its work so that you may be mature and complete, not lacking anything.*
>
> —*James 1:2-4 (NIV)*

There is no end to what the Lord may use to correct one's mindset and course.

All of the time lost to delays during my period of darkness was being steadily recovered due to the extraordinary grace now bestowed to complete the house project and jumpstart me. Even my workmen saw me as a new man!

The design of the house was intended to capitalize on the natural beauty of the hillside lot. A walk into the great room toward the angular window wall gave one the feeling of being inside a mountain resort, with everything else far below. The Chattahoochee River was visible through openings in the trees. The new driveway curved through the woods and was a pleasure to drive. The owners, Joel and Carla, loved their new dream home and never mentioned the "ski lift" driveway to me, even though they paid for it. I built them a stylized teak wall and steps in the entry foyer as my gift to them. The multitude of challenges associated with building the house were now becoming a memory. The entire experience had been brutally hard but was fully worth it.

I was humbled, grateful, and exhilarated. Wow! The joy of the Lord is for real, and what a strength it is! I had been given another chance—a chance complete with His empowering. The Lord had turned me so fast from near disaster and suicidal thinking to shouting from the rooftops that I almost thought I was dreaming, but my new life was surpassing all my dreams. And it was for real! Glory!

> *"For I know the plans I have for you," declares the Lord. "Plans to prosper you and not to harm you, plans to give you hope and a future. Then you will call on Me and come and pray to Me, and I will listen to you. You will seek Me and find Me when you seek Me with all your heart."*
> —*Jeremiah 29:11-13 (NIV)*

> *I have decided to follow Jesus;*
> *I have decided to follow Jesus;*
> *I have decided to follow Jesus,*
> *No turning back, no turning back.*
>
> *The world behind me, the cross before me;*
> *the world behind me, the cross before me;*
> *the world behind me, the cross before me,*
> *No turning back, no turning back.*
>
> *Though none go with me, I still will follow;*
> *though none go with me, I still will follow;*
> *though none go with me, I still will follow;*
> *No turning back, no turning back.*
> —*From the hymn, "I Have Decided*
> *to Follow Jesus," by Sadhu Sundar Singh*

A New Pentecost, the Abundant Life

The incredible experience of Pentecost catapulted faith and the church to new life, and both grew rapidly, but gradually, man's flesh, the love of the world and Satan's endless efforts against humankind undermined the faith of most people in the all-powerful but unseen God. Gratitude toward the Lord for centuries of His help and provision grew cold and was replaced by desires of the flesh—desires for whatever people thought they could have. Without eyes and hearts to see God's hand, humanity had little concern for the Creator or His ways, and apathy and selfishness abounded.

After many centuries of stagnant faith, the Lord saw the need for a "great awakening." He sent forth a new outpouring of the Holy Spirit at the beginning of the 1900s that brought about Pentecostalism, an expression of faith that was very different and quite challenging to the mainline churches. Despite much doubt and opposition, this outpouring gained spiritual momentum and bore great fruit for over half a century, and it still does today among the Pentecostal denominations. For many, signs and wonders replaced practices that had become too routine and even deadening.

Then, in 1967, through a small group of devout believers near Pittsburgh, a group seeking a new personal Pentecost, the Holy Spirit breathed fresh life of epic proportions into mainline churches. This group of churches, many of them liturgical, included the Roman Catholic, Episcopal, Anglican, Lutheran, Methodist, Evangelical and others. The Spirit sent forth a blazing fire that would become known as the Charismatic Renewal, and it spread like wildfire across America and around the world, even amidst Satan's tumultuous uprising that fueled the rebellious culture of the turbulent 60s.

The electrifying experiences with the Holy Spirit that came about with the Charismatic Renewal drastically changed the lives of many millions of men, women and children, as well as thousands of churches and even more Spirit-led prayer groups and communities. After years of waning interest or disillusion in church and faith, this Spirit-inspired awakening brought man and God close to each other, with life-changing results beyond anyone's expectations. Lay people and clergy alike discovered their rightful places in the life of the church and in faith, and everyone had a place. It was as if man had been connected directly to God's pipeline, and that pipeline was streaming with new life. The Holy Spirit was moving over the land, touching the thirsty and the hungry, the perishing and the starving, meeting their needs right where they were and inviting His people to come join in the work and the joy. Suddenly, we were all equal, on a level playing field, and experiencing all that was good, honorable and praiseworthy. What a different perspective on life. Gifts, works, and new life burst forth. Millions and millions of people experienced the emergence of a new, expectant faith, and that was just the beginning!

Some of the results have been:

- People on a disastrous course involving drugs, alcohol, abuse of sex and other serious sins have been rescued and redeemed, and then sent out to help others be rescued. We saw many freed from the hippie drug culture of the 60s, and have seen many freed since.
- Individuals bound up in insecurity, rejection, anxiety, doubt and fear have been set free to live balanced, capable and productive lives and have become living examples of God's freeing power.
- Countless men and women who had wandered aimlessly in life have come alive by God's grace and found real purpose and a plan for their lives. They are living life well, having discovered its true meaning.
- Many individualists who had lived only for themselves and this world's pleasures have worked hard to overcome self and ego and have discovered real life, a heart to help others and unexpected joy as they look beyond themselves and serve others.
- People who went through the motions for decades, attending church but experiencing no personal change, have found purpose and fulfillment building His Kingdom through the Holy Spirit. For many

people, their faith and church lives went from being the least significant aspect of their lives to becoming the most significant and fulfilling aspect.

Many talents, gifts and abilities have sprung up, been developed and been put to great use. Those whose lives were once filled with boredom, disinterest and mediocrity have been transformed to pursue virtue, goodness and higher goals. In so many ways, the Father, Son and Spirit have become real and present to humanity and given us new lives with a sense that we are where we should be, doing what we were created to do and living life with expectant joy.

Over the last thirty-five years, Nancy and I have been privileged to live closely together with several hundred redeemed, transformed men and women, both old and young, and have been in spiritual fellowship with thousands more. Their testimonies and reports are quite similar. What follows is an effort to put into words some of the changes that the Spirit brings about to transform, shape and mold us to be more like Him and better able to help build His Kingdom. I have included lists that are a compilation of what I've learned since I began living in the Spirit. However, these lists are by no means exhaustive. There is so much more!

What difference does living in the Holy Spirit make? ALL the difference—and all of it good!

What may change in your life? You may develop:

- A new love for the Lord and others, and gratitude for all His blessings
- A new awareness of the battle between good and evil, which is raging 24/7
- An openness to the Spirit's leading and guidance as you see your new life unfold
- New faith-tuned eyes and ears, as well as the mind of Christ (It's amazing!) *(1 Corinthians 2:5-16)*
- A desire or need to pray or maybe just to spend time with the Lord
- A prayer language, which will enable you to pray in the Spirit

- A new mindset and values (A transformation will begin, and you will find yourself making different choices than you would have in the past, and even taking on challenging service or ministry that you would not have considered before.)
- A new understanding of what IS important, and what is NOT
- A new awareness of sins of omission (God has given us responsibilities, and we must take the time to act.)
- New boldness and courage, and the grace to be a "stand-up" person
- A decreased attraction to material possessions/materialism
- An ability to say "no" to bad habits and an openness to good ones
- Development of the fruits of the Spirit: love, joy, peace, patience, kindness, goodness, gentleness and self-control *(Galatians 5:22-23)*
- Deliverance from stubborn old spirits (They are NOT friends, and you CAN get rid of them.)
- A new concern for others and a need to help (a good Samaritan outlook)
- An ability to separate what we hold sacred or precious from what is worthless *(Jeremiah 15:19)*
- Increased common sense (wisdom)
- A new peace that surpasses understanding, in all areas of your life *(Philippians 4:7)*
- A greatly increased awareness of the presence of God in your life (You can feel Him there.)
- The realization that God causes all things to work for good for His people *(Romans 8:28)*
- New order in your life (Things begin to fit into place.)
- God's favor in all areas of your life (This is huge!)
- A new reliance on the Holy Spirit for help (At any time, the Helper is ready.)
- A new grace to handle the hard things in your life, and even to count them as joy *(James 1:2-4)*
- An awakening of the spiritual gifts: prophecy, words of knowledge, discernment, healing, etc.
- A recognition of your life as a mission (We are builders of His Kingdom here on earth.)

- Increasing development of your "Spirit eyes," an ability to see circumstances through the eyes of faith *(Ephesians 1:18)*

You may also:

- Start learning to put the Lord first (It just begins to happen.)
- Hear the Great Commission as a personal directive, not a suggestion
- Experience Scripture as alive and personal, as if it has been written for you TODAY *(1 Thessalonians 2:13)*
- Worry less, and trust more

Remember the fearful runaway apostles at the crucifixion, and how the empowering of the Holy Spirit changed them into courageous, willing followers, enabling them to see the purpose of their lives and to die for the Lord as martyrs.

Things to do:

- Draw near to God, and He will draw near to you; be very intentional in seeking Him. *(James 4:8)*
- Develop a personal relationship with Jesus, and recognize Him as a person who is always available to you.
- Develop a personal prayer time and Scripture study.
- Get to know the Holy Spirit as a person, always within you and available to help.
- Ask for God's help, and trust Him with all your heart. *(Proverbs 3:5-8)*
- Avoid temptation and the near occasion of sin (putting yourself in situations that could easily lead to sin).
- Build and live your entire life around your faith (this is the key to bringing transformation to your family).
- Develop discipline, consistency, and perseverance.
- Remove idols (anything placed ahead of the Lord), including marriage, family, work, etc. He must come first.

- Be intentional with your faith and live it unconditionally, here and now, always and everywhere.
- Spend time with Spirit-led believers.
- Take your faith where it is needed most, beyond just the church (this will also cause your faith to grow fastest).
- Put on the "new man" or "new woman" daily, even when stressed, and say "no" to the old man or old woman.
- Work at humility and dying to self—an unending work. *(James 4:10)*
- Engage in the battle with Satan (he is very embattled against you).
- Know that your life has real purpose, and don't miss it—ask the Lord to show you the next step.
- Take up the Great Commission. *(Matthew 28:18-20; Mark 16:15-20)*
- Be on duty and on the alert to follow plan A. (You may be needed, right now!)
- Do the right thing, and trust the Lord with the results.
- Let go, and let GOD.
- Choose to want His will for your life (always a good starting place and valid to seek in prayer: Lord, help me to want Your will).
- Look outside yourself, your family, your work—if you are willing to be a rescuer, the Lord will direct you.
- Remember that you have been given much, and much is expected.
- Don't hold out or hold back on the Lord. (All we get to keep is what we give away, and we can't outgive God!)
- Recognize that this is a lifelong process and journey, a marathon, and the Lord sets the pace. *(Hebrews 12:1-2)*
- Be patient and be thorough in all that you attempt. There is time to do everything well.
- Keep pressing on because there is a "call" on your life; be faithful to His call. Our response to the "call" affects others, and they need our good response.
- Know that grace precedes the call, and anything the Lord calls you to do, He will give you grace to accomplish.
- Get prayed for as needed.

- Pray to be used in divine appointments, to provide prophetic words and prayers for healing, etc.
- Pray for more gifts to use in serving Him.
- Be present to the moment. (This has to be developed, but is so important.)
- Have joy in the journey!

Shout for joy to the Lord, all the earth. Worship the Lord with gladness; come before Him with joyful songs. Know that the Lord is God.
It is He who made us, and we are His; we are His people, the sheep of His pasture.
Enter His gates with thanksgiving and His courts with praise; give thanks to Him and praise His name.
For the Lord is good and His love endures forever; His faithfulness continues through all generations.
—Psalm 100 (NIV)

It is obvious that we have been imbued with power from on high. We are quite aware that we are in fact new creations; we can feel and see and know the difference. Many of us can hardly believe we were once the old selves we have been set free from, or can hardly believe the new person we are becoming. The contrast is incredible, and we can be ever changing for the better through the Holy Spirit.

Therefore, if anyone is in Christ, the new creation has come: The old has gone, the new is here! All this is from God, who reconciled us to Himself through Christ and gave us the ministry of reconciliation: that God was reconciling the world to Himself in Christ, not counting people's sins against them. And He has committed to us the message of reconciliation. We are therefore Christ's ambassadors, as though God were making His appeal through us. We implore you on Christ's behalf: Be reconciled to God.
—2 Corinthians 5:17-20 (NIV)

We find ourselves reaching out to help others experience this abundant life that the Lord has promised to anyone who asks.

Keep on asking, and you will receive what you ask for. Keep on seeking, and you will find. Keep on knocking, and the door will be opened to you. For everyone who asks, receives. Everyone who seeks, finds. And to everyone who knocks, the door will be opened.
                                                    —*Matthew 7:7-8 (NLT)*

We are also mindful that a great battle rages for the soul of each man, woman and child alive. We must have power from the Spirit to take on Satan—this is a battle that no one can win on his own.

Finally, be strong in the Lord and in His mighty power. Put on the full armor of God, so that you can take your stand against the devil's schemes. For our struggle is not against flesh and blood, but against the rulers, against the authorities, against the powers of this dark world and against the spiritual forces of evil in the heavenly realms.
                                                    —*Ephesians 6:10-12 (NIV)*

The stories in this book reflect acting in the moment as prompted by the Holy Spirit, and the broad range of results from the varied responses to these actions.

New Priorities

As we were nearing completion of the "conversion house," a couple relocating from Chicago came looking at the subdivision, and then through my house. They were in the market for a lot to build on, a designer and a builder—and all three were available.

God's grace was strong upon our business, and the couple made a quick decision to have me design and build them a house on the adjoining lot. This was also a hillside setting, but with a moderate incline by comparison. The construction went well, with no glitches (what a difference compared with the events of a few months earlier). The couple got their special house with all its nice touches, and the house nestled into the natural terrain as if it had always been there among the trees. My work of designing and building custom houses seemed to have returned to normal.

However, I was already beginning to feel the conflict between the Holy Spirit's deeper call on my life (a higher purpose) and the world's spirit, which I routinely encountered through my clients, their projects and their high level of success. For me, this sense of conflict, of being pushed and pulled, was a new, uneasy feeling, but I believe my clients were totally unaware of it. I realized that I was already thinking differently; my values were shifting. I didn't know where this was leading, but I could feel my passion for worldly "success" decreasing.

I want to share with you some details here because this was a pivotal place in our journey. A major fork in the road was coming. I believe you might be able to relate to this personally because of your own challenges, whatever they might be, and I hope this account of mine might be helpful.

Soon after the Chicago couple contracted for the design and building of their house, another man was drawn to check out Joel and Carla's house. His name was Phil, he was a psychiatrist, and he was interested in having me design and build a home for him on a rather severe downhill lot located in a new, high-end subdivision. Phil was artistic and inclined toward a creative, innovative design. Without delay, we agreed on a contract to design, and I began drawing my most ambitious plans to date. The design incorporated features that I had never before used, or even seen. The design was quickly agreed upon, and the house was soon under contract and construction.

I will be descriptive here to help you visualize and to better illustrate the Spirit's movement to the forefront of our lives. This is one example of how His ways are higher than our ways.

The focal point of the house design was an atrium set in the center of the home's ground floor level, with the living and entertaining area surrounding it. The atrium had a walkway surrounded by plants, shrubs, and full-sized ornamental trees. The atrium rose thirty feet to the ridge of the roof, with two sky domes, each four feet by eight feet, set into the roof to allow sunlight to pour in. In time, the trees would grow well past the second floor, up toward the sky domes. Open-tread mahogany stairs ascended from the atrium and joined the catwalk hallway that opened to the upstairs bedrooms. The house included many state-of-the-art touches, and the three-dimensional openness was virtually knee buckling. Like many creative artists, I had long believed there would be one very special project that would be a breakthrough and would lead to greater opportunities, and possibly a whole new level of work and clientele. This one had the potential to do just that.

The construction went very well, quicker than it might have considering the design, the heights and the unusual challenges. There was a whirlwind of activity over the final couple of weeks as I tried to keep it all moving toward completion, to be thankful that it was almost finished, and to not let Nancy and our family suffer too much neglect. Along with the scheduling and over-seeing responsibilities, I spent as many hands-on hours as I could, working to complete the mahogany stairway and handrails. Custom-built handrails, with all of the parts machined on site, had been a signature feature of my houses. I suppose they were my way of hanging onto my furniture-building experience. These were the most elaborate we had done.

After the house was completed and occupied, I went by to see how it looked furnished. Phil showed me in, and my visual sense was filled with the colors, the spaciousness, and the trees and plants bursting with life in the atrium. Then, suddenly, my eyes were drawn to the open mahogany stairs. Upon a closer look, I could see they were heavily pockmarked from bottom to top, with deep marks impressed in the wood, like something golf shoe spikes might have caused. This was the wood we had diligently fine-sanded and finished just days earlier As I stood next to Phil, perplexed, I asked, "What happened?" He looked over at Bruno, his full-sized Saint Bernard standing on the other side of him, and matter-of-factly said, "Oh, that's just Bruno's nails. He loves going up and down the stairs. So much to see, I guess." I still felt distressed, and then Phil settled it all by saying, "It's nothing. It's just us living in our house." And there it was. He was right, and no more words were needed. Any degree of ownership that I might have ever assumed of that house had just been removed.

I walked away grateful to the Lord for the challenging but completed house. I didn't take a single photograph, but I got a clear picture that my priorities were rapidly changing. I didn't know it at the time, but my brief visit with Phil and Bruno began a much needed detachment from the pride of accomplishment that had quietly held a strong grip on me throughout my life. The Spirit was even now replacing my ambition for the temporal with a hunger for the *more*—for the everlasting.

As I reflect back on that chock-full final week of construction and all that it entailed, my memories of that spectacular house fade, and my mind goes back to a brief Holy Spirit mission in which I had been used a couple of weeks before, while on my way to the house.

Something was in the air. I didn't know what, but I knew I needed to stay alert and pay attention.

See, the former things have taken place, and new things I declare; before they spring into being I announce them to you.

—Isaiah 42:9 (NIV)

Ground-Level Kingdom Building

For seven years, I had designed and built unique, custom homes, a lofty venture even under the best of conditions and in good times. I had begun with no architectural degree, no house construction experience, no financial stability, only talent, ambition, self-confidence and plenty of drive. The crippling recession of the mid 1970s and the humbling concrete experience during the building of the "driveway house" had seriously challenged the attitudes that had carried me along up to now. The vicious assault on my mind and spirit that Satan had launched to drive me to consider suicide had nearly overwhelmed me. Amazingly, the effects of the long and tormenting attacks by the demonic voice and my severe sleep deprivation were overridden and replaced by a new indwelling grace and the Spirit of the Lord Himself.

You, dear children, are from God and have overcome them, because the one who is in you is greater than the one who is in the world.
—1 John 4:4 (NIV)

Planning, thinking through and building these personalized contract houses had been all-consuming for me, but now the attention I gave my building endeavors lessened considerably. Claiming my attention instead was an ever-growing Kingdom-mindedness. I had learned much about designing and building during those challenging years, but my greatest help had come from "walking in the Spirit" and all that the wonderful transformation over the past two years had encompassed. The Helper, the Counselor, was always there, with any help that was needed. What would the world look like if everyone knew and experienced His abiding presence for themselves?

53

Following the completion of the atrium house, I had high hopes for new, prestigious clients, plus two houses lined up that I expected would take my business a long way toward financial recovery. Each was a large, complex project, and I believed that together they would take about a year and half to finish. I had already completed the blueprints for the first house and was expecting confirmation from the client to move forward. Instead, I got a call from the client's banker requesting my financial statement, even though the loan was to be in my client's name. I delayed responding, hoping that the bank would ultimately not require the statement. None of the banks for any of my other clients had, but this bank was persistent. Like those in construction and supply businesses, many banks had suffered large losses during the recession and had become cautious. My financial status on paper had been decimated over the last five years because of delinquent payments to multiple suppliers. Like many builders who were still in business, hanging on from house to house, I was hoping to survive and recover from the effects of the recession. In the end, I failed to respond to the bank's request. The bank would eventually approve my house plans and the loan but would not approve me to manage the construction money. What I had dreaded might happen did—the house project was irretrievably gone from me. Another contractor would build the house using the plans that I had designed and drawn.

The second house in my line-up had been agreed upon by my clients and me a few years earlier. I had built an "interim" home for them, and we had committed to a beautiful double lot for their final house. As the time drew near to begin designing and then building, a very disappointing letter arrived from the client informing me that he and his wife were going a different route, using others to design and build. They were very nice people, and we had enjoyed a very good builder-client relationship during the building of the first house. But now, as non-Christians, they didn't want to be exposed to the active new faith they had witnessed in me since my conversion. In two weeks' time both houses were lost, with all the work and income they represented, and with no replacements in sight. I had purposely held time open for those building projects. Since timing on large contract houses is crucial, my plans, which had seemed to be moving forward very well, had been derailed.

Now listen, you who say, "Today or tomorrow we will go to this or that city, spend a year there, carry on business and make money." Why, you do not even know what will happen tomorrow. What is your life? You are a mist that appears for a little while and then vanishes. Instead, you ought to say, "If it is the Lord's will, we will live and do this or that."
—*James 4:13-15 (NIV)*

I quietly grieved over this major setback for a couple of weeks, not complaining, just grieving. Deep down I knew that my time as a designer and builder of luxury homes in Atlanta had come to an end. The atrium house was to be my last hurrah as a home builder. The Lord was shutting a door that I couldn't open. I didn't know how I knew—I just did. It had to be a sense from the Holy Spirit. I also knew to accept this and not strive or struggle against it. The voice of the Counselor is often inaudible, but never to be ignored. The Spirit was showing me to "count it all joy."

For some time I had known that these big, all-consuming projects were adding far too much stress to my life and dominating the majority of my time and attention. I rarely got them out of my mind; they probably were idols for me. I was coming to understand that you really can't serve God and mammon.

But store up for yourselves treasures in heaven, where moths and vermin do not destroy, and where thieves do not break in and steal.
For where your treasure is, there your heart will be also.
—*Matthew 6:20-21 (NIV)*

I had not known any of my house clients before building for them, and of all my clients, only one couple gave any evidence of living as Christians. In reality, I had been using my God-given gifts to glorify myself and man. My personal life was way out of balance, as well; I was often not present physically or mentally for my family. The Lord was calling for that to change, and right away. Along with all of this, the biggest shift yet was well underway. When the Lord lifted me out of my depths of despair and hopelessness, He immediately burned into my spirit the new "higher call" to go into all the world and build His Kingdom here on earth.

He said to them, "Go into all the world and preach the gospel to all creation. Whoever believes and is baptized will be saved, but whoever does not believe will be condemned. And these signs will accompany those who believe: In My name they will drive out demons; they will speak in new tongues; they will pick up snakes with their hands; and when they drink deadly poison, it will not hurt them at all; they will place their hands on sick people, and they will get well."

—Mark 16:15-18 (NIV)

For me, I knew this was "the" word. Even early on, as a new believer, I knew this call to go and build His Kingdom would become the preeminent call on my life, transcending all other forms of building. This blazing work of the Holy Spirit was already breaking out at all kinds of times and places in my day-to-day life, with amazing results. This involvement in the work of the Spirit never replaced or diminished my regular work—it sometimes rearranged my hours, but it always enhanced our lives. (Anything the Lord orders He will pay for!) The sorrow over the loss of my home-building work was being more than replaced by the desire to pursue souls for His glory!

I would miss the big projects, the exhilaration of seeing beautiful structures fulfill my visions for them, and the power I possessed as a high-end builder, but I knew that such power fed my pride and had to decrease. That "power" was a perceived power, a "high" born of ambition that was capable of taking me in over my head. I realized that I must move straight ahead and not look back, just turn it loose—and amazingly, there was sufficient grace to do just that. Before long I came to accept that it was the Lord Himself who had brought my house building to an end, not the men who had pulled out of agreements. Already I was learning that the Lord is either actively calling the believer on or blocking him from going on. He has a plan and His plan is the one with grace, the one that works. Jesus wants to be Number One in our lives, in everything. I was beginning to recognize the truth of this Scripture:

And we know that in all things God works for the good of those who love Him, who have been called according to His purpose.

—Romans 8:28 (NIV)

The grace that had been on my design and contracting work had shifted, and now I was being empowered to use my woodworking gifts in another field. To walk effectively, we must go with the Lord's grace, His unmerited favor. The Spirit made it possible for me to take the men who had already been working with me, without a pause, and move directly into commercial woodwork, doing specialized installations in restaurants, banks, financial institutions, large offices, and other buildings for general contractors. I would now be a subcontractor, using none of my designing skills, not in charge, and rarely receiving a thank you. I was expected to get in, do good work, and get out, clearing the way for the next tradesman. It would be hard, dirty, gritty work, with hard-nosed people to deal with, on their schedules, but it was what the Lord had placed before me. He knew I needed this is as the ground-level place from which to work to build His Kingdom—the highest and best call offered to man.

Whatever you do, work at it with all your heart, as working for the Lord, not for human masters.
　　　　　　　　　　　　　　　　　　　　—Colossians 3:23 (NIV)

I would later have this Scripture above printed on my business shirts.

I had no idea what other work this might lead to later, but this present work would entail spending time on His "anvil" as He hammered out some of my old self and my pride and shaped me more in humility, acceptance and obedience (all challenging virtues that I had avoided cultivating), while making me more single-minded for Him. The years that followed included a multitude of divine appointments and opportunities in the midst of workplace settings. Many workers in construction greatly need to see Jesus' ways lived out among them. When the Spirit is "on" us, He can use us anytime. Being used by God in spontaneous and unexpected ways increases the adrenaline like nothing else—it's a thrill a minute. Glory! Especially when the tough ole guys get personally touched by the Lord Himself!

One contract flowed into another throughout this time, and there was no need to pursue sales; we got work just by word of mouth and the Holy Spirit's marketing. Then, as quickly as it started, the Lord turned it off, just like a faucet. As with the home building, I knew it was over. My three longtime workers knew it, also, and left to find other work.

Four years after I entered into commercial woodwork, the Lord would place a new call on me to consecrate all my design and woodworking gifts to Him. Nancy and I would begin our new business, Images of the Cross, making crosses and woodworks to glorify God. This would mean designing and building crosses in many fine woods, and all types of altar furnishings for churches, while not taking any secular work. To some people this call sounded far too specialized, and they would ask if there would be enough of this kind of work to sustain a business. But He knows what He wants and His grace is sufficient. We never doubted or questioned this new call. He had promised if we would do what He asked, He would keep us in business. Amen!

> *Commit to the Lord whatever you do, and He will establish your plans.*
> *—Proverb 16:3 (NIV)*

I had this Scripture above printed on our business envelopes.

Making crosses and woodworks to glorify God became my full-time career, and our business has been sustained for more than thirty-seven years. My gift and talent had been waiting to be used for His glory. What peace and joy this work has brought, and it has touched people like none of my previous work could. I realize now that I had to get all the other fields of building behind me and turn them loose before I could be entrusted with work to glorify God.

I have been able to work with many of the finest woods in the world: ebony, olivewood, bloodwood, satinwood, walnut, cherry, mahoganies, maples, jelutong, dogwood, nine different rosewoods, and many more. Watching the designs and the woods come alive and reflect the glory of the Lord has been something to behold, and the projects I have been able to participate in have far surpassed my expectations—and exceeded the pleasure and satisfaction of working on spectacular houses, as well. Of course, moving away from home building and into making crosses and liturgical furnishings is the only way I would have gotten to sculpt crucifixes.

The Holy Spirit marketing certainly came through and has kept us busy. We have been booked sometimes for nine months to a year in advance, but we have never had or lived in any abundance.

Then, a few years ago, He added to the liturgical woodwork the call and opportunity to write a book proclaiming His great redemptive works and the awesome adventure of living in the Holy Spirit, inviting me to build His Kingdom on a much broader scale. My first book was printed in 2012, and this is my second. The grace is there for both works: woodwork and writing.

I've come to realize that writing is much like building—even like sculpting.

Thank you for bearing with me through this discourse on building and how the Holy Spirit orchestrates all our plans when given the chance. It seems that one of the major questions in the minds of committed Christians is, "How do I know God's will for my life?" Regardless of your field of work or life experience, I pray you will find something encouraging in this story and in the pages to come, as I go on to describe many interesting Holy Spirit-driven encounters and the spiritual and mental awakening I experienced (and have seen in so many others). God's ways are astounding!

Oh, the depth of the riches of the wisdom and knowledge of God! How unsearchable His judgments, and His paths beyond tracing out! Who has known the mind of the Lord? Or who has been His counselor?... For from Him and through Him and for Him are all things. To Him be the glory forever! Amen.

—Romans 11:33-34, 36 (NIV)

Chapter 3

Sent Out, Going Out

As I emerged from that long captivity to darkness and unbelief, which had no higher purpose, it was awesome to find myself actually being used by the Holy Spirit! Nearly unbelievable! I felt remorse, and still do, for having been mindless and self-centered, blocking God out of my life for so many years. I never should have allowed that; it deprived my family and others of the blessings He had planned. I had lost much time and missed many opportunities. I had a lot of ground to make up.

A whole new awareness of others and their needs began to surface. I had spent a lifetime avoiding getting involved with others' predicaments, but on a dime, all of that was changing. I could no longer look the other way and walk or drive by as though I hadn't seen a need, nor could I claim to be too busy. Now, if an event caught my attention, I felt responsible for reaching out. What a new life! Guilt due to omission, or failure to act, was being replaced by a sense of fulfillment.

I came to realize that I had lived my life "in the natural" without eyes to see, ears to hear, or the mind or heart to understand. Suddenly all of these senses were being enlightened by the Spirit.

I pray that the eyes of your heart may be enlightened in order that you may know the hope to which He has called you, the riches of His glorious inheritance in His holy people.

—Ephesians 1:18 (NIV)

It was as though I had lived my life looking out of a window that had a shade pulled three quarters of the way down. My view of all of the better parts of life had been blocked, but I now had access to that view through the power of the Holy Spirit. I was beginning to understand that there was a depth and breadth to life that I had never known, or known about, before.

This was such a transition. Just weeks earlier, I'd had no idea that in our present age, the Lord interacts with man. Now, suddenly to be used in encounters with people I had never seen, to watch the Lord handle serious problems of all types right in front of my eyes, was astounding. How could anyone not get excited? How could anyone who had turned his back on the Lord for twenty years be used this way? It was only through mercy and grace. The Lord has many prodigal sons, and He is calling more all of the time.

I had heard other members of our prayer group describe the Spirit-led encounters they were having, but my main preparation for this "mission of the moment" came from the leading and help of the Holy Spirit and my own new experiences. This would be a learn-as-you-go thing, but His grace had already been activated. What gifts did I have that I could use to glorify God? Just weeks earlier, I didn't even know what spiritual gifts were. I needed to raise the bar and think higher—much higher. I had been given much, I was suddenly living the abundant life, and now much was expected. I would have to be more intentional in living my faith life than I had ever been with any other challenge.

It seemed as if the Holy Spirit was fast-forwarding my response to the call to make up for those twenty lost years. When anyone gets baptized in the Spirit, there seems to be a new, burning need to look beyond oneself and to notice and act on the needs of others. The Spirit might point people toward the homeless, the hungry, the unborn, the orphans, the destitute, the imprisoned, the physically afflicted, the hopeless, foreign missions or other people or needs. I was restrained by personal and business commitments and responsibilities, so I was not likely to head out across the world. However, I knew I had been commissioned, given an important mission—the Great Commission. The Lord had put on my heart the lost souls, the spiritually destitute, the downtrodden, the marginalized, the misled and deceived. It appeared that my mission would first center around those who were right where I was, whether at work, at home, or on the street. He wanted me to have a Plan A mindset and be on duty in the moment, to put on the new man, saying, "Yes, Lord send me," and then act on whatever happened. Being Spirit-led sounded about as far from my former project-oriented mindset as could be, but I learned that by His grace, I could do both my work in the world and my Spirit-led work, and His grace would be poured out over both. It became clear that success in Holy Spirit ministry was far more dependent on availability than ability.

I soon experienced times when the anointing of the Spirit was so clearly present for an encounter that the entire event seemed orchestrated, with each line of dialogue readily coming forth. I felt like a bystander listening in—except that I was the one speaking and ministering. Such is the way of the Holy Spirit, and any of us can be used if we keep ourselves available and on duty. The Lord seems to set His expectations high for those who experience radical conversions. Those who have been forgiven much love much. (See Luke 7:47.) I am mindful of Mary Magdalene, who was delivered of seven evil spirits and then became the first person to see and talk to the risen Jesus. He counts on the redeemed to live as the redeemed. If you are willing to walk the high wire of life for the highest of reasons, He just may be calling you to step into the mission.

"Alas, Sovereign Lord," I said, "I do not know how to speak; I am too young." But the Lord said to me, "Do not say, 'I am too young.' You must go to everyone I send you to and say whatever I command you. Do not be afraid of them, for I am with you and will rescue you," declares the Lord. Then the Lord reached out His hand and touched my mouth and said to me, "I have put My words in your mouth."
—Jeremiah 1:6-9 (NIV)

As you go out, know that you are an ambassador for Christ to reconcile anyone to Him.

Therefore, we are ambassadors for Christ, as though God were making an appeal through us; we beg you on behalf of Christ, be reconciled to God.
—2 Corinthians 5:20 (NASB)

Be mindful of the fellow travelers and their individual conditions. Many have never really felt God's love for them; some have been abused, demeaned or lost their way, and their minds, bodies or hope may have been ravaged. Others may have rejected help in the past that could have prevented their present condition. Some have broken important relationships and find themselves on a long, lonely road. Many are suffering the results of years of bad choices, beginning in their youth, and have nearly self-destructed. The desperate may be trying just to get away from where they are or a serious dilemma. I know that hopelessness can make people desire escape, and the spirit of hopelessness may well be the deadliest of the spirits.

Whatever the reason for each person's situation, each is still a child of God, made in His image, and He loves all people right where they are—maybe not their behavior or actions, but them. The Holy Spirit wants no one left behind.

> *The Lord is not slow about His promise, as some count slowness, but is patient toward you, not wishing for any to perish but for all to come to repentance.*
>
> *—2 Peter 3:9 (NASB)*

In our case, our "Yes, Lord, send me" response had been heard on high, and we had been activated. It was time to put on the "new man" daily and expect to be used.

> *Jesus called His twelve disciples to Him and gave them authority to drive out impure spirits and to heal every disease and sickness.*
>
> *—Matthew 10:1 (NIV)*

> *"As you go, proclaim this message: 'The kingdom of heaven has come near.'"*
>
> *—Matthew 10:7 (NIV)*

> *"Heal the sick, raise the dead, cleanse those who have leprosy, drive out demons. Freely you have received; freely give."*
>
> *—Matthew 10:8 (NIV)*

Hitchhiker Stories: A Lift from Jesus

Probably few of us have done any serious hitchhiking that involved time, distance and reliance on strangers. My one experience of having no obvious choice but to hitchhike—and hope—happened eons ago. Nancy and I were in our early twenties and had been married just over a year, and she was about five months pregnant with our first child. We were returning to Marietta from Nashville, where we had delivered furniture that I had built for my sister and brother-in-law. Without warning, a tire on my pickup truck went flat, and we had no spare. The furniture had completely filled the back of the truck, we had squeezed our suitcase behind the seat, and there had been no room left for the spare tire. I had thought that, surely, we weren't going to need it.

We were on a desolate stretch of highway about halfway between Manchester and Mont Eagle, Tennessee, about twelve miles from either town. It was Sunday night, approaching midnight. After walking up a long driveway to a lighted farmhouse, only to see all the lights go out as we knocked on the door, our dilemma seemed to worsen. Walking back down that driveway, the bleakness of our situation suddenly hit home.

Of course, it was decades before cell phones, and with no pay phones, neighbors or state patrol in sight, we decided to try for a compassionate motorist. This was a totally foreign alternative to us, and a little scary, especially with Nancy's compromised condition. We decided to walk north, since we remembered passing a service station some miles back that had still been open. Several motorists whizzed by, some moving toward the center line to avoid us. We heard an old car, across the highway, sputtering along in the opposite direction.

As we walked on, we again heard that sound—the old, sputtering car, struggling to keep going, only this time, it was coming in our direction. It

66

pulled up, stopping alongside us, and three rough-looking young men called out to ask if they could help us. They had seen our disabled truck, and then saw us walking, and decided to turn around and come back to offer help. Were they really going to help us, or were they up to no good? With reservations, but trying to trust, we climbed in among them.

They were on leave from the army and were heading back from Florida to their base in New York. Their old car was almost gone, and they had been stopping every now and then to pour water into the radiator to keep it from overheating. Although their tattoos and rough appearance didn't make them look the part of rescuers, they couldn't have been more respectful or helpful. They were especially sensitive to Nancy's "with child" condition, almost as if she were their own sister.

The old car kept plugging along and got us to the gas station. As we pulled in, the station attendant was just closing up for the night. When he learned of our problem, he told the young men that he would take it from there—he would take care of us and they could continue on back to their base. We thanked the three young men with real gratitude and again felt their compassion toward us as they told us good-bye.

The man at the station acted almost as though he had stayed open, expecting us. He locked up his station, drove us to our truck to remove the wheel, drove back to the station to repair the tire, and then again to the truck to put the wheel back on. He did all of this well after midnight on a Sunday, and didn't charge us anything. He stood watching us as we drove away, as if we were his own kids. His help to us was extraordinary—even back then, we knew that. We couldn't begin to understand why we had been treated so well, cared for so completely. We didn't have adequate words to thank him. Today we can see that all this help was directed by the Lord, eighteen years before our conversions. Even then, the Lord was watching over His kids, although we didn't know it. Prevenient grace, do you think?

Perhaps this event had more impact on me than I realized. I had not thought of it for some time, but it came to mind as I sat down to write about my own later experiences with hitchhikers. For years after this surprising experience, I had little sensitivity to hitchhikers, usually passing them by, not wanting to be bothered with them. Only after being baptized in the Spirit did

I feel a need, and have a heart, to help. Only then did I begin to empathize with their plight. It wasn't about my convenience, it was about their need, and the Holy Spirit quickened me to that need.

Being on the highway alone must feel like an extreme sort of homelessness (the area a hitchhiker is traveling through is often not "home"), and a lonely form of existence. Sometimes the Holy Spirit wants to help a wanderer along, not just with a free ride but with some added hope and joy. That encouragement may be the more important part. Many hitchhikers are trying not so much to get to a particular place as to keep moving, trying to get away from their pasts. If we are to be of any assistance, listening and caring are very important. I would soon learn that hitchhiker ministry is challenging, since there is often limited time to work with a person, and you have to be very sensitive to who they are and how they think. It's also potentially dangerous. If Nancy is with me, then we don't pick up hitchhikers.

No doubt we rarely provide a fix-all for hitchhikers, but we can help them, if we are open and willing to invest a little effort in them, and they can sense our genuine concern for them. There have been others along the way, but the stories that follow are about some of the hitchhikers who remain special in my memory.

> *"Give, and it will be given to you; good measure, pressed down, shaken together, running over, they will pour into your lap. For by your standard of measure it will be measured to you in return."*
>
> *—Luke 6:38 (NASB 1977)*

Red-Haired Hitchhiker

As my walk with the Lord progressed, I really expected Him to act everywhere, all the time, through the Holy Spirit. I was to be "on duty."

One morning, fairly early, I encountered a young man hitchhiking. He was standing on the side of the road, with bright red hair, a pretty lively spirit, and some urgency about him. The Lord told me to pull over and, "Get him." I pulled over, and he got right in. He said that his name was Jack. We began to head down the road. I was on the way to Buckhead, a suburb of Atlanta, to attend a meeting. Jack didn't have any particular place to go, so he was in full agreement with my agenda, however it worked out.

As we drove, he began to give me his story, telling me about how he had dropped out of the mainstream and become estranged from his family. He admitted to some dangerous drug use, and his arms gave witness to it. He was actually in the vicinity of his family's home, but had not contacted them at all. The family rift sounded like it cut both ways. Jack didn't want to get hurt again, but he also didn't want to pour salt in the old wounds of his family members. Even though Jack was really hurting, he definitely wasn't going near the family home on this trip.

Since he had no place to go, I wanted to help him, if he wanted help. I believed then that anybody who wanted help would be totally turned around and healed. I hadn't yet learned how hard it is to retrieve someone from Satan's long-term bondage, and how many ways he has to keep a grip on them.

When we got to Buckhead, I told Jack that I had two business appointments to keep. These would take awhile, but he could wait in the car if he wanted, and then I would try to help him. Jack willingly waited until I was finished, and then it was his turn. As we drove down the road, it began to dawn on me that I now "had" Jack until I could find a place for him. Not only had I made an investment in Jack, he had made one in me. I was suddenly aware that I had taken on a new responsibility.

At this point, I had only one place to bring him, and that was home. We arrived, sat down in the living room, and began trying to dig a little deeper into Jack's situation. Soon Nancy came home. She was rather surprised to walk in and find me at home talking with Jack. She was not expecting him to be part of her routine that day, and was not used to seeing people with needle-scarred arms in our house. But this type of thing was becoming more commonplace. Either of us might bring someone home to "get them help." She quickly got involved, and we began trying to find a place for Jack: a halfway house, a shelter, somewhere he could stay awhile and get his bearings. He indicated that he really wanted to get his life straightened out. Nancy and I both knew we needed to find him a place that day.

The pursuit of an available, appropriate place went on for most of the day. All the doors were closing. Finally, in the early evening, by way of several phone calls and information from various sources, we learned of a place south of Atlanta. It was a halfway house for ex-convicts and others with serious problems in a little place called Rex, Georgia, near the Atlanta airport. After we described Jack to them over the phone, we were told that if we brought him, they would take him in. It was getting late and Rex was almost an hour away, but Jack was too high a risk to keep overnight in our home, so we decided to take advantage of the only offer of the day.

It was 9:30 p.m. before we got there with Jack. The three of us walked in on a whole group of ex-cons and men in varying degrees of rehabilitation, trying to get their lives on track. It wasn't a comfortable scene for any of us to walk into, especially Nancy. I didn't feel very peaceful about having brought her along, but she was very capable in these types of situations. The ministry was headed by a man named Billy, whom we learned had been incarcerated years earlier with a very serious prison sentence. Supposedly, he was never going to be released, but a guard had pitched a paperback Bible to him while he was in solitary confinement. Billy had just consumed the Bible. Nobody quite knew how it got arranged, but soon afterward he was released from prison. Right away, he set out to start a halfway house for ex-convicts.

Billy began showing us around and introducing us to some of those in the group who had been there awhile. It was quite an interesting experience for all three of us. We could not have been treated more respectfully, and it was obvious that all of the men had the highest regard for Billy. He made it clear that he required Bible study twice a day, regular daily prayer time and lots of hard work. If anyone wasn't willing to do it all, he was out. This looked like just the place for Jack. Thankfully, he agreed to stay and try to make it work. Nancy and I were relieved! God had come through for all three of us. We prayed over him and said our goodbyes, leaving our phone number in case they needed us.

Over the next couple of weeks, we checked on Jack by phone. Billy said that he was doing great; he had really gotten in step with the program and had done all that was asked of him. He had grown in grace and the word of God, had a good heart and good intentions and was fitting in with the other men. It seemed as if Jack was well on the way toward recovery and making something of his life.

Then we got a distressing call. Some of Jack's old friends had learned where he was and had come for him. As his new friends from the halfway house watched from a distance, Jack got in the car with the old friends and left it all behind. Billy and the men at the halfway house were really disappointed. They believed Jack had had a real chance to turn his life around. None of them saw him again after that.

There were a lot of lessons in this experience. The biggest one for me was that we are called to do what God sends us out there to do—to deal with the people He puts in front of us and tells us "to get." We are rarely a "cure-all" or "fix-all" for these wounded people. We have a part to play, but ultimately, it is really between them and the Lord, and the outcome depends on what they are willing to do. I think the experience with Jack taught me that I wasn't called to bring hitchhikers home anymore. I could minister to them, but that ministry wasn't to involve bringing them home and finding them a place to live. I had to stay within my boundaries and resources and do my part, not try to be the whole answer. I had too many other commitments and not enough resources for that. We also learned that "old friends" and old habits are the biggest dangers to the wounded person and huge roadblocks to their being truly transformed and becoming the "new man."

Hopefully, Jack received enough of God's goodness and grace during his brief time at the halfway house with Billy and his men to rescue him later.

He got a good look at what works, and was already working, with those transformed ex-convicts—those "new creations" he was getting to know and respect and fit in with.

Maybe one day, if he hasn't already, he will want that transformed life for himself enough to turn from his bad-spirited old friends and their destructive ways and turn totally to Jesus. That's our prayer for Jack.

I have set before you life and death, the blessing and the curse. Choose life, then, that you and your descendants may live.

—Deuteronomy 30:19 (NASB)

Lewis and the Bowling Ball

One morning, I was headed to Mt. Paran Church of God, just north of Atlanta off I-75. It was a normal Saturday morning routine of mine to pray with a group of men there, six to eight of them, to experience what the Lord might do in the Spirit. Sometimes we would have prophecy, sometimes lots of prayer, sometimes impromptu readings of Scripture, being open to the Holy Spirit and whatever He would do for an hour or so. On the way there, I saw a man standing on the side of the road, trying to hitch a ride, and the Lord said, "Get him."

Pulling over, I asked the man where he was going. He said he was going south, heading for Florida, so anywhere I could take him further south would be a help. He was an interesting old guy, very pleasant, probably in his sixties, but with a whole lot of mileage. His name was Lewis. He said he had been on the street for a long time, and it had taken its toll. My attention was drawn to what he was carrying. He had three different items: an old tattered bag with some clothes, a plastic laundry bag with a sport coat, and a very worn, dirty vinyl bag with a bowling ball. This was my first hitchhiker with a bowling ball, so I asked Lewis about it. He explained that he had been carrying it across the country for the last fifteen years, while living on the street. During that time, he had never used it, but it was his prized possession; he hadn't been able to bring himself to turn it loose. I thought that maybe it maintained some attachment to his former life (before homelessness) and memories he wanted to hang onto. He had hauled this heavy bowling ball all those years, morning to night. I could almost feel his shoulders and back aching from the continual strain.

Lewis began to tell me some of his life story and about where he had been. It was a sad story; Lewis sounded like one who had met with hard times at every turn. He spoke of Christianity as though it was intended for others and beyond reach for him. I could almost picture him as a Christian and a typical family man. I wondered if his family had any idea where he was, and how long it had been since he had seen or talked to them. Did they pray for him and worry about his condition? He seemed to be just trying to deal with the day and keep moving, drawing the least attention possible.

As we got closer to Mt. Paran, I began directing the talk a little to see if Lewis would be open to going with me. I thought that maybe we could pray over him. I didn't tell him that part—just asked if he could go with me to prayers. At the last minute, he agreed. He was probably smarter about what that might mean than I realized. He may have suspected something good would happen if he went, or at least, that he shouldn't close the door to the possibility.

So we went in, and I introduced Lewis to the men. They were all very gracious to him, accepting him right into the group (believing the Lord had sent him), and we all gathered around the altar rails. The Spirit present at Mt. Paran seemed to be really ministering to Lewis' spirit. We all prayed over him and were about to send him off when the men decided they wanted to raise some money for Lewis so he wouldn't have to hitchhike to Florida. They gathered $35, out of their pockets, and quietly handed the money to me for a bus ticket for Lewis. As we left, I told him what they had done, drove him to the station, and gave him the money for the bus ticket. Lewis was really appreciative and, I believe, surprised. I don't think he intended to ask for anything; he knew he had already received a special blessing. For a non-Christian, he seemed to have an unusual level of acceptance of what life brought—good or bad.

Then a memorable thing happened. As I was leaving him at the station, Lewis shocked me with a major decision: He wanted to give me his bowling ball. That ball was almost sacred to him, but he wanted me to have it as a token of his appreciation. Unfortunately, I forgot to be alert and be the "new man" and reverted to reasoning as I had in the past, not "seeing into" what was happening. I just wasn't thinking beyond myself at that moment. Since I didn't need or want it, I didn't see that I should take that old bowling ball and tattered bag. So I thanked Lewis for the thought but told him that I thought he should hold onto his ball; it was probably too valuable to him to give away. He immediately saw right through me, that I was too proud to take his gift. I could feel his disappointment as he headed toward the bus. It probably felt like rejection of him and all he had—as though everything about him was dirty and worthless. While offering to help Lewis along, I had instead miserably failed to consider him and his real need.

I have reflected on that many times since, and kick myself for not accepting Lewis' heartfelt gift that he needed to give. I did not allow Lewis to give his sacred bowling ball and return an act of kindness. I blocked his good intentions and probably confused him as well—and his understanding of Christians. I had totally spoiled his chance to feel self-respect from bestowing his gift.

If I had taken the bowling ball, I would have thought of Lewis every time I saw it, remembering to pray for him. It would have helped me to remember that everyone needs to be able to give—that both giving and receiving are meant for everyone. Through this experience, I've tried to learn to not deprive anyone of giving, no matter what they have, and gaining some self-respect as a giver. As the Lord teaches us, *"It's more blessed to give than to receive." (Acts 20:35, NIV)*

Even without the bowling ball, I often think of Lewis. I helped him a little in a surface way that day, but failed him in a much deeper way. Receiving respect and being treated like an equal may be the aspects of life that homeless or street people long for the most, and rarely experience. It would take many years and crossing paths many times with disenfranchised people on the street for me to learn that, and even longer to live it. There are two sides to every encounter with strangers, and God has His hand on both. I would learn that no encounter should ever be taken for granted.

Let each of you esteem and look upon and be concerned for not merely his own interests, but also each for the interests of others. Let this same attitude and purpose and humble mind be in you which was in Christ Jesus: Let Him be your example in humility.
—Philippians 2:4-5 (APMC)

Nathan and the Revealed Word

It was a Saturday morning and there he was, stationed at a popular major intersection on I-75 South, hoping to catch a ride. I remembered my experience with Lewis, who had been standing in almost the same place a few months earlier, and how the Lord had blessed him. I quickly pulled over and invited the young man to get in.

He was in his late twenties, tall and lanky. He said that his name was Nathan. He didn't look like a typical hitchhiker, and he appeared smarter than most, perhaps even well educated. Although Nathan said that he had family in the area, he had been sleeping out in the woods, unwilling to let them know he was nearby. It was immediately apparent that his family relationships were severely strained, if not broken.

Nathan was hitchhiking south. I told him how far I was going and what I was doing, and that I'd be glad to help him get farther down the road. Since we had about ten miles to go before my destination, Mt. Paran Church of God, I asked Nathan to share a little about his trip and his life. I always figure that hitchhikers have their stories to tell (it's never just the ride that they need).

With that, Nathan's story began to unfold. He told me about his life and all that had happened to him. He acknowledged some drug use, but said his real problem was the lifetime of mistreatment he had received from his family and their failure to understand him. Nathan went on to expound on how he felt about the rotten deal he had been given by each of them. He developed this story in such detail and with such apparently pained feelings that I felt confident he had retold it to many others along the way. It was clear that Nathan was caught up in a lot of self-pity and bitterness. His only real interest seemed to be in recounting how tough life had been on him.

During our ten-minute drive, I tried to interject some encouragement here and there about what the Lord could do and how Nathan could be reconciled with his family, but he showed little interest in listening or in making an effort to change things, and just let his sorrowful story roll on.

We were approaching the exit to Mt. Paran, so I told Nathan that this was where I would be turning off. He was welcome to go with me to the church and to prayers, or I could let him out there on I-75 and he could hitch another ride. Either way would be fine—it was his choice. I was not making a real effort to encourage him to go with me. He had already drained away most of my patience, which was always short with people who could, but wouldn't, try. At the last second, Nathan surprised me and decided to go to the prayer gathering.

As we walked into the church, we were greeted by the regular Saturday morning group. Most of them had been present when Lewis had come with me, and they remembered their ministry to him. They received Nathan into the gathering like a new friend, with nothing more than a first-name introduction. I think they suspected that the Lord had brought him there for some kind of ministry. If Jesus had sent him, that was plenty good enough.

With no further conversation and without hesitation, we all knelt down around the altar rails to pray, and Nathan knelt right there among us. We prayed silently for about ten minutes, with not a word spoken by anyone, and then the silence was suddenly broken. Ben, the acknowledged spiritual leader of the group, had quietly stood and walked over next to Nathan. Ben was an elder at Mt. Paran, a consummate gentleman, very intelligent and knowledgeable, calm and collected, full of wisdom. Ben also was frequently used by the Holy Spirit in a strong exercise of the gift of prophecy and words of knowledge.

Ben laid his hands on Nathan's head and began to deliver a word of knowledge. He recounted the story of Nathan's life just as Nathan had told it to me as we drove down I-75, virtually word for word. Ben repeated the details of how Nathan had grown up feeling his family had mistreated him and that the whole world and life itself had been against him. Through the leading of the Holy Spirit, Ben didn't leave out any of the particulars that Nathan had shared with me, none of which Ben or anyone else in the group (except for me) had heard before.

When Ben had finished sharing this word of knowledge, the Holy Spirit inspired him to bring forth a prophetic word concerning what the Lord thought of Nathan's attitude, self-pity and bitterness, and what the Lord expected Nathan to do about it. As the Holy Spirit revealed it to him, Ben described how Nathan had placed himself and his family in bondage through his self-concern and disregard for all of them. Ben told how bitterness had taken root and grown into a huge vine of self-pity that was consuming Nathan and choking the life out of him. Through Ben, the Spirit went on to tell Nathan that he was to repent of his thoughts and actions, go and ask his family members for forgiveness, and ask to be accepted once more into the family. Wow! These were hard words even for us to hear. The Holy Spirit had spoken—and it must have been like a piercing sword, straight into Nathan's heart. With that, Ben quietly returned to the altar rail, knelt down and resumed praying.

After a time of praying and reflecting on the Lord's intervention, we concluded and all stood up, but Nathan was missing. He apparently had heard all he wanted to hear and decided to start walking back to the highway. We hoped he went north toward home and didn't continue running away. I went on to confirm the words that Ben had spoken to Nathan, sharing with them Nathan's discourse as we had driven down I-75. None of the group had doubted, but the way in which the Holy Spirit had delivered definitely built our faith—and encouraged each of us to step out and use our spiritual gifts more readily.

The Holy Spirit had spoken into Nathan's heart that morning in a way that probably no one who Nathan knew would have been allowed to do. His defenses and the spirits of self-pity and bitterness were too entrenched. By means of the spiritual gifts, God cut right through it all to reach Nathan's heart and sense of reason. None of the group will likely ever forget this powerful delivery of God's tough love. Hopefully, Nathan won't either. We pray it was the key to unlock those chains that Satan had on him. We hope that it set him free to be grateful and seek God's plan.

> *Thank God in everything [no matter what the circumstances may be, be thankful and give thanks]... Do not quench the Holy Spirit. Do not spurn the gifts and utterances of the prophets—do not depreciate prophetic revelations nor despise inspired instruction or exhortation or warning.*
> *—I Thessalonians 5:18-20 (AMPC)*

Black Muslim Prophet

One morning, as I was taking a trip in my El Camino to a little place several miles north of my shop, my eye was drawn to a tall, lean man standing under a bridge abutment trying to hitch a ride. He had the look of the "Uncola Man" frequently seen around that time in TV commercials. Dark-skinned, well over six feet tall, with a shiny, bald, shaved head and a rangy build, he was very distinctive looking. The Holy Spirit highlighted him and just said, "Get him." So I pulled over next to him and called out, "Where you going?"

"Anywhere," he said.

"In that case, get in," I replied.

When someone tells you that they are open to going anywhere, they don't have a lot of plans. It puts you on triple alert—this guy's looks already had. He climbed into the El Camino, and with effort, got himself into the passenger seat. He was scrunched in tightly, with his knees against the dash and his head virtually against the ceiling of the truck. He looked extra tall and very uncomfortable. I sensed, though, that he would have been uncomfortable regardless of the amount of space in my passenger seat. His discomfort was somewhat distracting to me. I didn't know exactly why.

I told him my destination and we started down the road. Hoping to make both of us more comfortable, I asked him where he would like to go, if he could go anywhere. (At least, it was some effort at conversation.) He said he would take a sabbatical, but he would need $200, which he didn't have. I asked, "What kind of sabbatical?"

"Well, I am a Black Muslim prophet," he said, and then he explained that the sabbatical was offered by his Black Muslim group.

"A Black Muslim prophet, huh?" I answered. He kind of muttered an acknowledgment that he was. Neither of us was overly impressed with the other. But he was my first Black Muslim prophet hitchhiker. That was special.

As we drove down the road, I tried to interest him in a conversation about the sabbatical and his beliefs. Even Black Muslims can be evangelized. After confirming what he already knew, that I couldn't help him with the $200, I tried to pursue the issue. I told him that his belief was fine, nothing wrong with him being a Black Muslim prophet, except there wasn't any salvation in it—it would only lead to death. To my surprise, just about that time, I realized we were going in the wrong direction. I had made a wrong turn and we were now traveling away from our destination instead of towards it.

I told the prophet what I had done, that I'd made a wrong turn while talking to him, and explained that we needed to turn around. "Just hang on," I said. We turned around and began heading again in the right direction. Feeling a real burden for his soul, I resumed talking to him about being a Black Muslim and the need for him to realize that Jesus was the only answer in his life or anybody else's. We had not gone much further, just a couple of minutes' driving, when I realized that I had made another wrong turn. I was rather embarrassed and felt a little dumb (this was a route I had taken several times before), but then the Spirit revealed something very important. I kept my voice pleasant but didn't hide my surprise, and told him what had happened.

"You are not gonna believe this, but I just made another wrong turn. Seems like ever since you got in the truck, there has been a spirit of confusion over everything." I had new peace through this discernment, even as we went in the wrong direction.

As soon as I said the word confusion, the prophet jerked his head around and looked at me, wild eyed, and blurted out, "What are you trying to do? Kill me?"

I said "No, brother, I am trying to help you, not trying to kill you or hurt you or anything else—just help you. We are going to turn around and get headed in the right direction, just like I promised."

A second time, in a loud, more anxious voice, he asked, "What are you trying to do? Kill me?" His face was filled with anxiety and fear.

I said, "No, no, we just have a spirit of confusion here in the truck and it's causing strange things to happen. But we are going to be fine. Just hang on."

The prophet then pronounced, as if talking to himself, "I'm getting out of here!"

"No, no, just stay put, right where you are, we're turning around right here. We'll be fine." I was doing my best to settle him down while paying attention to my driving and the traffic.

We had come into a congested business district that was bustling with midmorning activity. I was driving about five miles an hour, making a U-turn to the left, when the passenger door was flung open and the prophet just leapt out. He actually jumped out of the moving truck. With his knees touching the dash, and with his height, I don't know how he got out without tripping and getting run over. But he sprang out wildly and took off, loping up a nearby hill as fast as he could.

I stopped the truck and called out after him, "Jesus loves you, brother. He really loves you." Looking back over his shoulder as he ran, he had the wildest look on his face that you can imagine, and quickly disappeared over the hill, fast as he could go. It was the last I saw of the Black Muslim prophet!

It was an incredible teaching for me on the power of truth over demonic spirits. The Black Muslim prophet obviously was very much under the spirit of confusion. That spirit did not want him to entertain any more Jesus talk, and did not want any more truth being spoken to him. For the demons, it was a lot safer just bailing him out of the moving truck than allowing him to stay. They didn't want to take any chances on losing their control over him. The stronghold of darkness certainly didn't want the spirit of confusion challenged. I guess he'd been running away from Jesus his whole life (that was probably why he was a Black Muslim), and the demons feared that Jesus was closing in on him that morning. I could relate to him. I had run from Jesus for a couple of decades myself.

Resist the devil and he will flee from you.

—James 4:7 (KJV)

Healings for Mario

One day, Nancy and I got a call from a charismatic woman who lived out of town. (By "charismatic," I mean that she fully believed in all of the gifts and fruits of the Holy Spirit.) The woman said that her grandson, Antonio, had recently been taken to our local hospital with meningitis and desperately needed prayers from someone who believed that the Lord heals through prayer and the laying on of hands.

Because of our activity in our church prayer group, the call came to us. We recruited another couple, Fred and Lynn, and headed straight to the hospital. Antonio was about nine years old, and just days earlier had become sick with a fast-moving, aggressive meningitis. His prognosis was poor, his condition life threatening. His father and mother, Mario and Elaine, were at the hospital and in a very distressed state about their son's condition. Trying to talk with them before praying, in hopes of learning more about the situation to better know how to pray, didn't make matters better. In fact, tension appeared to be building, especially with Mario, the father. He seemed to have a lot of unresolved issues in his life, and perhaps the most significant was that he wasn't churched. He had grown up in church and was very familiar with it, but like many, he had dropped out as an adult. His interest in church and his faith had been replaced by the pursuit of material things, which at this point he probably considered more important.

The exchange between Mario and our friend Fred had become really edgy by the time we got around to praying. Fred and I had been somewhat heavy-handed and direct with Mario, and the tension was thick. We were zealous about seeing Antonio healed and getting Mario to see truth, but working toward both objectives at once made things a little strained. In the end, Antonio's serious condition carried the moment. We began praying over Antonio, asking his parents to join us in prayer and to place their hands on their son. When the prayers appeared complete and seemed to have covered all we had come for, we put the situation in the Lord's hands, concluded the prayer, and prepared to leave. We had not been there long, but the experience had been quite intense and Spirit filled. We invited Mario and Elaine to visit our prayer meeting sometime, believing this to be the next step toward their healing. We left feeling good about Antonio, "believing for" his healing, but not feeling good about Mario. We knew his pride had been hurt—and that was largely our fault. We were hopeful about Elaine and what she might do if Mario didn't make life too hard for her.

Within two weeks, Elaine showed up at the prayer meeting by herself. She gave us a great report: Antonio had been totally healed just days after we prayed over him. The doctors had been very surprised and couldn't account for his rapid recovery. Elaine told them about Antonio being prayed over, convinced that Jesus had brought about the healing. She was ecstatic and was personally open to more of what the Lord might have for her and her family. She did go on to say, however, that even though Antonio had been healed, and her husband Mario was thankful for that, he was irate about some of the things that had been said to him at the hospital when we came to pray. He was especially upset about the suggestion that his separation from God might have something to do with Antonio's illness. Elaine went on to say that Mario "wasn't about to come" to the prayer meeting.

We knew that Jesus is in the healing business and we wanted to see Antonio stay healed. It was obvious that Mario needed an overhaul. We had Elaine sit in proxy for Mario (in place of him), laid hands on her, and began praying. Then we just asked the Lord to heal the whole family at once. God was far more patient with us than Mario had been. Looking back on it, our manner and style toward him at the hospital that day had been harsh and insensitive—immature, at best. We hadn't taken into account his stressed state of mind due to his son's condition. Hopefully, we would be more understanding if the same situation arose today, but we did what we knew to do at the time. God worked around our shortcomings and healed little Antonio anyway, in spite of our "help."

Elaine became a regular member of the Thursday night prayer meetings, straightaway got baptized in the Holy Spirit, and was on fire for the Lord. We all joined her in continuing to pray for Mario's salvation and for the family— whatever it took. Just a few weeks after that, Elaine walked in to the prayer meeting with Mario. A change had come about in him. He was venturing to "come and see" for himself the great things that had been happening for his wife, and was wondering if there could possibly be something there for him. We saw his coming as an answer to Elaine's prayers, and ours. We were far more patient with him this time. Amazingly, he responded as if among trusted friends and family.

Mario became a regular on Thursday nights and soon got baptized in the Holy Spirit and was even more dramatically on fire for the Lord than Elaine. His fiery, passionate nature was good, dry wood for Holy Spirit fire. Mario was an entrepreneur from New York with two small businesses, one a taxi service, the other a car wash. One of his earliest inspired "new man" thoughts was to hang some of our crosses up for sale in his car wash office to get the Good News out. I imagine it became the holiest-looking car wash in town. He prominently displayed the crosses there for several months. We didn't sell any of the crosses, but that didn't bother any of us. Mario got the chance to answer a lot of questions and tell of Antonio's miracle healing, and he got a taste of being "in the world but not of it." I felt really honored to be asked to hang our crosses at his business, especially after roughing him up a little (verbally and spiritually) on our first meeting.

Mario was merging his old life and what he knew about business with his new life, trying to make something good happen. The Lord is probably amused by many of our impulsive ideas and efforts—but certainly He is pleased that we feel compelled to act on them.

Probably the best part of this experience was that Mario recognized the Lord's transforming blessings, and he cared enough about his family to swallow his wounded pride and his anger and ask the Lord to give the family a whole new direction. Mario's new faith and zeal may have melted the hearts of lots of hardened men who had turned their backs on the Lord. As far as we know, the whole family remained healed and moved forward together in their new life in the Lord.

And after he brought them out, he said, "Sirs, what must I do to be saved?"

They said, "Believe in the Lord Jesus, and you will be saved, you and your household."

And they spoke the word of the Lord to him together with all who were in his house...

And he brought them into his house and set food before them, and rejoiced greatly, having believed in God with his whole household.

—Acts 16:30-34 (NASB)

In the Name of Jesus, Walk!

One day, Nancy and I received a call from a friend of ours, a Spirit-filled Methodist minister. A woman he didn't know had telephoned him to request a visit and prayers for her daughter, who needed urgent help. As the mother told it, the daughter seemed to be locked in a chair, couldn't move and was unresponsive, staring straight ahead. Our friend was overcommitted already and asked us to go in his place and see what could be done. We got a quick "yes" from the Holy Spirit and told our friend we would go right away.

This prayer request had a strange feeling about it—it seemed spiritually loaded—so I called our longtime friend Bill to see if he and his wife Dian could join us. After hearing a short explanation, Bill also sensed the urgency of the situation. We agreed that since the address given for the woman was only a few miles from Bill and Dian's home, their place would be ideal to "go out" from.

Nancy and I arrived at Bill and Dian's and, without hesitation, the four of us began to pray about this ministry. Within minutes it was confirmed to all of us, in our spirits, that the wives should stay back and intercede in prayer while Bill and I went to the address and prayed over the woman. This felt like the right approach, as the mission appeared rather ominous and we had a sense that there was demonic oppression involved.

With some degree of uncertainty, Bill and I drove slowly down the narrow street lined with small apartment buildings on both sides, the area getting more depressed the further we went. We finally spotted the correct number and pulled over to park. It was time to see what the Holy Spirit would do. But as we quietly walked toward the apartment, we didn't feel we really belonged there. This would require the Holy Spirit's leading, and our patient listening.

Our knock on the door was met with an immediate response from the mother, who graciously welcomed and ushered us into their home. She was a healthy looking, pleasant woman of faith in her mid-fifties, but she was very worried, and it showed. Her name was Doris and she pointed toward her daughter, Wanda, and introduced us.

Wanda was probably in her mid-twenties, a waif of a woman. Curled up tight in a nearly fetal position, she looked as though her life was evaporating right in front of our eyes. Her mother told us that this was the second day that Wanda had been in this position without moving. Neither Wanda nor her mother thought she could stand up. Wanda also wasn't talking. She was just staring straight ahead, looking almost terrified, as if in a trance. Her body was there in the chair, but she was scarcely present.

We began to gently talk with Doris and Wanda about God's love. Doris had no problem with that, and it seemed she already knew the Lord quite well. For Wanda, this was going to be a rather slow process, but it was starting to work—it was as though she were beginning to thaw. Bill's gifts of love and personal ministry were soothing her spirit and her mind and bringing her to life. Observing her closely, we both had a strong sense that this problem was not physical, but entirely spiritual.

We took authority "in the name of Jesus" over all demonic forces holding Wanda incapable of moving, standing or walking. We then told Wanda to stand up. Standing was a huge challenge, as she had been locked in that fetal position for almost two days. With our help, she was with difficulty able to stand—very still. Then, very slowly, she began to move her legs, one at a time, like someone stepping out on thin ice. Gently, we told Wanda, "Walk!" Gradually, she began to slowly walk, then to walk in a large circle, at a normal pace, with the biggest, broadest smile imaginable. She was much like a little child walking for the first time. It was an exhilarating sight to witness—a release from bondage right in front of our eyes. Perhaps it was a little like Lazarus coming out of the tomb.

Then we encouraged her to run, and that was even easier. She jogged around the perimeter of the room several times, each time a little faster, like a trained runner in good condition, almost effortlessly. Wow! We were all four amazed—nearly overwhelmed by the power of God's touch on Wanda and how she had been set free from the evil grip holding her immobile. We shouldn't have been surprised. After all, similar events are recorded in the Book of Acts, and God's desire to free us never changes!

After reassuring Wanda and Doris that the healing had come from Jesus and He had great plans for them both, we gave them our phone numbers and prepared to leave. They were most grateful for God's love poured over them, and they stood there together on the porch as a mother and daughter with a new beginning—savoring the wonderful thing the Lord had just done. Doris' appreciation was probably even greater than Wanda's and certainly must have deepened her already strong faith.

We didn't know what had happened to cause Wanda to be in that comatose-like condition, and we didn't ask. That wasn't what we had been sent for, and getting to the heart of the problem could have been another ministry of its own. We knew Whom it would take to set her free, and we asked for Him, Jesus, to do just that. Our visit at their apartment took less than an hour and then we were heading back to our wives, who had been praying for us all.

Our God is quick to answer, especially when He is asked to release His people from Satan's bondage. When Jesus sets you free, you are free indeed!

"Silver and gold have I none, but what I have, that I give you.
In the name of Jesus Christ of Nazareth, get up and walk!"

—Acts 3:6 (WEB)

Holed Up

The ongoing involvement in the parking lot ministry had resulted in the development of a real bond between Bill, Jerry and me. We had observed the fruits of working together in the Holy Spirit and giving Him space to call forth the gifts needed for the occasion. From time to time, we got into each other's way a little bit—but we were learning. Our Catholic-Baptist mix was a sign to others of God's power through unity.

One day, Jerry got a call from a very distraught mother about her son Johnny, who was holed up in his house, alone and depressed. She feared he might even be a danger to himself. It made sense that she thought to call Jerry. The mother and son had belonged to the same church as Jerry for some time, but Johnny had drifted away. The mother remembered Jerry's own story and contacted him.

Jerry had been a long-haired, rebellious, roughneck motorcyclist, the son of a devout, prayerful couple. His parents had prayed tirelessly for Jerry and for a "good woman" to come into his life and turn him around. Once the Holy Spirit laid hold of Jerry through Helen, who became his wife, he turned into a new man. He was now a Bible-toting, gospel-living crusader for Jesus, a picture of physical and spiritual strength, ready to attack evil. Now many were glad that they were on the same side he was.

Jerry told Bill and me about the mother's distressing call. He knew the man, Johnny, was an ordained minister, but did not know him well and over time had lost track of him. We all agreed that Johnny needed a visit—the sooner, the better.

Early one morning, we gathered for prayers at Bill's house and asked the Holy Spirit to anoint us for the mission and give us revelation knowledge. We opened the Bible, Russian roulette style, letting the Holy Spirit decide where we should read. After carefully reading the passage of Scripture, we headed off with a great sense of purpose to the address.

The house was located in a blue-collar area of old, small houses with small yards, all crowded together in a haphazard configuration. The neighborhood was mostly still asleep as we arrived, but a few of the surrounding houses had activity. The local dogs had discovered that we were there, but Johnny's house was conspicuously silent. Hoping for the best, but fearing the worst, we rang the doorbell. There was no response. The house was locked and looked deserted, eerily quiet.

After much ringing of the doorbell and knocking on the door and a prolonged wait, the three of us stood there looking at each other, thinking we might have misheard the Lord about this visit (or at least, about the timing). The neighborhood dogs, now gathered at the fences, had decided that we definitely did not belong and were letting everyone know it. Deep down we all knew that the Holy Spirit never misses, so we continued to wait. Then we heard a slight noise. The front door was being unlocked and opened very slowly—just a little. A pitiful-looking, disheveled man stood hanging onto the door. The room behind him was dark. This beat-down shadow of a man, Johnny, recognized Jerry right off, and Bill and I were introduced. Then Johnny, reluctantly, with a rather shamefaced look, asked us to come inside.

Of course, on entering a house that is filled with depression and heavy spirits, you can really feel them and can almost smell them. It's a spirit stench like no other. All of the signs of a failing life, a life given up on, surrounded us—with one exception. Visible through the doorway was a large Bible, open on a table in the next room.

The Holy Spirit had me tell Jerry to go to it, leave it open to where it was, and read the verse that his eyes fell on. Jerry walked to the Bible, looked down intently, and read the exact verse that we had just read together at Bill's house before starting our venture a short time earlier.

> *But Zion said, "The Lord has forsaken me,*
> *And the Lord has forgotten me."*
> *"Can a woman forget her nursing child*
> *And have no compassion on the son of her womb?*

Even these may forget, but I will not forget you.
Behold, I have inscribed you on the palms of My hands;
Your walls are continually before Me."
　　　　　　　　　　　　　　　　　—*Isaiah 49:14-16 (NASB)*

Wow! The exact verse! What a sign. We hadn't missed it after all. We were right where we were supposed to be at this moment in time, and we knew we needed to get to work. The three of us began to work on Johnny. We reasoned with him, encouraged him, reminded him of who he was and God's promises, prayed for him, and listened to where the Spirit was leading and what the Spirit was revealing. It was arduous and intense, and we definitely sensed that Johnny's future hung in the balance. He was surprisingly open and receptive.

After a time, when the Holy Spirit's intentions for this trip seemed accomplished, we stood up. Johnny looked better—not great, but better. He no longer looked like a danger to himself. Some level of hope and returning reason were noticeable. The next step would be up to him. It seemed time for us to leave. We each hugged Johnny, blessed him, and left quietly but thankfully, grateful that the Holy Spirit had touched us all in this time of dire need. We all left our phone numbers, but Johnny never called any of us.

Several months later, Bill was out walking near his own home when a truck slowed down and pulled alongside him. The driver was Johnny. Bill told us later that he looked peaceful and happy. Johnny told him that he was back in the ministry, that everything had turned around for him and he was doing well. He also wanted Bill to be sure to tell Jerry and me that when we arrived at his house that morning and rang the doorbell, he had the barrel of a loaded pistol in his mouth, ready to pull the trigger.

God's timing is perfect.

He drew me up out of a horrible pit [a pit of tumult and destruction], out of the miry clay (froth and slime), and set my feet upon a rock, steadying my steps and establishing my goings.

And He has put a new song in my mouth, a song of praise to our God.
　　　　　　　　　　　　　　　　　—*Psalm 40:1-3 (AMPC)*

Chapter 4

Prophetic Words (Words of Knowledge)

One night at a large gathering of the Alleluia Community, we were all shocked by an announcement from Larry, a dentist in the community. Larry stood up with his wife Mary and their three daughters to tell us alarming news. That day he had been diagnosed with a deadly prostate cancer, and had a PSA level of 159 ng/mL (a normal level for his age would have been 4 ng/mL). The doctors told him that he likely had only six months to live, at most, and that he should go home and get his affairs in order.

Larry and his family looked distraught, and everyone else in the gathering did, also. He asked for our prayers and those started immediately. Larry quickly became the most prayed-over person in Augusta; he was prayed over at meetings, at home, at his office, and in passing. People sought him out just to pray over him.

A couple of days after the meeting in which Larry announced his diagnosis, I had an unexpected, clear vision. It was like watching a movie in full color on the big screen. I saw Larry walking his daughter Rachel down the aisle. He was in a tux, and she was in her sparkling wedding gown. And they both looked great! It could not have been clearer in any way.

The next time I saw Larry, I told him, "Larry, I saw you walking Rachel down the aisle!" Larry scoffed at me and growled out, "Rachel's eight years old."

My response was, "I know Rachel is eight, but she sure wasn't when I saw the two of you walking. She was no girl, not even a really young woman, but a mature young lady—and you were walking her down the aisle."

Larry seemed to seriously doubt what I was saying. I would guess he was about 90% skeptical of that word, and yet I knew that he had heard me and wanted to believe.

This became a standard practice when I ran into Larry, and it happened countless times. Whenever I saw him and had the opportunity, I would say,

"Larry, I saw you walking Rachel down the aisle." Larry passed this word on to Mary, Rachel and the rest of his family. As time went on, they all began to hold onto that word with hope and faith. This was especially true when Larry's cancer would flare back up, his counts would rise, and he would start treatments again.

In 2002, Larry was told that he had six months to live. In August of 2018, he walked Rachel, a 24-year-old beauty, down the aisle. Larry looked the best we had ever seen him look.

Larry's wife Mary told me later that she shed tears when she saw me arrive for the wedding. I shed mine when I saw Larry and Rachel step into the aisle.

This prophetic word became such a key part of their lives that Rachel had a wedding picture made of her with her dad and me, just to remember what God had promised for her great day. He keeps His Word!

Soon after Rachel's wedding date was announced, I saw Larry. I smiled and said, "Larry, I hear you're walking Rachel down the aisle!"

With his dry sense of humor, he responded, "Yeah, I hope I don't drop dead at the altar."

As I have said, he certainly didn't. Larry remained in the same condition for the next year, and then the cancer reasserted itself quickly and took him.

Larry didn't live that final season in fear or anxiety. He used the time in a very productive way to get his family well positioned to carry on without him. This was his time to go—nearly eighteen years after that first diagnosis.

Prophetic words can be life giving, and sometimes even life saving. My first experience with a prophetic word was on October 17, 1969, when I was driving on the highway and a voice said, "Buckle your seat belt!" I did (for the very first time) buckle up. Ten minutes later I was in a high-speed, deadly, head-on collision at the top of a hill. I never even saw the car that hit me. I was a total unbeliever at the time, with no passport to Heaven. Years later, after my spiritual awakening, I realized those four words, "Buckle your seat belt," had spared my body and my soul as well.

Over the last forty years, I have received many prophetic words that have literally directed the path of my family. Words like, "Which had you rather have, your pride or My will?" I knew instantly what that meant when I heard it, and I chose His will, which launched a new business venture. My business is now thirty-seven years old.

A word two years later released our family from waiting any longer to relocate to Augusta to join the Alleluia Community. "Unless you are willing to turn loose what I have given you, you won't be able to take hold of what I want to give you." The discussion was over. We moved.

These are just three examples among many prophetic words and words of knowledge that I have received over the years from the Lord, either directly or through others who spoke them to me. Not one of them was off the mark.

Years ago, a word of knowledge was given to the Alleluia Community music ministry. We were already in our van, ready to drive three hours to a conference. Dale, an elder of few words but with sharp spiritual gifts, especially discernment, came to pray a "go out" blessing over us and our mission.

When he had finished the blessing prayer, he told us he had a word for us. "You will encounter a person with a witchcraft spirit [a controlling, manipulative spirit], who is disruptive, five feet, eight inches to five feet, nine inches tall—and the person is not one of you." That was it. Dale left.

As we drove down the road, we discussed it for awhile. When we arrived at the host church, no one was there to let us in. Someone finally came but didn't have the key to the building. After more delay, we finally got into the building, but then things got worse. In particular, there were disruptions with the sound equipment as we began to set up. Our leader, Bob, had left the church with the priest that we had just met; they had gone to get something we needed. When Bob and the priest returned, Bob told us that the priest was "the one." Bob had discerned this, but in addition, the priest's height matched the description given by Dale.

The priest had decided that he was supposed to lead all of our music, and that Bob would be sitting down with the rest of the group. The priest also had some songs that he felt strongly about including in the program, and he wanted to sing a couple of solos himself.

Our group began to put the pieces of Dale's word together, and we all began to quietly pray against the spirits of witchcraft and disruption, and for the release of the spiritual bondage over the priest. We prepared to do what we had come to do.

As the meeting began, the priest seemed to completely forget everything he had told us about his changes to the music plans. Bob led us through our program, as had been planned.

Afterwards, our group was asked to pray over the congregation, and the priest came up to us and asked to be prayed over for the Baptism of the Holy Spirit. We prayed, and he received—and he looked and acted like a different person, one who had been set free.

All of the prophetic words mentioned here have been important, sometimes directional, sometimes correctional, some to inform, some to give courage, some to address fear or pride, but all were intended to be taken in and acted upon. I have scores of friends who pray for and depend on the wisdom of such words—and the Holy Spirit does not disappoint. Scripture tells of numerous occasions when prophets were sent to address kings with words from God.

Across the community, there have likely been several hundred such instances like these I have described. Without these words being given and acted upon, the community probably would not resemble what it is today. The Alleluia Community even devotes the first prayer meeting of the year to receiving prophetic words and printing them out so that we can more fully reflect on and understand them. Usually if one listens to, receives, and acts positively on prophetic words and words of knowledge, that person will be entrusted to deliver those kinds of words to others. It's a wonderful thing to know you're being used to build others' faith or trust, to embolden them to step out and act on their faith, or sometimes, to deliver a word of adjustment or correction that is needed but simply won't be received any other way.

The Holy Spirit knows what each of us needs and can deliver in His way.

Of course, the words that are stunning are the ones we tend to remember the most. The following event rocked our community one night.

The crowd was arriving at our gym for the community's regular Thursday night prayer meeting when, just minutes before the meeting was due to begin, a phone call came informing us that our sister Sue had unexpectedly been struck down by a brain aneurism. She was in a local hospital and near death. Her grave condition immediately became the focus of our prayer meeting; everything else was put aside. Meanwhile, a small group rushed to the hospital to be with her in prayer.

Sue's condition deteriorated rapidly, and all the news was dire. She soon flatlined, and her doctor told the family that neither he nor the hospital could do anything more for her. He was leaving so that her family and friends could be alone with her at the time of her death, and he went home.

About an hour into the prayer meeting, as we continued to storm heaven, begging the Lord for Sue's life, Leo, a brother who frequently delivered prophetic words and words of knowledge, rushed to the microphone to say, "Look at your watches—Sue is being healed right now!"

A phone call was immediately made to those at the hospital who were praying. Their report was that Harriet, a close friend of Sue, had said to her comatose sister (at exactly the time the prophetic word was given at our gym), "Sue, we love you." With that, Sue sat straight up in bed and replied, "Harriet, I love you, too!" Sue had returned to life!

For weeks she underwent numerous tests and scans at Emory Hospital in Atlanta. The doctors there finally proclaimed that her healing was a miracle.

Three weeks after Sue had flatlined, as the community was having our usual prayer meeting, in came Sue, with her husband Larry's help. Instantly, the gym was charged with excitement, and a portable microphone was quickly taken to Sue. We all listened intently.

Sue told us how the Lord had saved her life, and she thanked us for all the prayers and love shown to her and to Larry, and she told us how great it was to be back. She was articulate and talked for a few minutes. A couple of times, she interrupted herself to say, "Oh, Jesus wanted me to be sure to tell you, when I saw you the next time..."

Surely the Sovereign Lord does nothing without revealing His plan to His servants the prophets.

—Amos 3:7 (NIV)

We also have the prophetic message as something completely reliable, and you will do well to pay attention to it, as to a light shining in a dark place, until the day dawns and the morning star rises in your hearts. Above all, you must understand that no prophecy of Scripture came about by the prophet's own interpretation of things. For prophecy never had its origin in the human will, but prophets, though human, spoke from God as they were carried along by the Holy Spirit.

—2 Peter 1:19-21 (NIV)

Not Yet

The Fox Theatre on Peachtree Street in Atlanta was undergoing restoration of some of its storefronts, and we had the woodworking job. It was a small job, and we had been there but a few days. Our work was independent of the other trades, so we had not come to know anyone else on the site. One Friday afternoon, I had a couple of men working in the storefront area, and I was preparing to head back to Marietta. I had my truck double parked on Ponce de Leon Avenue, just off Peachtree Street and next to the construction barricade. Only the ongoing construction on the Fox would have made this permissible. Climbing into my El Camino, I started the engine, reached for the gearshift, and then the Voice said, "Not yet."

I've learned that when the Holy Spirit speaks, I had better listen. This was not an audible speaking, but it was clearly the Voice who spoke. So I took my hand off the gearshift and sat there with the engine running, waiting to see what was about to happen.

Soon, a siren could be heard in the next block, farther down Peachtree Street. It was still some distance away but sounded as if it were coming in my direction. I kept sitting there, and sure enough, an ambulance came into sight and turned at the light onto Ponce de Leon. As I watched in my rear-view mirror, the vehicle came past and pulled up directly in front of me. The EMTs jumped out, grabbed a stretcher and ran inside the building. So that was what the "Not yet" was about. It was beginning to make sense. We were all responding to an emergency call.

With that, I turned off the engine and ran inside the building behind them. It's funny—when you run into a building like this, the people there tend to think you belong to another group. The EMTs thought I was part of the construction crew, and the guys on construction thought I was with the

EMTs. Nobody paid any attention to me, so I was able to get right next to the man who was hurt. He had fallen off a ladder while doing sheetrock work and was feeling a lot of pain. The EMTs quickly determined that his ankle was very likely broken—they were almost certain.

They propped him up, someone gave him a cigarette, and the EMTs began to work on him, preparing him to be moved to the ambulance. I knelt down next to him, slightly out of his line of sight, and started praying in the Spirit. He didn't have any idea what I was doing—he didn't know who I was or how I had come to be there. Since no one was asking, I just went on doing what the Spirit told me to do. I had my hand on his shoulder and kept praying in the Spirit all the while the EMTs were working on him. People had begun to watch. As they lifted the stretcher to carry him out, I stood quietly by. Looking one of the EMTs in the eye, I asked if he thought that the ankle was broken. Probably thinking I was the construction foreman, he said, "That's the way it looks."

The EMTs began to carry the injured man out on the stretcher, and I followed right behind them. Reaching the ambulance, they slid the stretcher into the back, and I returned to my truck, mission accomplished. I was ready to leave. The two EMTs were situating the injured man for the ride to the hospital, and the doors of the ambulance were still open, with the patient's feet in plain sight. Then, abruptly, both EMTs left the man in the ambulance and went back into the building. As I reached to turn the ignition key, the Holy Spirit again said, "Not yet."

All right! Sure! The ambulance door had been left open for me. So out I came, quickly, and climbed into the ambulance. The man was lying on the stretcher, smoking a cigarette and trying to process what had just happened to him. He looked startled when he saw I had climbed into the ambulance. I guess he put it all together then and realized I was the unknown guy who had knelt down next to him on the building floor. Any comfort he was feeling appeared to leave him right then.

Knowing there was only a small window of time, I quickly told him, "Brother, I know this seems really strange, but I believe the Lord wants to heal your ankle—and before you get to the hospital, if you will just ask Jesus yourself, I think He'll heal you."

Silence.

With that, I climbed out and returned to my El Camino. As I closed my door, the EMTs both returned to the ambulance. Everything was quiet. The ambulance pulled away toward the hospital, and I pulled out behind it and headed toward Marietta.

As these events unfolded, my two men had been working out in the front of the Fox and had seen the ambulance come past and heard the siren abruptly go quiet. They had come around the corner to check it out, and then gone into the building and observed some of what happened. Neither of them was used to any of this and didn't understand it, so they had kept their distance, just observing. Caught up in what the Spirit was doing, I hadn't noticed them there.

My two men had worked on the storefront all day Saturday, so when I arrived on Monday, I was interested in seeing what progress they had made. As soon as I saw them, it was clear that they were more pumped up than usual—quite excited. One of them quickly said, "That guy that fell on Friday and you prayed for... Well, he and another guy worked here all day Saturday with no problem."

The man had not only had his ankle healed on Friday, but on Saturday, all four men—my two men, the injured man, and his coworker—had received some healing of their faith. We all learned something about the rewards of asking Jesus.

"Keep asking and it will be given to you... Everyone who keeps asking will receive."

—*Matthew 7:7-8 (ISV)*

Fr. Walt, Delivering the Mail

I spoke a good bit about Fr. Walt in my first book, *Swept Up by the Spirit*. He was as attuned to the leading of the Holy Spirit as anyone I have ever known. Nancy and I were around him frequently during the first several years after our Baptisms in the Holy Spirit, as our process of transformation began, until Fr. Walt was transferred to another church some distance away. Our home became a way station of sorts for Fr. Walt, a place he could drop in spontaneously. Spirit-led spontaneity was a special characteristic of his life. Nancy and I considered his presence alone to provide something like an antenna for the Lord's voice, and even quiet times with Fr. Walt were special.

Sometimes he would abruptly stand up and start walking toward the door, rubbing his hands together and saying, "I've got go, my hands are getting hot. There's somebody I'm supposed to pray over." He would quickly head toward his truck, not yet knowing which direction to drive.

Fr. Walt's primary impact on us was as a role model—yes, he could and did teach Scripture and Catholic doctrine, but he changed our lives by just being a great, proactive example to us. He was totally unassuming, didn't regard himself as better than anyone else, and consistently lived his faith. He was always on duty, ready for the next Holy Spirit assignment. Because Fr. Walt lived this way, many of his actions that delivered extraordinary results were undertaken just at the Holy Spirit's nudging, with no assurance of where they would lead. This emboldened some of us to try to respond to the Spirit in the same way, and when we would, it often worked for us, too!

One event stands out in my memory. Nancy and I were part of a prayer gathering of about fourteen people, along with Fr. Walt. The group was comprised of young couples in their thirties and early forties. There were some singles also in the mix. We were seated in a circle of chairs, which was typical in our prayer meetings.

Without a word, Fr. Walt stood up, moved in front of one of the men, laid hands on his head and began to prophesy over him. The prophecy consisted of three or four insightful sentences, which were affirming as well as directive. Upon completion, Fr. Walt moved to the man's wife and prophesied a message to her with similar clarity and authority. Fr. Walt proceeded around the entire circle of fourteen, never pausing or slowing down, methodically approaching each person with the same intensity and care. He was like the Holy Spirit postman delivering the registered Jesus mail.

The words he had for Nancy and for me and the others, whom we knew well, were totally right on and anointed and very meaningful to each individual. Every message was personal and worthy of being embraced, remembered and cherished. At the time, our church was in the midst of true renewal by the Holy Spirit, so this impressive use of the spiritual gifts didn't affect us as much as the valuable information that was delivered.

When Fr. Walt had finished sharing the messages, he sat down and went silent—and then moved on with the next part of the program. We all knew we had just experienced a very personal visit from the Holy Spirit. The messages and the messenger touched us deeply.

After forty years of walking in the Spirit, with much exposure to prophecy and words of knowledge, I've never seen anyone exercise such continuous use of these spiritual gifts as Fr. Walt, and I might never again. At the same time, the Holy Spirit could instill gifts that exceed those we saw in Fr. Walt at any time.

Forty years later, I did feel a similar power of the Spirit in the anointed return/repentance exhortation given by Rabbi Jonathan Cahn in September 2020 in Washington, D.C. I am sure many were moved by the Spirit that day. Hopefully, the word delivered will bring forth the response that is needed.

Never Look Up

Soon after entering the business of house building, I was told by tile suppliers that Harold was the best tile man in Atlanta. He worked on my second house, setting the tile, and I was sold. He did all of my tile work from then on. He, his partner and his son did great work and were good to work with; they quietly came and went with no hassle. He was truly an outstanding craftsman, a first-class person, and a good addition to our subcontractor lineup.

Harold was also the most committed Christian among my subcontractors—very solid in his faith, he would refer to being in church but didn't talk a lot about it. He had an evangelical spirit, but by nature he was a quiet, introverted person. I was still a nonbeliever, and Harold was careful to never push his faith on me, although I sensed his deep concern for me. I'm certain he was bothered by my self-assured manner, which he probably recognized as stemming from pride. If that's what he thought, he was right on.

Harold had been handling all of the tile work in my houses for about five years. One day he was setting tile in a bathroom and I was leaving to check on another house I was building at the same time. I looked in on him and told him I would be back soon, but at that, he abruptly stopped his work. Down on all fours on the floor, he looked up and delivered this profound statement, which must have been burning in his mind, "A hog will stand in one spot and eat acorns all day long and never look up to see where they came from."

Message delivered, Harold went right back to tile setting. We said nothing else.

As I rushed out, I was instantly challenged by the words and by Harold's courage to deliver them. That was a very gutsy thing he had just done, and again, I sensed his concern for me. I went on to my next house but couldn't get the words out of my head. Those words were for me—I was the hog with the ungrateful spirit. The message kept playing over and over, and not just that day. I've shared this little story scores of times and reheard those words many more.

After I came to the Lord (while still building that house), I told Harold that his message had affected me more than he could know. He seemed surprised. I later came to see that the Holy Spirit's timing in using Harold to deliver the word of admonition was exact. I had never before been in such trouble during the construction of any of my houses. I believe that the Lord used those simple words of truth to begin to marinate my prideful and ungrateful heart, and Harold's courage to speak them would later give me courage to deliver challenging words to others.

Do not quench the Spirit. Do not treat prophecies with contempt but test them all; hold on to what is good...
                                                    —1 Thessalonians 5:19-21 (NIV)

There is a time for everything,
and a season for every activity under the heavens...
a time to be silent and a time to speak...
                                                    —Ecclesiastes 3:1 and 7 (NIV)

Wake-Up Calls

One morning a customer walked through the front door of my business. He was a serviceman in his early thirties, looking in peak physical condition and wearing camouflage fatigues. His name was Willard. He had called ahead after finding my business listing in the yellow pages of the phone book. He had come in hopes of having a lectern designed and built to give to his pastor. Since this was going to be a serious and somewhat costly venture, I wanted to make sure our understanding was totally clear. I also sensed that the Holy Spirit might have led him to me for other reasons as well.

As Willard talked and I listened, he told me that while he was still a young boy, he had lost his father and had been raised by a very moral and strict uncle who was unwavering in his principles and had taught him to always do the right thing. This started as a business conversation between two men who had just met, but suddenly it was becoming a deeper talk. Willard proceeded, "Recently the Lord has been waking me up at night."

Wow! That little statement got my attention. Willard didn't add details as to why He was waking him up, so I listened for the Holy Spirit's direction. On a clear leading, the Spirit had me ask, "Willard, do you have a relationship with a woman?"

Willard replied, "Yes, I have a fiancée who is also in the service but stationed in Germany, so I rarely am with her."

I continued, "When you are with her, you are both upright and moral in your sexual behavior?"

Willard replied, "We try to be."

As the Holy Spirit led me, I pressed on and said, "You try to be, but you're not able—right?"

With that, Willard just burst into tears.

I went on to tell him, "That's sin and you know it—it's got to stop, you were taught better than that."

The words just leapt out and brought conviction right on the spot! Willard knew the word to be true, since he had been raised to know truth. Even I was surprised by the intensity of the words. It was as though I was standing in and speaking for his uncle, whose authority was still very present. He continued to sob as I knelt down next to the chair he was sitting in, my hands on his shoulder. His strong body shook and tears ran down his face as he nodded in agreement. In a halting voice, he said, "My fiancée's not going to like hearing this. She's not the believer that I am."

I went on, "You're the one responsible, and you are to stop any sexual activity until you get married—that's why the Lord has been waking you up at night." It took several minutes for him to get his emotions together, but Willard got the message very clearly that morning and he knew what he had to do.

He soon came back and ordered a very nice lectern that cost him about $2,000. He returned a couple of times to bring money while it was being built. He never again looked distressed, throughout the rest of our interactions or at any point during the building and delivery of the lectern. He took a second part-time job to pay for the lectern, but he was happy to do so. He had gotten far more than his money's worth. He had regained his direction.

Train up a child in the way he should go, and when he is old he will not depart from it.

—Proverbs 22:6 (RSV)

Pressanna

Nancy and I were on a brief getaway to Hilton Head Island in South Carolina. This is normally a beautiful area, but on that early summer morning, it was even more so. The weather was nearly perfect, in full Technicolor, with everything blooming and growing, bees humming, butterflies flitting around. It brought to mind that old jazz line, "Summertime, and the living is easy..."

We were headed for Shoney's, looking forward to a nice brunch. The quickly filling parking lot indicated that many others were planning the same thing. Fortunately, we were ushered right to a table in an area that was not yet filled with customers. As soon as we settled into our seats, a waitress was at our table with a water pitcher, filling our glasses. She was going from table to table, handling the refills. She was a most impressive figure, looking as glorious as the beautiful day outside. A radiant Black woman, large and immaculately groomed, she was emanating joy from head to toe. She looked like someone on a mission, just sparkling as she went. She filled our glasses and exchanged pleasantries, moving easily among the tables.

Sooner than we expected, she was back at our table, checking our glasses, and I was especially drawn to the name plate pinned to her neat uniform. The name read "Pressanna." I couldn't resist commenting, since I was getting a nudge from the Holy Spirit. "What a pretty name, Pressanna. I don't believe I've ever heard it before."

Without a pause, she replied, "My father named me; he was trying to tell them Priscilla, but between the nurse and him, this was the name that showed up on my birth certificate. So I grew up with the name Pressanna. All my life I was asked about it and I hated it. I just hated that name Pressanna." Then her face brightened considerably and she continued. "One day not long after

I met the Lord, He spoke to me. 'Pressanna, I am the One who gave you your name. It means: Press on, Anna. Days ahead will get hard but I want you to press on. Press-on-Anna, Press-on-Anna.'" With pride of ownership, she said, "Ever since then, I've loved my name—my name is Pressanna."

We thanked her for sharing her story with us. She and her pitcher of ice water had to keep moving and she eased away.

About that time the hostess seated two other couples at the next table. We exchanged introductions and learned that they were from Canada, and right away we realized that they also were Spirit filled, with lots of faith. Nancy and I told them about Pressanna. They were moved by the story and looked forward to meeting her.

Pressanna soon returned, pitcher in hand, and we introduced the two couples to her. Her presence blessed them as she filled their glasses. Having seven believers now assembled together seemed somehow special. Then I got that nudge, and I asked, "Pressanna, will you sing for us?" She stopped in place and with a surprised voice, said, "How did you know I sing?"

Just following the Spirit's lead, I replied, "The Holy Spirit told me you sing in church and not only that, you have a gift of prophecy, too!" Pressanna just stood there, very still, looking as if she had been found out.

I said, "We don't want you to risk losing your job, but if you could just sing for us, we would really be blessed." We all stayed silent.

After a minute, she said, "I'll go fill a few more glasses, then I'll come back and sing to you." She eased off into the now full restaurant.

After a short while, Pressanna returned, and we all got quiet and waited with great anticipation. Pressanna leaned back against the wall, pitcher in hand, telling us, "I'm going to sing you the song the Lord gave me that I wrote last weekend. I've only sung it once at church." With great passion she began and just overwhelmed us immediately. Her glorious voice, her inspired original song, her obvious deep love for Jesus, and her heartfelt delivery just blew us away! Wow! Her anointed offering lasted several minutes and she did not hold anything back. To our great surprise not another head in the crowd turned; apparently no one else heard her. It was our own private, Holy Spirit-inspired concert. With no rush, Pressanna humbly concluded, smiled, and glided away to pour more water. We all dried our eyes, knowing we had just experienced a Holy Spirit "gotcha" moment, a special dessert that the Lord Himself had prepared just for the seven of us.

***

The following morning, Nancy and I were to depart Hilton Head. We were packed and had just enough time to take one last walk on the beach. Savoring the time, we saw a woman coming toward us, walking a dog. As we approached each other, we shared a greeting, as many do when walking the beach, and then struck up a conversation.

Within minutes, our casual conversation led to this woman opening up to us about some confusion and difficulty in her life that had been building for a long time. It soon became apparent that she was only interested in relating her problems, not in listening to us. Then I felt the Holy Spirit give clear direction to me: "Pressanna has a word for her." We gave her directions to Shoney's, told her to ask for Pressanna, who had the gift of prophecy, and that whatever Pressanna told her to do, she should just do. If she would act on Pressanna's word, good things would happen.

We had to leave, but we had tried to follow the leadings of the Holy Spirit and act upon the word. After the results from the day before, how could we do any less?

What a wonderful blessing it is to watch the gifts of the Spirit unwrapped and opened up before us.

When you assemble, each one has a psalm, has a teaching, has a revelation, has a tongue, has an interpretation. Let all things be done for edification.
                    —*1 Corinthians 14:26 (NASB)*

...forgetting what lies behind and reaching forward to what lies ahead, I press on toward the goal for the prize of the upward call of God in Christ Jesus.
                    —*Philippians 3:13-14 (NASB)*

Hardwood Lumber, With a Touch of the Spirit

I was twenty years old the first time I drove onto the property of Atlanta Hardwood Lumber Company. It was a big-time, sprawling, hardwood lumber supplier located at the southeastern edge of Atlanta among multiple trucking lines and heavy industry, and only did commercial sales. My little old pickup truck looked totally out of place there.

For the past few years, I had been buying my lumber from a high school industrial arts supplier in North Carolina that shipped by trucking lines, and sometimes my orders were slow to arrive. This was my first experience with a large commercial distributor.

I came that day hoping to purchase a small amount of cherry, maple and walnut for custom furniture I had been commissioned to build. My order consisted of just a few boards of each wood; it would total around one hundred board feet. I hoped they wouldn't think of me as a nuisance or disqualify me as a customer because of the small amount I needed. After the thirty-mile drive to get there, I really didn't want to be turned away empty handed. I knew that my order was a drop in the bucket to them, but it was really important to me.

As I entered the impressive-looking, wood-paneled sales area, my eye fell upon one of the offices, indicated by a sign to belong to a Mr. Hill. He was a middle-aged man, dressed in a nice suit, seated at his desk with a phone to his ear. He was speaking loudly, with confidence, about "his" supply. The sign over his door read, "West Coast Lumber Sales." I later found out that he sold large-volume orders of redwood, fir, western cedar, etc. Mr. Hill was obviously not the salesman I needed.

The receptionist escorted me to Mr. Les Boyd's office, which was next to Mr. Hill's. Mr. Boyd was in his sixties, also dressed in a suit, and had a very pleasant demeanor, like that of a good-natured uncle. He welcomed me right in, yet in spite of his warmth, I felt embarrassed to show him the small list of lumber I needed.

But Mr. Boyd totally surprised me. He set me at ease, slowed down the pace of the interaction, and treated me like an important customer—as if I were there to buy a boxcar load of lumber. He patiently shared some lumber knowledge that I really needed and treated me with respect that I didn't expect and doubted that I deserved.

Mr. Boyd then stood up from his desk, told me to come with him and led me out into "the yard." Multiple huge open warehouses opened onto this immense area, stacked high, pallet upon pallet, with every kind of hardwood imaginable. Every board was rough on the surfaces and along the edges, but I just knew that underneath was something wonderful. The pungent smell of the wood thrilled me; I'm likely addicted to that smell. I would have been happy just to wander around awhile, looking up at all that wood and soaking in the sights and aromas.

As we stepped into the yard, Mr. Boyd caught the attention of the yard men. He lifted one finger and a man quickly came to get instructions and fill my order. I could hardly believe it all. I hadn't been treated so well as a customer even when I bought my first car.

For years after that, I returned to Atlanta Hardwood and bought my lumber from Mr. Boyd—he was my go-to man. He was never any less gracious than he was the very first time. It never occurred to me then, but perhaps he thought of me like an industrious son or grandson. The company continued on through the years, transferring ownership over to some of its employees, moving to a different location across greater Atlanta, but still maintaining the same good lumber supply and service as always. For the last few decades, they have been known as Sweetwater Lumber.

I have bought tens of thousands of board feet of lumber from Sweetwater but never have been a big-volume buyer. Yet they still treat me as special, as though I am an important customer.

My first experience with Mr. Boyd was a milestone for me, teaching me how to relate to others while conducting business. He showed me by example that it isn't the size of a sale that matters—it's about taking the best possible care of the customer. I will always be grateful to Mr. Boyd for freeing me up as a young man from thinking of myself as a second-class or insignificant customer. I hope to someday do for someone else what Mr. Boyd did for me.

Twenty years after meeting Mr. Boyd in the great hardwood world, I met Jesus and the Holy Spirit. Naturally, this added a wonderful new dimension to all my relating. Ever since, my lumber dealings with Sweetwater have had a Holy Spirit element that touches their employees. Like me, it seems that they expect something special to happen whenever we connect.

As part of a recent order, I requested about forty board feet of 16/4 (four-inch thick) cherry. I was dealing with Doug, a young shipping department head with whom I've had limited conversation on the phone. Doug is always respectful and very efficient.

As soon as I asked for 16/4 cherry, Doug told me he was sorry, but they didn't have any. I said, "But you've always had 16/4 cherry."

He responded rather sadly, "I know, but it's no longer available. We haven't had any for several years. The mills run the logs into 12/4 and 10/4 because the 16/4 doesn't sell as fast." I was surprised and quite disappointed. He continued, "I'm looking here at our inventory and it's showing zero." But being the helpful man that he is, Doug added, "I'll double-check on the yard when we pull your other lumber, but I'm pretty sure we won't find anything." I could tell by his voice that he held out little hope for it.

Doug called back in a little while to tell me that the rest of my order was in stock and being pulled, but no luck on the 16/4 cherry.

By now the Holy Spirit had all but told me that two boards were tucked back in the bin waiting to be found. I said, "Doug, I feel bad asking you to do this, but could you take one last look? I really believe there are two boards up there just waiting to be found."

He responded with enthusiasm, as though they had just been located, saying, "If you think they're up there, I'll sure look again."

A few minutes later, Doug called back, sounding excited, and said, "I climbed up the ladder [referring to a point high in the warehouse] and looked back in the bin as far as I could, and I saw the ends of just two boards. They look like they're about the size you need. I've got the men pulling them for you."

I thanked him for his willingness to help, told him that I wasn't surprised, and added, "Doug, I guess you realize those boards may not have been there when you looked the first time."

With obvious joy, he said, "I know, I know!" I could hear the faith in his tone. Maybe the discovery of those two boards blessed not only Doug, but his coworkers as well.

Sweetwater delivered the lumber to my shop a few days later. I couldn't wait to run those two dusty timbers through the planer, and sure enough, they came out the other end looking exceptional, even after only being planed. They are even prettier now in their finished form—their grain really came forth in the pair of six-foot candle stands that anchor an Episcopal church sanctuary we were hired to complete.

About three years later, I got an order to build a tabernacle for a Catholic adoration chapel. The remainder of those two special cherry boards was just enough—and just right—to build the two arched sides of the tabernacle.

The 16/4 cherry boards are like many of us who once were lost but now are found. Redemption in Jesus changes everything. It leads to a whole new life, and can bless so many others. Glory!

And my God will meet all your needs according to the riches of His glory
in Christ Jesus.

—Philippians 4:19 (NIV)

Chapter 5

Habits, Dysfunction, Evil Spirits, Bondage

Let's take a brief look at some particular tormentors, keeping in mind that this is not a comprehensive study.

We are likely to encounter plenty of bad habits, dysfunctional behaviors, bondage, and even evil spirits on our journey—sometimes even in ourselves, when we least expect to—but the Lord can set us free, and we will be free indeed.

> *"...You will know the truth, and the truth will make you free."*
> —*John 8:32 (NASB)*

Bad habits may take root very gradually. Any one of us can be subject to them, and likely are now or have been in the past. We may have picked up these habits from a family member, a friend, a classmate, someone we looked up to when we were young, or maybe even someone we idolized, such as a celebrity we never met. If dealt with early, such habits may be quickly eliminated, but if left untended, they can throw us off balance or get us into trouble. We need the Lord to show us how to make the needed correction.

Bad habits may open us up to dysfunction that leads to poor choices or puts us on the wrong path without our awareness. Dysfunction in the form of unreasonable fears, fixations, and obsessions (and in some cases, even phobias or paranoia) may develop. These may grow into major hindrances, distractions or diversions, much like texting can impair driving by taking our minds off what is important so that our attention is focused on the distraction instead. Evil spirits can slip in and take over the territory and open us up to spiritual bondage. Surely any person who denies the presence of demonic activity is especially vulnerable.

In our everyday lives, we will likely encounter such evil spirits as pride, fear, anger, resentment, insecurity, rejection, unforgiveness, deception, complacency—the list could go on and on. Most of us will be targeted by a few of these spirits over time; being human almost ensures this. These are dangerous spirits that can masquerade as an individual's own persona and dominate our behavior. C. S. Lewis' masterpiece, "The Great Divorce," shows graphic examples of such. Fear may well be the most dangerous and damaging of all spirits. I pray regularly against the fear of life, fear of death, fear of failure and the fear of seeking the approval of man.

Spirits that have been attached to someone for a long time may be more difficult to discern and expel from the person. I refer to these as "squatters on the property" who enter through doors or windows left open to the world and to evil spirits. They come in and try to claim ownership or tenure, and deliverance ministry may be required to evict them. Old spirits such as anger might hang on and surprise us; we might think they are gone when in fact they have just temporarily gone underground to avoid detection. These are sometimes referred to as "the tigers in the basement" that appear upstairs unexpectedly. Anger is no friend to anyone and should never be held in reserve "just in case it is needed." Do you ever get surprised by your own anger when you are driving? I still do, although not as much as I did in the past. Anger has not totally left me yet.

Pride persists in many of us, and it sometimes shifts from worldly pride to spiritual pride. What an ugly comrade. Pride is a lying, deceitful "friend" who aims to bring us down, and really is no friend at all! He is always setting us up. Pride goes before a fall, as we know, and overcoming it is a lifetime's work. Pride and fear are the extremes that the Devil uses to thrash us if we give in to either.

A longtime tormentor of mine is a spirit of perfection. This spirit disguises itself as the ultimate judge of excellence, but in fact is a merciless, critical spirit, insatiable, never satisfied, and even capable of immobilizing a person. This spirit tries to ruin someone's outlook on a really good work by causing that person to dwell on the most minute imperfection. Satan's efforts to overtake a person's scrupulous intent with a spirit of scrupulosity is similar.

Of course, indulgence in harmful or hurtful practices, such as excessive alcohol use, drug abuse, smoking, profanity, deviant sexual practices, and other bad behavior often is preventable in the early stages and should be brought to an end, if possible, before these behaviors reach the stage of addiction or bondage. At that point, the person's actions literally fall captive to the spirit.

A spirit of delusion, which denies the truth of a situation and creates an illusion of the truth that might be more appealing, can attach to us because of our efforts, even subconsciously, to escape reality through fantasy. This spirit can be very subtle but very controlling and can wreak havoc with lives. Our culture's present-day fascination with fantasy and virtual reality is causing people to replace and destroy their own real lives and their futures. Living a life of fantasy can never deliver success or true joy and can lead to serious bondage.

Character assassinations such as, "You're a loser and you always will be," or "You'll never amount to anything," or "Why can't you be like your brother or sister?" and all the other degrading statements and terms that have been thrown at people, usually early in their lives, can take root and hold people in bondage for decades. These are total lies that masquerade as truth. Such demonic words have blocked many from the great journey the Lord has for them. But the chains that result from these words can be broken and the person can be set free through deliverance ministry.

Poor practices can be accepted at home on the basis of unsound or unfounded thinking, ideas like, "Men don't do housework—that's women's work," or, "Women aren't supposed to do anything outside the house." These thoughts, when embraced and followed, can lock a family in imbalance and hold them for generations until the myth is unmasked. Pride and a dug-in mindset that is against change are usually the driving forces behind these binding situations.

Procrastination can block people from moving forward, and they can stay stranded indefinitely because of their inaction or slowness to act. Unwarranted fear of failure often drives procrastination, causing a person to ponder on and plan many courses of action but in fact do little or nothing. This spirit can hold a person in perpetual bondage if not overcome by truth, good decisions and action based on those decisions.

Since we live in both God's world and Satan's world, it is imperative that we understand the workings of both. Throughout Scripture, Jesus refers to Satan as the adversary or prince of the earth and speaks of the grip Satan has on human events. Satan is far more involved in our personal lives than we may realize and is quite aware of our weaknesses and the sins that attract us. He has no problem putting those in our path, in plain view. If we don't emphatically say NO and turn abruptly away, he will intensify his efforts. Casual tolerance of temptation can be deadly. Jesus speaks far more about evil spirits than He does about healing. Of course, deliverance from evil spirits and healing are never far apart. We all need to be well balanced and on the alert in order to combat Satan and all forms of evil, even in ordinary times. We should never lose sight of the assurance that *"greater is He who is in you than he who is in the world." (1 John 4:4)* Of course, the indwelling and empowering of the Holy Spirit, along with the heart and desire to be healed or changed, are the keys to all good transformation.

> *Wash away all my iniquity and cleanse me from my sin.*
> *For I know my transgressions, and my sin is always before me.*
> *Against You, You only, have I sinned and done what is evil in Your sight;*
> *so You are right in Your verdict and justified when You judge...*
> *Create in me a pure heart, O God, and renew a steadfast spirit within me.*
> *Do not cast me from Your presence or take Your Holy Spirit from me.*
> *Restore to me the joy of Your salvation and grant me a willing spirit, to sustain me.*
> *Then I will teach transgressors Your ways, so that sinners will turn back to You.*
> —*Psalm 51:2-4, 10-13 (NIV)*

Our own personal handling of free will and the choices we each make will determine whether we live in freedom and health or in bondage and travail. These choices can even determine our direction and ultimate destination. We definitely want to be part of the solution—not the problem.

> *So I tell you this, and insist on it in the Lord, that you must no longer live as the Gentiles do, in the futility of their thinking. They are darkened in their understanding and separated from the life of God because of the ignorance that is in them due to the hardening of their hearts.*

Having lost all sensitivity, they have given themselves over to sensuality so as to indulge in every kind of impurity, and they are full of greed. That, however, is not the way of life you learned when you heard about Christ and were taught in Him in accordance with the truth that is in Jesus. You were taught, with regard to your former way of life, to put off your old self, which is being corrupted by its deceitful desires; to be made new in the attitude of your minds; and to put on the new self, created to be like God in true righteousness and holiness.

—Ephesians 4:17-24 (NIV)

And do not grieve the Holy Spirit of God, with whom you were sealed for the day of redemption. Get rid of all bitterness, rage and anger, brawling and slander, along with every form of malice. Be kind and compassionate to one another, forgiving each other, just as in Christ God forgave you.

—Ephesians 4:30-32 (NIV)

The following stories show how the Lord's intervention sometimes caught a person's attention and brought about positive change, but also illustrate times when Satan's deception and bondage kept a person entrapped.

The Visitation

Our church was conducting a Life in the Spirit seminar, a short course about the Holy Spirit that ends with prayers over all participants for the release of the Holy Spirit. A large group of about 120 people signed up, and Nancy and I were table leaders of a small group. The members were quite diverse, with varied backgrounds and life experiences. Our challenge was to relate to each of them on his or her own level while delivering the empowering message of the Holy Spirit.

In our group was a man named Jim, in his early forties. He appeared prideful and deceitful, neither trusting nor trustworthy. He didn't look or sound like a true convert to faith—but here he was. We soon came to know him as a distracting type with an abundance of questions and comments, many of which were not relevant. Attracting attention seemed to be his main motivation. He also seemed to consider himself an immense gift to women. We decided that the best way to try to help him was to invite him to our home for dinner and spend a couple of hours with him, away from the seminar group. At least this way, he wouldn't be a distraction to the sessions.

The following week, Jim came for dinner. It was a beautiful, warm spring night. Flowers were blooming and the windows were open, but Jim seemed oblivious to this beauty and to the dinner and was full of negativity. He talked almost continually. He acknowledged that he had used both alcohol and drugs, but what he really wanted to talk about that night was his former wife (they were divorced) and all of her problems, dysfunction and shortcomings. Apparently, despite all of this, he still wanted her, but he didn't have a clue about how to recover their relationship.

After a long couple of hours, Nancy and I were both feeling that the time had netted little. We saw no progress and we were glad the evening was nearly over. We weren't really disappointed, since we had gone into the evening expecting little. As Jim prepared to leave, I said, "Let's just have a quick prayer before you leave." This was basically our way of saying goodnight, and standard for us at the end of an evening with friends. We all joined hands and I led us in a short, spontaneous prayer of blessing and protection.

Upon finishing the prayer and opening our eyes, we realized something had happened to Jim. The color had drained from his face and he looked frozen in place, immobile. He suddenly couldn't walk at all, so Nancy and I carefully helped him to sit down on the sofa, as if he had a serious back injury. He began to shiver and shake uncontrollably, as if he were freezing. We closed the windows and Nancy got a blanket and put it around him as his shaking increased. Then he asked for a glass of warm milk. He could barely hold the glass to drink because his shaking and teeth chattering had intensified.

This strange phenomenon continued for the next couple of hours. Nancy and I sat with him, staying quiet, praying or sharing encouragement as he went through this ordeal. We were both sure it was spiritual, not a situation requiring any medical attention. Jim then drifted into a quiet stupor. He was still unable to stand or walk. At about eleven o'clock, Nancy excused herself and went to bed, certain that whatever was happening, the Spirit was in control. It was long after midnight, nearly four hours since the shaking had started, before Jim could stand and take a few careful steps. He then decided to leave, and as he slowly walked toward his car, I had concern about his ability to drive. He lived just a few miles from our house and assured me he would drive very slowly and carefully and would be able to make it home.

When we saw Jim at church a few days later, he looked very different: pensive, subdued, and cleansed. He told us that the Lord had detoxed him that night, right on the spot. He had not had any alcohol or drugs since, nor any desire for them. Before that night at our house, he admitted he had used both alcohol and drugs every day for the past sixteen years—he had not missed a single day.

Jim's alcohol and drug abuse over the years had undoubtedly brought much pain and hurt to him, his wife and others. In a matter of hours, he had been detoxified and given a priceless gift of deliverance from addiction. Now it would be up to him and his free will to decide if he would maintain it.

Jesus said, "Neither do I condemn you; go and sin no more."
—John 8:11 (NKJV)

The Sign and the Bankers

After more than twenty years of marriage—years spent living according to the world's values and reacting to challenges or obstacles in a worldly way—Nancy and I were now "walking in the Spirit" and experiencing a whole new way of life.

Nancy had a position working two days each week as a drive-through teller at a large bank in the area, and she worked well there, with speed and efficiency. Now, with her new call to evangelize, she had been reaching out to her customers with faith, encouragement and an occasional prayer as they pulled up to her window. We thought it would be beneficial to have a small sign made to help equip her in evangelizing.

I had one professionally painted. It was a small stand-up sign, eight by twelve inches, and red with white letters in script on both sides. It was quite classy. Since Nancy's two working days were Monday and Friday, one side read, "May the love of the Lord help brighten your Monday and bring peace and joy to your week ahead." The other side read, "Friday brings hope for a weekend to remember—the Lord brings joy to each day that we let Him."

As soon as the sign was completed, Nancy took it to the bank and put it in her teller window. Fellow employees admired it right away. Some customers began to comment favorably on the encouraging addition. She even got to pray for more people, without any disruption of her bank responsibilities.

Nancy and the Lord had been using the little sign very effectively for about a year, and then it happened. A female customer whom Nancy had waited on a few times drove up to her window and then abruptly stopped. She seemed to be totally absorbed in the sign. After a long pause, she asked, "Is that your sign?" When Nancy assured her that it was, the woman just drove off.

Although Nancy sensed the woman was really bothered, she didn't expect her to make a complaint to the bank. But that is exactly what happened.

Nancy was told that she would have to remove the sign or quit. She responded that she didn't believe she could remove the sign, as her faith meant too much to her, and she wouldn't quit because that would imply some wrongdoing on her part. Her supervisor told Nancy that if she refused to take the sign down and refused to quit, he would have to fire her. Nancy told him that she would let him know her decision the following Monday.

Nancy and I discussed the dilemma and prayed over the weekend, really wanting to know God's will in the matter. By Sunday we agreed that she wasn't to remove the sign or to quit her job—whatever came about, so be it. We had real peace about the decision and its results.

On Monday morning, Nancy told the banker her decision, and she was promptly terminated. We felt no remorse; instead, we felt quite good about standing up for our faith at the expense of the job. Nancy would not work again outside the home for a dozen more years, and she never applied for unemployment benefits.

Blessed are those who have been persecuted for the sake of righteousness, for theirs is the Kingdom of Heaven.
—Matthew 5:10

The weekend after Nancy's termination we went to eat dinner at Houlihan's Restaurant. It was the site of my first commercial woodworking job, which had recently been completed, and we were celebrating. Just as we were finishing our meal, the couple at the next table got up to leave. Nancy recognized the woman as the bank customer who had complained about the sign—the complaint that led to her termination.

Instantly, Nancy jumped up and followed the couple outside, leaving me sitting there, unaware of what was going on. The woman turned and recognized her. Nancy told her that she wouldn't be at the bank to help her anymore, since she had been fired on Monday. With that, the woman burst into tears, sobbing and repeating over and over, "I didn't mean for that to happen." She was clearly very shaken. Nancy began to minister to her and spoke with her for a few minutes, assuring her that everything would be all right. By that time, the woman's husband and I were both standing nearby, quietly watching.

Although Nancy was no longer with the bank, and we had peace about that, our troubles with the bank weren't over. The next week we got a call from David, a young loan officer there, who told us that Nancy's employee loan of $1,000 was now due because she was no longer employed by the bank. I gave him a backhanded response, telling him that we would get around to paying off this loan like we would get all the others paid.

The following Friday, I walked into the house not long before 5 p.m. and found that an envelope from the bank had arrived in the mail. Upon opening it, I learned that the $1,000 loan had been paid by means of a small savings account our son Craig had in our name at the bank. The banker had simply switched the funds over to pay off the loan. This action by the young banker was the straw that broke the camel's back. Nancy and I considered the action both unmerited and unethical. We both just lost it, and I immediately called the bank.

David, the young banker, became the target of my anger, and I verbally unloaded on him for violating our trust and acting without our knowledge or consent. My verbiage was not profane, but it was very condescending and scathing. I hadn't talked like that to anyone in a very long time. Once I finished with David, I asked who his superior was, and he told me it was Mr. Brantley. I then took it out on Mr. Brantley, heaping on even more condemnation. Mr. Brantley was calm, pleasant, offering his sympathy, but would not reverse the bank's action. With nothing resolved, we ended the call, and then everything went quiet as a great awareness settled over me. I had just violated commands of the Lord and had dishonoured two men in the process. The eerie silence was soon replaced by the worst raking over the coals I had ever experienced from the Lord. The message was, "You don't ever talk to anyone like that again, no matter what they have done. As My follower, you don't talk down to anyone."

I quickly picked up the phone and called the bank to ask forgiveness. The phone rang and rang, to no avail. A recorded message finally informed me that the bank was closed and would reopen at 9 a.m. Monday.

Well, that was the longest weekend I had yet spent as a Christian, and I got no consolation the entire time. I was dead wrong, and I would have to be the one to make it right. All day Saturday I was repenting, and Sunday found me counting down the hours until the bank would open. At 9 a.m. on Monday morning I was dialing the bank's number, asking to speak to David. My call was strictly to ask forgiveness. When he came on the line, I told him that it didn't matter what he had done, as a Christian, I was wrong to talk down to him like that. David was very gracious and told me that no one had ever called him at the bank to ask for forgiveness. He readily granted it. I then asked him to connect me to Mr. Brantley because I needed to ask his forgiveness, also. David explained that he would be happy to transfer my call, but Mr. Brantley was not at work, he was in the hospital. When I asked why, David replied, "Mr. Brantley has had a long-term heart condition but has had no problems for a long time." He went on to say, "He was fine on Friday but something must have really upset him because he was rushed to the hospital Friday night."

Well, there it was. My unbridled anger had been turned loose and somebody was paying. I asked David whether Mr. Brantley could have visitors and which hospital he was in. He said that yes, Mr. Brantley could have visitors, and he gave me the name of the hospital. I told David I was on my way.

Minutes later I made a very humble entry into Mr. Brantley's room. There he was, flat in bed, with his wife seated in a chair by his side. They were both around seventy years old. I introduced myself cautiously and asked if he remembered talking to me on Friday. He knowingly smiled and assured me that he did, but he didn't dwell on that in any way. Right away, I asked for and received his forgiveness. He and his wife were very gracious, welcoming my prayers with them for his healing and for their family and their future. They said the doctor had assured them that he would be fine and home soon. As I left the hospital, I felt relieved that I had been restored by the Lord's mercy and by their forgiveness.

When the Lord called me to become a new creation, He meant in every area, not just in some. I would not be allowed to go on living the wonderful life, living in the power of the new man, while still reacting under pressure like the old man.

This was the first time my anger and impulsive reaction had been reprimanded so severely by the Lord. I knew I had better pay attention and get rid of those caustic old behaviors. The demonic spirit of anger tries to stay entrenched and to taint the lives of God's redeemed.

You must all be quick to listen, slow to speak, and slow to get angry. Human anger does not produce the righteousness God desires.
—James 1:19-20 (NLT)

Let no unwholesome word proceed from your mouth, but only such a word as is good for edification according to the need of the moment, so that it will give grace to those who hear. Do not grieve the Holy Spirit of God, by whom you were sealed for the day of redemption.
—Ephesians 4:29-30 (NASB)

No discipline seems pleasant at the time, but painful. Later on, however, it produces a harvest of righteousness and peace for those who have been trained by it.
—Hebrews 12:11 (NIV)

Rob's Anointing

Rob, Nikki and their family looked like the ideal family, with a good marriage, young kids and a nice home. Rob was well educated, with a good career, and he and Nikki were solid in their faith and church lives. They were part of a group of twenty or more young couples, all in their thirties, with good jobs. Most of them were corporate employees with the potential to move up in their fields. The church itself was located in an economically booming, desirable area north of Atlanta.

Rob began teaching Scripture on Sunday mornings at the church. Most of those attending the classes were cradle Catholics and had little exposure to stirring teaching about the Bible and how it pertained to each of them. But Rob had such an anointing that the word became personal and alive each Sunday. The Scripture study soon became packed with people, and everyone caught fire. This study, along with the charismatic prayer group and share group, had our large church hopping. New people were regularly being baptized in the Holy Spirit, and spiritual life was flourishing.

After a season of this anointing, Rob received a call from the corporate headquarters of his employer. They wanted to interview him for a possible job promotion and transfer to their headquarters in Delaware. The potential offer was intriguing, but Rob knew that not all things that looked good in the natural (in the physical world, that is) were part of God's plan. He knew to pray diligently for discernment and direction before making any major changes, especially since many other people were benefitting from his teaching.

I was one of the people praying with Rob when he headed out for the interview. When he returned from Delaware, he called me from the airport and came right over for prayer and to sort out what had happened. The corporation had in fact offered him the promotion and transfer. As we prayed and listened, we both felt that accepting the job promotion would endanger his family's current, very good situation, and the family's departure would also be a loss to the church community. We both felt that the Lord wanted him to turn down the offer and stay put. Rob did decline the offer, to the dismay of the company.

Unfortunately, Rob's parents were dead set on seeing him climb the corporate ladder. It would justify the expensive education for which they had paid. When they heard that he had turned down the offer and promotion, they raised a terrible ruckus about Rob throwing away his chance. Rob gave in, recanted, and asked the company if he could still accept the offer. They readily agreed and gave him the promotion.

Rob and his family soon moved to Delaware. We moved to Augusta a few years later and lost touch with Rob and his family, but on a return visit to Marietta and our old church, we ran into Rob, who was in town on a visit. He looked like a hollow shell of himself—not a glimpse of the Spirit was detectable. We had heard that he and Nikki had divorced. When we saw Rob, he was with Lola, who along with her husband Bill had also been part of the Scripture class. Now Lola and Bill were also divorced.

It had been about twelve years since Rob and his family had moved. We asked Rob if he had been teaching Scripture in Delaware, but the answer was already obvious. "I haven't taught at all since we moved from Marietta," he said. Lola also looked totally devoid of her former vibrancy. She told us that Rob was helping her move to Delaware the next day to live with him.

Nancy and I left shocked—not that Satan had knocked them off course, but shocked by how far off course.

But those who want to be rich fall into temptation and are trapped by many senseless and harmful desires that plunge people into ruin and destruction. For the love of money is a root of all kinds of evil, and in their eagerness to be rich some have wandered away from the faith and pierced themselves with many pains.

But as for you, man of God, shun all this; pursue righteousness, godliness, faith, love, endurance, gentleness. Fight the good fight of the faith; take

hold of the eternal life, to which you were called and for which you made the good confession in the presence of many witnesses.
—1 Timothy 6:9-12 (NRSV)

Rob was a good man with good intentions whom God chose to receive an incredible gift to teach Scripture. This gift was opening the spiritual eyes of many bright and active young men and women and represented a threat to Satan's ability to impact their future.

Rob was not spiritually mature enough to effectively contend for the gift God had given him. Satan stole it away through the world's empty promises.

He said, "The knowledge of the secrets of the kingdom of God has been given to you, but to others I speak in parables, so that, 'though seeing, they may not see; though hearing, they may not understand.' This is the meaning of the parable: The seed is the word of God… The seed that fell among thorns stands for those who hear, but as they go on their way they are choked by life's worries, riches and pleasures, and they do not mature. But the seed on good soil stands for those with a noble and good heart, who hear the word, retain it, and by persevering produce a crop."
—Luke 8:10-11, 14-15 (NIV)

910

"910" was the affectionate name given by street people to refer to a ministry that was soup kitchen, shelter, shower and clothes closet in one. It was located at 910 Ponce de Leon Avenue on the east side of Atlanta in an ethnic, artsy area with many small businesses. To the street people, who were mostly homeless, 910 was a home base.

Nancy and I, along with some of our ministry group, had served there before, and we were assigned to man the soup kitchen one Saturday each month. Our group consisted of eight to ten adults, both men and women, and included more than enough people to handle all of the required tasks.

One particular Saturday, we arrived ahead of time. I was looking forward to this opportunity. The founders of this ministry (Ed and his wife, Murphy) believed in ministering to the whole person, body, mind and spirit, and I was especially excited. All prayed up and ready for a rescue mission, I wanted to evangelize and pray over these hurting people. I knew we had sufficient numbers to handle the serving of food and drinks, and I wanted to help feed souls.

Murphy began to give us information and instructions, after which she was going to leave everything to us. Her directions were not what I expected. Straightaway, she singled me out to be the dishwasher of the day. I would wash all of the plates, bowls, glasses, silverware and cookware. The only paper products used by 910 were napkins. They used regular dinnerware and silverware that had been donated to the ministry.

Murphy told me that Johnny would show me what to do in the dishwashing area. Johnny was a recovering street person who lived and served at 910. Leading me to the large triple sink with drain boards where everything was washed and left to dry, he demonstrated how the first sink was used to "knock off" the food (his way of explaining it), the second was for washing, the third was for rinsing, and the drain board was used for quick drying. This set-up, with its very hot water and strong water pressure, seemed like an impressive arrangement to me and something I had never encountered before.

It was good that the dishwashing area was so well equipped because within minutes, the dirty dishes started stacking up in the pass-through window from the dining hall. Used soup bowls, glasses, plates and silverware were filling the window. As fast as they could be thoroughly washed, dried and made ready for another use, they were replaced by the next stack of dirty dishes. That process was repeated for about an hour and a half, until the dining hall emptied of those who had come to be fed. Once all of the eating utensils and dishes were washed and put away, I was given the heavy cook pots and skillets with their crusty, cooked-on residue. These were more work to clean than all of the dishes before.

My great evangelistic plans had long since gone down the drain with the dirty dishwater. Surprisingly, though, I got into step with this fast-track program. I accepted the dishwashing as my job and was able to get beyond the discomfort of the unknown. I really love work, especially physical work, and I like to bring order out of disorder, so this job was (to my surprise) a natural fit for me.

Near the end of the morning, as I was closing in on the last of the large cook pots, Murphy walked up behind me and called my name. As I turned toward her, she laughed and said, "Smile," and snapped a photo of me.

We completed our 910 mission that weekend and I reflected on that busy morning several times over the next few days. The following week, we received a copy of the regular 910 newsletter, and in it was the photo of me in the midst of the sinks and cookware, looking over my shoulder with a big smile. Under the photo, Murphy had added a caption. It read, "Gary's wife, Nancy, says he never enjoys washing dishes this much at home."

Amen to that! The Holy Spirit instantly revealed a deception that had led to long-term bondage for me. The fact was, I had never washed the first dish at home. I had always considered dishwashing to be "women's work." Many males of my generation were under that deception. Outdoor work was the man's responsibility and housework was the woman's, regardless of personal circumstances.

Once I was convicted of my bondage to this untruth, right there in front of me, it was broken. What I hadn't learned in twenty years of marriage, the Spirit showed me in twenty seconds. There was no denying or questioning the truth. I should lend help where help was needed, even at the sink. That day I began washing our dishes at home and have been the primary dishwasher ever since, for over thirty years now. Since I started twenty years late, I'm still playing catch up. I grieve over the early years when that service would have been such a help to Nancy, when she had all the "woman's work" of young motherhood. I didn't see or do my part until that bondage was broken.

Ten years later, after relocating to Augusta, Nancy was hired to manage the local soup kitchen, The Master's Table. Her weekly schedule had her rotating on duty every third Sunday. Each of those Sundays for five years, I would go with her and help in some way. My service of choice was always the dishwashing. I usually got it. The sink arrangement was almost just like the one at 910. The time spent with those big sinks and hot water helped to open my mind and hammer home my healing and the new freedom I had been given to handle my broader responsibilities.

Over the years, I have gradually added to my range of housework tasks. Inside the house, I'm still a distant second to Nancy, but I can be of considerable help. And it has made me a better man.

I guess it follows that, as I have become freed up in these areas, some of my fellow brothers have, too. I love to point out to them this great opportunity for service and growth. A change of mindset from "women's work" to "men's household responsibility" adjusts and balances our lives considerably, both in workload and in outlook. When done in the right spirit, our help is accepted very well by our wives—even appreciated.

The Holy Spirit set me free through the simple truth, delivered by someone I had just met.

> *"And you will know the truth, and the truth will make you free."*
> — *John 8:32 (NASB 1995)*

The Man in Charge

My crew of a half-dozen men and I were heavily involved with a commercial woodwork job at Perimeter Center in Dunwoody, Georgia. We had been moving steadily from one location and contract to the next for about three years. We had been blessed with the Lord's favor and good referrals. This particular job was in the central area of a new, state-of-the-art office complex with nice woodwork and stylish touches throughout, even in the elevator. We had been working there steadily for about a month and were closing in on completion, expecting to finish the work the following week.

It was late Friday afternoon when the doors swung open and in strode "the man in charge" and his two attendants, almost in lockstep. I had never met or talked with him, but had heard others speak of him. He was "the whip" for the development. He was walking in the middle of the threesome, of course, with a younger man on each side hurriedly taking notes on a clipboard, one or the other recording each word he spoke. He was in his mid-sixties and wore a long trench coat almost to the floor. If he had been wearing pearl-handled pistols, he would have looked like General Patton.

With a good deal of posturing and flourish he walked right up, asked who was in charge, and then thrust his hand toward me and announced that he was Mr. Diamond, the man in charge of the complex. He rolled quickly through meaningless pleasantries, verbalizing his great appreciation for our good work—at which he never even looked. It all sounded hollow, scripted and very much like a set-up.

Then he told me the tough news he had come to deliver. He had to ask us to work Saturday and Sunday—whatever it took—to completely finish the job before Monday. This was absolutely essential, he said. The job must be completed before Monday morning. Of course, he wasn't asking, but telling. I

135

responded by explaining that my men and I had worked there all day for each of the past three Saturdays in an effort to move the project along, and I had just given them the following day (Saturday) off. I told him that since Sunday is the Lord's Day, we would not be working on Sunday, and wouldn't be back that weekend, but we would return Monday morning to finish things up.

With that, Mr. Diamond became livid. His expression changed to what looked like pent-up hatred. He stormed away, his attendants trying to keep up, as he lashed out at us, shouting, "This job *will be finished* before Monday morning, even if Jesus Christ Himself comes this weekend."

When we arrived at the site on Monday morning, we found that a different crew had in fact worked on our job over the weekend. Nothing was completed and no one was there. We had to rework almost everything they had touched, and I was charged for the time they had wasted. We completed the job that week. We never again heard from Mr. Diamond, and we never got another contract offer with that company. I would not have accepted one anyway—I don't work for blasphemers.

> *Do not be deceived, God is not mocked; for whatever a man sows, this he will also reap.*
>
> —*Galatians 6:7 (NASB)*

Mike, the Tormented Scholar

When Mike walked into my shop on Broad Street, he struck me right away as a committed homeless person—not because he was panhandling or scamming, but because he seemed to have accepted homelessness as his life. Over time, I learned a few things about Mike. He had not been in Augusta very long, but had been on the streets for fifteen years, beginning in Detroit. Before that he had worked at a regular job, but indicated that he had no intention of ever working again. This was about all he would reveal of his former life. He never mentioned any family. He was about fifty years old and lived mostly out in open fields or in the woods. Quite intellectual and very well educated, he would read for hours each day in the public library. He was very introverted, always paranoid, and talked only to pass on or gain information, not to develop relationships. Mike would drop by in streaks—I wouldn't see him for weeks, and then would see him almost every day. He would come into my shop while I was working and just stand. He seemed to see it as a place where he was accepted and could enter and spend a few minutes. Mike was White and an extreme racist; he wouldn't eat at soup kitchens because of the mixed-race crowd. He would not accept or wear any previously worn clothes, and he didn't ask for money. He carried plastic bags in both hands. These bags were used at night to surround himself and to serve as a warning system while he slept.

Mike was a sepia grey color most of the time, as though he had been sleeping in a coal bin, and he had a stench to match. I took him home a couple of times just so he could have a shower, while Nancy washed and dried his raggedy clothes. Then I would drive him back downtown, where he would begin the process of dirt accumulation all over again. He said he tried to do this (get a fresh start) once a year!

From time to time, I would get a late-night phone call at 10:30 p.m. or later. It would be Mike. He would have found a quarter left in a pay phone and would call to talk, mostly about the latest current events or politics. He diverted all my efforts toward spiritual talk back to intellectual or scientific topics. He was passionate about information and consumed and retained it well, but he resisted any attempt to get personal. His comments were never rash or flippant, but thought through and carefully worded, almost as though he was being taped.

One night, he was at my shop at closing time, on an evening when the area was being pummeled by a cold, driving rainstorm. I could not hazard leaving him in my shop overnight with all of my woodworking equipment, and I couldn't risk taking him to our home because of our family, so I just delivered him where he told me—to an open, empty field outside town. It was painful driving away, leaving him in that condition. I felt guilty having a nice home in which to find refuge and comfort while he was left outside in the cold rain. Unfortunately, it was the life he had chosen many years earlier and for which he seemed to have steeled himself. He likely saw it as the price of his independence from conformity.

I eventually relocated my shop several miles away from my previous location and I lost track of Mike. Years later, an article appeared in the local paper—Mike had died. His last "home" was in a different field, behind a shopping center on the safer, more prosperous, west side of town. He had taken shelter there for a long time. His intelligence, presence and homeless plight (although in some ways brought about by choices he had made years before) had caught the attention of other people, and a small memorial gathering was being held in his honor. The article said that Mike had died in a motel room, which was rented for him for a week as a gift from a benefactor. What a wonderful gift to a homeless person who had nothing.

I considered Mike to be a friend. We had little in common other than the time and space that we briefly shared. Mike's circumstances challenged me to be more sensitive to the disenfranchised. I hope I helped him along somehow, at least by boosting his self-esteem and giving him some awareness of God's love for him.

"The poor you will always have with you..."

—*Matthew 26:11*

The Ticket

Paul was a tall, gangling, confirmed bachelor in his early forties. Soft spoken, reticent, he had a frequently apologetic demeanor. I first encountered him while working with his church's building committee to plan furnishings for the sanctuary. He was quite intelligent, perceptive, with good, clear thinking, but he had trouble making himself heard.

Paul had a longtime position that paid well, owned his own home, and was serious about his Catholic spirituality and devout in practicing his faith. Although I didn't really know him, it was clear to me that something was missing. With all he had going for him, he still seemed somehow incomplete.

After seeing him at various church functions and interacting with him only on a surface level, I was surprised one day when Paul asked if I would be open to giving him some counseling. He realized that he needed help with socializing and thought I could help him. Since I had been doing a good bit of this already with other men, I agreed to give it a try. We began a routine meeting every other Friday at 6:30 a.m.

This worked out very well for both of us, and I was impressed when I saw that Paul really wanted help changing and was open to constructive criticism. He tried hard to act upon it. Much of this process wasn't easy for him, but he was trying. He epitomized the concept of "set in his ways." To his credit, he asked for and received help from other counselors as well.

One Sunday at church, Paul appeared with a tall, attractive European woman. He wanted me to meet her after church. Celina was from Poland and was visiting Paul. She seemed serious and spiritual and very righteous. Paul had met her in Europe when he was there as a tourist. She was a tour guide for his group. Even on first meeting, she struck me as someone who was tenacious about things of importance.

Paul wanted me to pray for them and suggested we go behind the church, away from the crowd in front. We walked to the back of the property and stopped next to a large dumpster that was being used for construction waste from the church renovation. As we came together in prayer, seeking the Lord's direction (while standing by this massive steel roll-off), I was struck by the magnitude of the moment. We were asking for the Lord's leading for their future, either together as husband and wife, or individually. All three of us felt the weight of the prayers, and I definitely sensed that the Lord's plan was for them to be together. The Holy Spirit was very present and seemed to be moving their relationship to a new level. Celina returned to Poland, but her heart remained in Augusta.

Our counseling sessions continued regularly and Celina's name was mentioned frequently. One day, Paul admitted that they were both serious about marriage and he believed Celina would say yes if he asked her. In fact, they had an understanding that if he would send her a plane ticket, she would come right back and they could finalize plans for marriage. The love he felt for her was obvious, but so was his fear. He wanted the married life that Celina represented, but he was somehow bound up, unable to act on that deep desire. That old enemy, insecurity, had stepped forward and was trying to undermine his reason.

Paul knew that Celina was very serious minded. She knew what she wanted, and she had made known that the Lord was now leading her toward marriage and a family. She clearly felt that Paul was the one the Lord had picked for her, and she was ready. Being plainspoken, she also let Paul know that she didn't intend to wait indefinitely. Through many sessions with Paul, I had learned he was never impulsive, but very deliberate and given to procrastination, sometimes because of a fear of failure. Also, it was obvious that he didn't respond well to being pushed. He liked to act on his own timetable.

After a couple of weeks, I asked if Celina was still ready, still waiting for the plane ticket. Rather sheepishly, he admitted that was how things stood. He saw my next question coming, as I asked, with some urgency, "So, when are you going to get her a ticket?"

As though he had run out of excuses, Paul replied, "Right away." If it hadn't been for our prayer time next to the dumpster weeks earlier, I wouldn't have pushed him on this serious issue.

Several days later, he called me and I asked, "Have you gotten her ticket?"

In a restrained voice, he replied, "Yes, I got her ticket." Then he went silent.

Sensing that there was more to his answer, I followed up. "You got her the ticket but haven't sent it to her?"

Sounding ashamed, he said, "Well, not exactly. But I do have it and it's lying on the dresser."

"How long has it been lying on the dresser?" I asked.

"Well, I guess about four days now." Paul's voice was getting weaker.

Now I was beginning to sound like a drill sergeant, and I brusquely asked, "How is she going to use it with it lying on your dresser?"

Almost like someone anticipating a dreaded shot, Paul replied, "I know, I'll have to get it mailed."

Well, he must have gotten a Holy Spirit shot in the arm because later in the day, he called back with an update and a confession. He had taken the ticket to the post office to mail. The postmaster gave him three options: fastest air mail, regular air, or least expensive. Paul chose the least expensive option, mailed the ticket and returned to his car.

As soon as he got into his car, the Holy Spirit convicted him of his unacceptable choice and sent him right back to the postmaster. By that time the envelope had made its way well into the mailing room, and the postmaster had to find it and change the stamps to "fastest air." But the process that day seemed to bring some real freedom and healing to Paul in several areas.

The ticket arrived in Poland and Celina soon arrived in America. Paul proposed, she accepted and wedding plans were made. The wedding followed later at Celina's home church in Poland.

Procrastination is one of the most disruptive and costly of spirits. Very quiet, it presents itself as a friend that requires (and may even encourage) no action from you. That inaction, if left untended, can negate so much, including God's great plan for a person's future.

When God wills something, the timing belongs to Him—not to us!

***

Many years later, it's a joy to watch Paul and Celina and their three kids at mass each Sunday. They are all growing in holiness and faith and trust in their Lord. They are happy and fulfilled, right where they're supposed to be. Paul even looks complete now.

That ticket on the dresser was their ticket to what the Lord had for all of them. What a shame it would have been if it had never been redeemed, and God's plan had been missed altogether.

Any mention of the ticket still gets an immediate reaction from Paul, but now he can smile about it with deep gratitude.

Hope deferred makes the heart sick, but desire fulfilled is a tree of life.
—Proverbs 13:12 (NASB)

Dwight

Since I was eleven years old, I have loved baseball—as a player, as a fan and sometimes as an addict. In recent years, after undergoing significant healing and some withdrawal, I'm less addicted. This means that I can attend to other things while the World Series is on, and only give in to this old love on occasion.

For several years, our community retreat was at the Junaluska Retreat Center, in the mountains of North Carolina, on the same weekend that the World Series was wrapping up. On one retreat, as we concluded our Saturday night community session and walked through the retreat center's sitting area, there it was on television, being played out right before our eyes—the World Series. Without slowing down, Nancy excused herself and went up to our room and to bed. I surveyed the group and took a look at the TV. It was late in the game, and the outcome was uncertain. The spectators were gathered around in chairs, some quietly maneuvering for better seats as others were vacated. All of the "box seats" were filled, so I settled for a grandstand seat on the far side of the room. After about twenty minutes (and just like in Scripture), I was called up to a better place. A great seat opened up, second from the TV. Since no one else was getting up to take it, I eased on in.

The group of spectators, which included several Alleluia brothers and a few sisters, knew baseball to varying degrees. The conversation was peppered with baseball trivia, both old and current. We were enjoying the break from our own intense weekend and were unwinding. There was nothing serious at stake here for any of us. After a few minutes, my attention was drawn to the man sitting beside me, between me and the TV. He was nice looking, sharp, personable and knowledgeable, about sixty years old, dressed in a white dress shirt and slacks. I first pegged him as perhaps a Methodist minister, since Junaluska is a world headquarters for the Methodist church. We all began to realize that he was the trivia ace. He knew the most trivia and seemed very comfortable in the setting.

Between pitches, he and I shared more about ourselves. His name was Dwight. Before long, he confided that he lived in the area, but hoped to soon be moving to Atlanta. When I asked, "Why Atlanta?" he replied that it had the greatest sports bars and the most beautiful women—and that he was very single. Wow! Why had he told me this? What was happening? All of a sudden Junaluska, that bastion of Methodism and goodness, had become a sports bar, complete with talk about beautiful women. I sat in stunned silence, temporarily losing track of the score and the sport we were watching. Almost before I could get back into the game, it was over and the players were leaving, replaced by Bob Costas and Joe Morgan. As the field emptied of people, so did the lobby. All of my Alleluia friends were heading off to bed. I told Dwight, my new acquaintance, that it had been enjoyable talking with him, and I also began to leave.

The Lord doesn't mince words with me, so three fourths of the way across the lobby, the Voice quietly spoke to me, asking, "Where are you going?"

My first thought was, "Going to bed. The game is over, it's 11 o'clock, and it's time to get to bed. Tomorrow will be a very full day."

With that, the Spirit had me look back across the lobby and there was "my man," standing alone, still next to the TV, with his back to me. The Voice said, "The game is not over—it's just starting." Got it! And I had been within a heartbeat of totally missing it!

Saying goodbye at 11 p.m. and then reacquainting oneself two minutes later can be awkward and appear a little strange, but God's grace is sufficient. It was clear to me that the challenging question the Lord wanted put to Dwight was, "Where are you with the Lord?" I explained to him that this was what I had been sent back to ask him. He was more than a little taken aback. Both the abruptness and the "God factor" caught him flat footed.

The next two hours were some of the most intense and challenging that I've ever experienced in witnessing. It didn't help that "Saturday Night Live" was on the TV then, in the background. To try to move past Dwight to turn it off could have broken the momentum. Better just to mentally block it out and work around it. It was as if Dwight's life was hanging in the balance. It was clear to me that there had been a great battle between the spirits for this man's soul, for a very long time. My spirit was quickened all the more when he said that he was not a guest at Junaluska, but had driven to the retreat center just to watch the World Series, as his own TV was broken. This encounter had really been set up by the Lord.

About an hour into this great odyssey, my friend and fellow Alleluia member Paul came back and joined us, carefully assisting in the Spirit's work. Our man finally (and cautiously) consented to allow us to pray over him. It was good. Paul and I left feeling we had tried hard to deliver the "Jesus mail" to Dwight.

The next week, back in Augusta, some of our Alleluia friends told me that they had seen this same man on Sunday at Junaluska, standing in the back of our meeting room during the closing session of the retreat. I was encouraged that our prayers had not scared him away. Maybe Dwight had received just what he needed and it was turning his life around. Perhaps that had been the biggest victory of the weekend. Glory!

In the months following, I reflected often on that World Series encounter, wondering if Dwight had in fact begun to get his life together. On the same weekend the following year, we returned to Junaluska for the annual Alleluia Community retreat. As we arrived, some of our friends began rushing up and telling us that the guy from last year's World Series was there. I had no trouble remembering him, and minutes later, there he was in the flesh. Not so much in living color, though. He looked rough, beaten down and disheveled, not at all the cool and confident man he had seemed during last year's World Series. Dwight tagged along over the next couple of days, staying close by and gradually unfolding more of the real story. He reluctantly confessed that he had actually been homeless the first time we met, living out of his old car (which was filled with all of his belongings) and using public restrooms to wash up so that he would look presentable. He was concerned about his future, had no plans and was not optimistic about anything. As we concluded our community weekend, several men and women gathered around Dwight and another drifter type, Tom, who had also latched onto us. We laid hands on both of them, prayed over them, and then drove off to Augusta, leaving them standing there looking pretty pathetic. We didn't feel great about the chances for either of them.

About ten days later, a worn-out old car slowly rolled up in front of my shop and came to a stop. Out climbed Dwight, all of his possessions stashed in the car. He had decided to make a move, driving four hours to Augusta unannounced. He just went to the address on the business card I had given him. Dwight had relocated to Augusta. How about that! And to live with us. Oh, Hallelujah! Nancy was less thrilled with his move than I was (that's saying a good bit) but got with the program and showed Dwight his new quarters. Over the years, she had been involved in enough ministry with street people to be able to deal with it.

As time went on, Dwight became very uncomfortable with our lifestyle and would come to compare it to a monastery—that was his definition of order and schedule. (We didn't deserve such a high evaluation.) The pieces began to come together, little by little, as we talked to him and later, to his adult daughter, Shannon, whom he had reluctantly agreed I could call to better understand his plight.

Shannon recounted how her father had been an outstanding young banker at the age of thirty, managing two branch banks, and was voted the civic man of the year in Asheville, North Carolina—no small honor. (He carried newspaper articles about that with him; they were among his personal treasures.) He had a good wife and two young children and a lot going for him. One day, though, his wife decided she'd had enough of his womanizing habits and just loaded up their two kids and all their belongings and left Dwight to himself—and to all the other women of the world. Shannon felt her mother was right in doing what she did.

But Dwight never recovered. His career straightaway crashed and burned like a meteor. He basically never worked again and became a womanizing drifter, staying with one woman and then another as long as they would put up with him and he with them (such women often delude themselves into thinking of this lifestyle as a ministry). Possibly, his wife's departure with their children was such an embarrassment that he couldn't face his business peers. He apparently didn't have the character or incentive to even try. Shannon said she had been expecting a call from someone—a bar, a jail, a husband—to come and get her father because he was in trouble again. It was a cycle that had been repeated over and over for years. You could just feel the embarrassment and pain in Shannon's voice as she relived it again. And you could feel that void in her own life for the father she had never had. It was not the type of father-daughter relationship that most of us desire. Still, she was prepared to come and retrieve him. But her protective husband put his foot down. He just couldn't let her do it. For her own good, and for the good of the family, he said no. So then, Dwight became our extended guest—and whether he knew it or not, the bar had been raised.

Along with the help of some community brothers, we rushed Dwight into a crash program for total rehab, taking him to as many men's functions as we could and keeping him separated from the women. We didn't violate his space or pressure him overly to participate, but he knew what was expected. Still, he wasn't changing much. After about three weeks, Nancy had had enough of Dwight's unwillingness to help out or try to get work. His all-day presence in our home was wearing thin. His confidence was starting to return, but so were his pride and cynicism. We both knew he had to vacate our home. Three weeks had been our limit.

Ken, also a member of Alleluia, a single man in his forties who lived across the street, agreed to take him in for an indefinite period of time. Being left to himself and his own devices all day while Ken was at work didn't help Dwight's rehab. After a month in Ken's house, Dwight began to get critical and cocky, sometimes caustic, especially about women. He even began to express his views of community women, evaluating them on the basis of his worldly criteria. That was crossing the line. Male chauvinism began to show its ugly face. His history, three decades of selfishness and aimlessness, was holding sway. We all knew it was over. His chance in Augusta was up.

Dwight didn't seem surprised when I told him he had to leave Alleluia. He seemed to expect it. It was obvious that he had been told to leave many places throughout his life. Grudgingly, he left as he came, dragging off in his old car without a "thank you" or a smile, looking bitter and depressed, disappointed in us all. He was convinced that people had let him down again, as he was certain they always had. He could have been a character in C. S. Lewis' insightful novel *The Great Divorce*—rejecting the light and returning to his familiar darkness.

Months later we got a brief note from Dwight. He was in Michigan, temporarily staying with a benevolent old aunt who had taken him in many times before. She was usually his last resort, when no impressionable younger women were available to come to his rescue. She would likely let him stay until she couldn't put up with him anymore, and then send him away.

Dwight was living proof of what is warned in the Book of Proverbs about the results of adultery, fornication, slothfulness and pride, all significant sins. Evil spirits allowed to have influence can undermine an individual's talent and potential every time. Shannon described her father as a borderline genius who knew a lot about many things, but just wouldn't apply himself to anything except womanizing. Dwight even knew a lot "about" Jesus—but he never had submitted himself to Jesus.

Lord, have mercy on him.

Drink water from your own cistern and fresh water from your own well. Let your fountain be blessed, and rejoice in the wife of your youth. As a loving hind and a graceful doe, let her breasts satisfy you at all times; be exhilarated always with her love. For why should you, my son, be exhilarated with an adulteress and embrace the bosom of a foreigner? For the ways of a man are before the eyes of the Lord, and He watches all his paths. His own iniquities will capture the wicked, and he will be held with the cords of his sin.

—Proverbs 5:15, 18-22 (NASB)

Hogwash

Many dramatic events happen on Broad Street in the killing zone of Planned Parenthood; it's a cutting edge between good and evil. Since the "prayed-up" sidewalk is holy ground, it frequently becomes a place of encouragement or ministry to someone you have never seen before. They just walk right into the Holy Spirit zone. Since evil also frequents the area, you never know which is coming next—an opportunity for ministry or an ugly encounter.

Early one morning around 6:30 a.m., while it was still very dark, I was walking up and down the sidewalk in front of Planned Parenthood carrying a seven-foot cross. No one else had arrived yet. Then, angling across Broad Street on foot in my direction was a tall, older White man. I had never seen him before, not even from a distance. His body language appeared hostile as he passed about twenty feet from me. He looked quite angry about my presence there with the cross.

I called out to him, "Hi, Brother," and my greeting was met with scorn and an evil scowl as he growled out, "Hogwash!"

I responded, "Jesus died for you, Brother."

He quickly kept walking and calling out into the darkness, "Hogwash! Hogwash!"

His words seemed amplified on the still vacant Broad Street. The whole event seemed surreal—like I was witnessing an impending car wreck. In my street exposure, the many hundreds of times I had publicly carried a cross, I had heard and seen many things, but never this particular, blatant reaction. I prayed for this misguided and hardened old man during the following week, asking for a breakthrough in his understanding and a release from bitterness.

We had a second encounter a week or two later. This time, the man walked toward me, acting even more hostile and belligerent. I couldn't get him to talk with me, but he did stop momentarily. I got a good look into his eyes this time. He looked intelligent enough—not a mental case, I'm almost sure—but he was filled with bitterness and hatred and scorn. Again, his comment to me was "Hogwash!" He spat out the word in such a way that it sounded like the most vile profanity, expressing a total contempt for the cross and for me. He walked away quickly, putting distance between us. It was obvious to me that he was in Satan's grip, and this situation wasn't just recent or temporary.

The third and last time I saw him, he came down the sidewalk pushing an old shopping cart that was loaded to the top with scraps of wood and junk he had been picking up to try to sell. The whole pile might have brought him a dollar or so. This time he walked right up in front of me, almost as if to defy the cross, trying to intimidate me. By this third meeting, I was really concerned for his soul and where he would spend eternity, so I asked him to let me pray over him and lay hands on him. With a quick move, he fearfully backed away, saying "No!" emphatically. I asked him to just reach out and take hold of the cross, but since demons are terrified of the cross, he rushed away, pushing the cart of junk, shouting, "Hogwash! Hogwash!" into the darkness surrounding him.

I stood there saddened by the devastation that Satan had wrought in this man. He looked like one being led off to his execution. He was made in God's likeness and image but had chosen hatred and defiance of God, along with a cart full of junk, over the inheritance of a King's son that he could have had— an inheritance that had already been paid for in full and promised to him.

The demons had taken over this man's spirit and mind so thoroughly, it would take a powerful act of God to free him. I didn't expect to ever see him again, and I haven't. I had a sense that his time was running out.

Blessed is the man who walks not in the counsel of the wicked, nor stands in the way of sinners, nor sits in the seat of scoffers; but his delight is in the law of the Lord, and on His law he meditates day and night. He is like a tree planted by streams of water, that yields its fruit in its season, and its leaf does not wither. In all that he does, he prospers.

The wicked are not so, but are like chaff which the wind drives away. Therefore the wicked will not stand in the judgment, nor sinners in the congregation of the righteous; for the Lord knows the way of the righteous, but the way of the wicked will perish.

—*Psalm 1:1-6 (RSV)*

Chapter 6

The Spirit Has a Plan: Divine Appointments and Encounters

Jim, a friend of mine, was having a noteworthy birthday. It seemed like a good idea to take him out to lunch, as this was a special day and he is a special friend.

Jim likes a place that he and his wife Jane used to go, the Village Deli, so we decided to go there. We arrived and parked at the shopping complex where the restaurant is located. As we left my vehicle and walked toward the deli, Jim was slightly ahead of me. It was then that I saw her, a woman on the sidewalk, about half the distance to the deli. She was standing outside of a retail shop, apparently waiting for something. She was a capable-looking, nicely dressed Black woman, maybe in her early sixties, a typical-looking shopper. I had never seen her before.

As I got closer, she might as well have had a sign around her neck that read, "Woman in need of prayer." My attention was drawn straight to the cigarette she held in her hand, not quite out of sight, next to her leg.

By now she was focused intently on me, as if I had a sign that read, "Man sent to pray," and she was expecting my arrival. I walked straight forward, approaching her, and said, "Bless you, sister!"

Without hesitation, she replied, "Lord knows I need it!"

I pointed at the cigarette and told her, "I know, those things are killing you!"

With that, she blurted out, "I can't get rid of them. I've been trying. They're driving me crazy. I can't even sleep."

I asked her name in a confidential tone (it was Gladys) and told her mine. I then asked, "Gladys, would you like to ask the Lord to take away all your desire to smoke?"

Emphatically, she burst out, "Yes, yes!"

Then I asked, "Is it OK to lay hands on you and pray for you?"

She nodded yes, repeatedly.

As I signed her forehead with the cross, Gladys gave two affirming yelps and jerks that slightly lifted her body; you see these sometimes in Pentecostal people of faith when the Spirit touches them.

I gave my best effort to deliver a Spirit-led prayer over Gladys about the ravages of smoking and her body being a temple of the Holy Spirit (this clearly resonated with her). I beseeched the Spirit to help her give up smoking, forever.

Gladys opened her eyes and looked deeply touched by the Spirit—shaken, in fact! Then I asked, "Do you want to give me your cigarette?" She readily gave it to me.

After a quick hug and blessing, I walked toward the deli, cigarette in hand (my first), and noticed the restaurant's "No Smoking" sign.

The entire event happened so fast that even though I had stopped and prayed, I found myself entering the deli right after Jim. In the speed of the encounter, I had overlooked asking Gladys to give me any cigarette pack that she might have had. I feel sure she would have given it to me.

If we are on duty and paying attention with our spiritual senses to what is in front of us, the Spirit does almost all of the rest.

Praise be to the Lord, to God our Savior, who daily bears our burdens. Our God is a God who saves; from the Sovereign Lord comes escape from death.

—Psalm 68:19-20 (NIV)

Numerous events in Scripture describe what many believers call a "divine appointment." This is most often a meeting involving three or more people, but at least involves a person of faith, the Holy Spirit, and a third party who has a need that the Lord wants to meet. Time is usually of the essence, and a quick response to the Holy Spirit's prompting is absolutely essential. These meetings can happen anytime, anyplace.

I will briefly paraphrase a story from the Acts of the Apostles (18:26-39). The apostle Philip is spoken to by an angel and sent south to a particular desert road, with no other information. On the road he sees a eunuch, the treasurer for Candace, Queen of Ethiopia. The eunuch is sitting in his chariot reading the book of Isaiah. The Spirit says to Philip, "Go up and join this chariot."

After a brief verbal exchange, Philip is invited into the chariot to explain to the eunuch the Scriptures and God's great gift of salvation, given to us through Jesus' crucifixion, death and resurrection.

Then, since the eunuch has experienced this great new awakening, he wants Philip to baptize him in the water nearby. Philip complies, baptizes the eunuch, and then is snatched up and whisked to the place of his next mission. The eunuch sees him no longer but goes on his way, rejoicing in his new life.

This is a classic divine appointment. Philip is told only the direction to go and the road to take. He knows he is on a mission for the Lord and he trusts the Spirit to provide all the necessary elements, which of course He does, including the water for baptism, which might not even have been there until it was needed.

Often in our divine appointments, we are sent to a location and then someone arrives; unbeknownst to them, they are there to receive something from the Lord. Sometimes they come directly to us. The key in each case is to be on duty and led by the Spirit, and to be obedient to His prompting. All of the details will be supplied as they are needed. This is living our faith "in the moment," often outside of church, as it should be lived. The Holy Spirit is always ready to do His part, sometimes even supplying the transportation to the encounter.

Scripture has many "divine appointments," such as the one involving Peter and John and the lame beggar at the temple called Beautiful (Acts 3:3-9). In this encounter, the lame man (who has been lame his entire life) is healed and begins to dance and praise God. In another divine appointment, Ananias is sent to Saul (Paul) to remove the scales from his eyes, baptize him in the Holy Spirit and send him on a lifetime mission trip (Acts 9:10-19). We read of another such appointment when the angel comes to prison to release Peter (Acts 12:6-11). All the guards are put to sleep, the chains fall off Peter's hands, every door swings open and Peter is set free to become the "rock" on which the church is built.

There are many, many accounts in Scripture of a man or woman being used to assist in a God mission. The Spirit knows exactly what He is doing. If He calls us to go, if He sends us, the grace is on us to accomplish the mission.

We all know that God is perfectly capable of dealing with anyone and their problems or needs without help from us—but instead He includes us in the words or actions that He wants to deliver or the works He needs done. Divine appointments are important to us, and to the Lord.

Much like when a father includes his young son as his "helper" on a project around the house, or a mother includes her little girl as her "helper" in cooking the family meal, the Lord invites our participation to get us involved, teach us and prepare us for what lies ahead.

Apparently, it is the Lord's desire that we work together to build His Kingdom here on earth, learn the "what" and the "how," and take up some of the work for Him, once He knows our hearts are in it and that we will do our best. Why should we worry? His Grace is sufficient!

If we expect to be with Him and work with Him forever, now is a great time to start.

Remember, as hard as it may be to believe, Jesus Himself tells us that we will do even greater works than those He performed in His earthly life.

> *"Very truly I tell you, whoever believes in Me will do the works I have been doing, and they will do even greater things than these, because I am going to the Father. And I will do whatever you ask in My name, so that the Father may be glorified in the Son. You may ask Me for anything in My name, and I will do it.*

> *"If you love Me, keep My commands. And I will ask the Father, and He will give you another advocate to help you and be with you forever—the Spirit of truth.*

> *The world cannot accept Him, because it neither sees Him nor knows Him.*

> *But you know Him, for He lives with you and will be in you."*
> —*John 14:12-17 (NIV)*

The following stories describe just a few of my experiences; these stand out from among many others. I know quite a number of men and women who live with an "on-duty-to-divine-appointments" mindset.

A New Year, A New Day

It was New Year's Eve, and the usual nighttime prayer meeting was being held at our local church. Our small group had a tradition of gathering on this night to celebrate and focus on our new life—rather than celebrating in the old way, the world's way.

During the meeting, Steve, one of the men, stepped out to go to the restroom. As he was returning, he heard an unusual sound coming from a nearby room and stopped to investigate. He discovered a young woman crying. She was all alone and in the dark, on the floor.

Steve was a father of two himself, and he approached her with care and concern to see how he could help. He soon realized that she was a stranger, and she needed lots of help. She was in a drunken state, almost unable to stand up. As he labored to communicate with her, he learned that her name was Susan and that she had no idea where she was. With some gentle coaxing, Steve assisted her to her feet and was able to help her over to the room where our prayer group was gathered. Of course, as soon as they came into the room, we recognized her condition.

Susan was an attractive blonde college student who had come home for the holidays with the primary intention of partying, and she was now under the full effects of that partying. She told us that she didn't know how or why she came to be at the church. She thought she remembered driving past the property, then making an unplanned U-turn and driving up the very long, winding driveway over the hill to the church building, which is not visible from the road. She soon found herself inside the dark building.

Instead of a DUI, a wreck, or worse, Susan had the gift of a lifetime waiting for her from the Lord.

As our group of about eight men and women began to minister to her, showing her unconditional love, Susan very quickly started to sober up (surely this was a work of the Spirit) and began to awaken spiritually. She was very truthful with us and confessed to being distraught because nothing in her life was going right for her. This was not the first time she'd had a problem because of alcohol. She also shared that her father, although successful in business, had struggled with alcoholism for many years.

Susan was very open to receiving help that night. She seemed quite aware of the dangerous state of her life and her desperate need for a new direction. Her unplanned visit to the church and our ministry to her seemed totally set-up and orchestrated by the Holy Spirit. After we had listened to her, talked things through, and prayed over her at length, we felt that she could safely drive home. As we all prepared to leave, we exchanged phone numbers and invited her to come the next night to a "share group" meeting to be held at a nearby home. We felt encouraged that we would likely see Susan again (but, of course, you never know).

The next night an energized crowd assembled, and among them was a joyful, enthusiastic Susan. The drunken, distraught young woman from the night before had disappeared—without a trace. Wow! She also brought another woman to the gathering, her mother Barb. At one point during the meeting, all members of the group held hands and prayed the Our Father (Lord's Prayer). Barb was jolted by the Spirit and converted on the spot! Barb had undoubtedly said the words of this prayer many times during the decades she had attended church, but on this night the words were faith filled and came alive to her. Her spirit woke up!

Over the next season, Barb could hardly contain the joy she had discovered in this new life. She ignited spiritually, like a parched tree engulfed by a forest fire. She had endured much in an abusive, alcoholic relationship that seemed to have reached a dead end. Suddenly there was hope and joy and a new life.

Susan and Barb, who looked almost like sisters, had been longtime church-goers, but they had never before been among born-again people who exuberantly lived their lives in the Holy Spirit. In a matter of minutes, they each had felt the love and presence of the Lord like they had never felt it before, in all their years of attending church. Susan said no to alcohol, and they both became regulars in our Spirit-filled activities. Their individual lives and family life were changed forever. Even Brian, Susan's father and Barb's husband, was so influenced by the transformation that he saw in them and in their home that he began to make changes for the better.

Sometimes just the opportunity to witness and experience the "real thing"—God's ways lived out—is all that is necessary for people to begin to make choices that transform their lives.

> *This is why it is said:"Wake up, sleeper, rise from the dead, and Christ will shine on you."*
> —*Ephesians 5:14 (NIV)*

> *He who was seated on the throne said, "I am making everything new!"*
> *Then He said, "Write this down, for these words are trustworthy and true."*
> —*Revelation 21:4 (NIV)*

Middle Seat

I was traveling by plane from Washington, D.C., to Atlanta. I consider virtually any trip as a possible evangelistic opportunity and was hoping (really, almost expecting) that the Lord would send someone for me to evangelize. As I boarded the plane, I wondered who this person might be. I was an infrequent flyer, which was likely obvious, so the flight attendant invited me to choose any vacant seat. There were several from which to choose. The plane had rows of three seats on each side. I chose a middle seat (not my favorite), which gave me two opportunities to engage with someone. The seats on both sides of me remained empty, but then, just as the doors were about to be closed, a woman walked down the aisle and without hesitation took a seat next to me. Her arrival had the look to me of a Holy Spirit placement; she looked like she knew just the right seat for her.

She was an attractive Black woman in her early forties, nicely dressed, as though she had been attending an important event. As she got settled, we spoke, and the Bible on my lap probably put her at ease to talk with me. Within minutes, it became apparent that she was a good Christian woman with strong faith, but she had a heavily burdened spirit that day.

Her name was Pamela, and as we talked, she told me she was on her way home to Alabama. She was just returning from burying her husband at Arlington Cemetery, just across the Potomac River from Washington. He was a decorated war veteran and had died after a long illness contracted during his military service. She reflected on their rich life together and what an awesome husband and father he had been. I just listened to her sharing about him, letting her talk as much as she needed to, and then asked if I could pray for her. She was totally receptive to that, and as I reached out my hand toward her, she firmly took it. Before I finished praying for her, she was fast asleep, and she held onto my hand, with her head resting on my shoulder, throughout the entire flight to Atlanta.

I believe that experience was a healing balm for Pamela, and probably for the flight attendants. They seemed mindful of what was happening. They were very available to serve us but didn't disturb Pamela's peaceful rest. Neither of us needed any service. We both already had what we had requested.

...but those who hope in the Lord
will renew their strength.
They will soar on wings like eagles;
they will run and not grow weary,
they will walk and not be faint.

—Isaiah 40:31 (NIV)

The Man

Nancy and I were staying at a hotel on the weekend of our youngest son's wedding. It was Saturday morning, the day of the wedding, and we were starting this special day with a continental breakfast. As we stood there drinking coffee and eating doughnuts, four pleasant-looking businessmen in their fifties approached to get their own breakfast. They looked like men who could be "talked to," something I see as a call of mine. I usually start the conversation and see if the Lord has something planned or set up. In an upbeat manner, I greeted them and then asked the four together, "How is your day going?"

One started to respond, but stopped, and then another, and then one man finally spoke up for them all. "Not very good," he said. "We came here on Monday to work out a problem with the business. We've been at it all week—and right now it doesn't look like we're any closer to getting it solved than when we started on Monday." They didn't seem surprised or overly disappointed.

Before I could respond, out of the corner of my eye I saw The Man coming down the hall. I recognized him right away, even though I had never seen or talked with him. He was like a type that I had worked for before—you may have worked for this type yourself. His boastful, in-charge swagger and the suddenly tensed body language of the other four were dead giveaways. He was the boss and we better all know that!

In part because the four men had been so open with me, I sensed a green light from the Holy Spirit to act quickly on a leading. As The Man approached his subordinates, planning to walk past and ignore me, I said to him, "Excuse me, I was just talking with your men. They tell me you've been here all week working on a business problem, and it's no better now than when you started. I know this is none of my business, but I also have a business and had problems with it a while back. But I got an answer, put it into practice, and it sure worked for me!"

The Man, looking quite irritated at my intrusion, growled, "Oh, yeah? What's that?" He could just as well have said, "Who cares?"

I wasn't surprised or bothered by his response, since I was on a mission from the Spirit. I was to deliver the mail. With real enthusiasm, I replied, "Just give the business to Jesus. Whatever He tells you, just do it!"

The Man, clearly someone with a hot temper, pride and pent-up resentment, instantly exploded and burst out, "Je-sus! Je-sus!" He immediately stomped away, leading his men and adding rapid expletives as he rushed them off. I knew before speaking to The Man that it would be hard for him to hear, and much harder for him to receive. I also knew that the other men might pay a short-term cost, but I sensed that the Lord wanted to address The Man's arrogance and pride right then, for his sake and for the sake of all the others who had to relate to him, both in business and personally. Ugly spirits are like puss in festering sores and need to be gotten out. It's not likely The Man would have received such a message from anyone he knew, but words of knowledge have a way of getting through.

An arrogant man stirs up strife,
But he who trusts in the Lord will prosper.
He who trusts in his own heart is a fool,
But he who walks wisely will be delivered.

—Proverbs 28:25-26 (NASB)

The Time

Dale, one of our Alleluia Community elders (we refer to our leaders as elders), was near death and was in the intensive care unit in a hospital in downtown Augusta. Because of his serious condition, Nancy went to the hospital on Friday to check on him and on his wife, Carolyn. I was at work and agreed that we would go to see Dale together on Sunday.

While at the hospital on Friday, Nancy met and talked with a young woman named Julie in the waiting room. Julie was there for her fiancé, Josh, who had recently been afflicted with a fast-moving, life-threatening blood disorder and was now in the ICU. The prognosis for his recovery was grim, and their wedding date had already been set. Nancy was very impressed with this sharp young woman who was faced with such a daunting challenge. Nancy came home as concerned for Julie and her fiancé as she was for Dale.

Nancy and I returned on Sunday to visit Dale and his family. We wondered if Julie's fiancé would still be there, and if we would see Julie herself. As in many hospitals, only two visitors at a time were allowed to visit a patient in the ICU. After a short wait, I was able to go in to pray over Dale for God's will for him. I sensed he might not have much time left on this earth. I came back to the waiting room and told Nancy about Dale's condition. After she heard the report about Dale, she wanted to introduce me to Julie, who was standing next to her.

Julie fulfilled all of Nancy's earlier description and more. In addition to being a beautiful young woman in her late twenties, she had a gracious spirit and she appeared to be a seasoned Christian. The three of us talked for a few minutes about Josh and his swiftly deteriorating condition. A sizable group of friends and family members, including parents, aunts and uncles, were standing a few feet away. Worry, distress and mounting hopelessness seemed to hang heavily over them. Then one of them suggested they all go get lunch in the hospital cafeteria. The entire group, except for Julie, headed down the hall.

Only Nancy and I remained with Julie, who was about to go in to see Josh, and I felt led to ask her, "Could I go in with you to offer a prayer over him, even though I don't know him?" Julie agreed readily, saying, "Sure, that would be great."

So in we headed. As we arrived at Josh's bedside, I was struck by his still strong-looking but almost lifeless body lying in the bed. He had been an impressive male counterpart to Julie. I was also taken by the apparent purity of both of them. The upcoming wedding date was on the horizon, but death seemed to be standing in the way. Since I had never seen or talked to Josh, I tried to get my bearings so that I would know how to pray effectively for him.

Julie already knew what was needed and she felt it was important to act boldly while she had the opportunity. She spoke encouraging words to Josh, telling him that he could let go of this world and put himself into Jesus' hands. Her message set my course. I realized right then that I wasn't there to pray for Josh's healing, but to help Julie and Josh with his safe passage into the Lord's hands. Julie and I each reminded Josh of the great life he had already experienced (the Holy Spirit supplied my part) and of the Lord's great love for him and Julie's love for him, too. It was obvious that Josh was a strong and longtime follower of Jesus. We reminded him of the great promises to him that were about to be fulfilled, the very hope for which he had lived. Julie reminded Josh that he didn't need to worry about her, she would be fine. She had the Lord with her (He had her!), and Josh could be at peace to go to Jesus. That was God's will and plan. Our words for Josh just all fit together, almost as if they had been orchestrated.

She was almost a bride. She had looked forward to decades of a good marriage and family life, and was now losing both her marriage and the love of her life. But Julie looked as though she had chosen to release Josh and be at peace. Only grace could have accomplished that in her! Josh looked as if he was already in the Lord's arms.

After a few moments of silence, I blessed them both, signed him with the cross, thanked Julie for the special opportunity, and left them together as I rejoined Nancy.

That afternoon, back at home, we received news that Josh had gone to be with the Lord an hour or so after we prayed. Julie and I had been called to carry out evangelical "last rites" for Josh that day. Certainly it was nothing planned or official—just believers' last rites. Our faith alone prepares us for our mission, and being on duty and available enables God to use us in any given time and place.

> *There is an appointed time for everything. And there is a time for every event under heaven—A time to give birth and a time to die; A time to plant and a time to uproot what is planted.*
> *—Ecclesiastes 3:1-2 (NASB)*

> *...In a moment, in the twinkling of an eye, at the last trumpet; for the trumpet will sound, and the dead will be raised imperishable, and we will be changed.*
> *—1 Corinthians 15:52 (NASB)*

Infectious Faith

Our monthly prayer breakfast is held in a different location in Augusta each month. Different faith denominations, with congregations of various ethnicities, take turns hosting. The prayer breakfast is about unity. This particular morning, the breakfast was being held at a Lutheran church in South Augusta. The Holy Spirit had been felt in power this morning, raising our expectations about what the Lord might be doing. The breakfast always begins with prayer before eating, followed by dining and fellowship, and was coming to a close. We were preparing to leave and head off to work. Only a small group remained behind, mostly to clean up.

As I walked toward the door, I noticed a middle-aged man sitting at a table ahead of me. His name was Daryl, and I occasionally ran into him at such events. I had not seen him earlier that morning. I stopped to speak and said, "Daryl, I didn't know you were here. I didn't see you out there when I was sharing."

Daryl replied, "That's because I wasn't here. I just got here a few minutes ago." He went on to explain. "I was trying to be on time but haven't been able to do that with anything the last several days."

I took that statement to mean he had a ministry need, so I sat down across from him at the table. "What's been the problem?" I asked.

Daryl confided, "I've had this infection on my leg and ankle, been to several doctors. They don't know what it is or how to treat it—nothing they've tried has worked. It's only gotten worse." By that time Mike, the pastor of the church, had sat down next to us and was listening intently.

"Here, I'll show you," Daryl said. He pulled his pant leg up to the knee and revealed the most angry-looking, inflamed, infectious skin you can imagine. Fiery red and swollen, it looked like a combination of extreme poison ivy and a severe reaction to fire ant bites. It challenged the senses just to look at it.

This was obviously nothing to fool around with, so I flatly asked him, "You don't want it, do you?"

Daryl snapped back, "No, I don't want it!"

The Spirit was moving, so I tried to stay with Him. "I just heard something from the Holy Spirit that sounds pretty absurd, but I know you deal in some pretty absurd things." (Daryl frequently prayed over people who were beset with various problems.)

"What did you hear?" Daryl asked.

"I just heard that we are to take your cup of coffee, pour it over your leg, lay hands on you, and ask the Lord to heal you," I told him.

Daryl instantly agreed. "Go for it," he said.

Mike, the pastor, quickly retrieved a towel from the next room. We then had Daryl hold his infected leg in a horizontal position over his other knee, and we placed the towel under his lower leg and ankle, extending it the length of his leg. Then I poured his cup of coffee over his leg, making three passes to fully comply with the word I had received from the Lord.

We wrapped the towel around his leg to dry him off, laid our hands on his leg, and asked the Lord to heal him. Mike and I removed the towel and, to our amazement, Daryl's leg was absolutely free of any redness or infection. His leg was totally clear, white as a baby's skin. The Lord had instantly taken the infection away! We were stunned by the speed. Glory!

I've shared this story a few times and listeners are usually jolted by the instant results. I am still in awe that such an infectious condition disappeared so quickly and completely—but the Lord can do anything, and instantly, if He chooses to! Listeners are frequently taken aback that we poured coffee right onto Daryl's leg, but I'm convinced that the coffee in and of itself had nothing to do with the healing—what mattered was our obedience in following what the Lord had prompted us to do.

The Spirit sometimes tells us to do what may seem absurd to us, but if He says it, He has expressed the way He wants things done, and whatever He has called for will work. He alone may understand the reasons. At times, He may be blessing the people praying as much as the one for whom we pray. The Spirit seems to work most efficiently when we operate in complete and rapid obedience, expressing no doubts and asking no questions. Daryl's painful and distressing infection was healed in far less time than it has taken me to write about it.

Whatever He tells you—do it!

His mother said to the servants, "Whatever He says to you, do it."
                                                        —John 2:5 (NASB)

Washed Clean

One Saturday afternoon, I took our car to a local self-service car wash on a busy thoroughfare, where today's culture is very much in evidence and can be both seen and heard as it passes by. On a typical Saturday when the weather is good, this car wash is quite busy, with lots of music coming from the various cars.

As I put my coins in and began washing our car, I was suddenly unable to ignore a man with a flashy red car about forty feet away in the center of the lot. His speakers were blaring out ear-splitting, caustic rap music, heavily laced with profanity. He was a Black man around thirty years old, solidly built, with his pants pulled well down, showing his underwear. I wanted to disregard this unpleasant scene that I suddenly found myself a part of and just wash my car and leave.

I used up my first soaping time, put in more coins, and continued to wash my car. The noxious song ended and was followed by another that was more violent and more sexually explicit. The man seemed oblivious to it all as he worked on his car. By this time, I was really disturbed, both by the scene and by the Holy Spirit. What if a woman came onto the property? I remembered the many times I had prayed for good people to wake up, stand up and be responsible. Was I just going to finish washing my car and drive away as if nothing were wrong, and then later regret not doing what I knew to do? Come, Holy Spirit, I prayed, what is the right course of action here?

Immediately, the Spirit sent me out across the lot to encounter the man. I was aware that he could and might try to deck me, but rather than dwell on that possibility, I thought about how to approach him so that he would hear me. The Holy Spirit had that part covered.

I reached the car feeling quietly confident. The man was bent over with his back to me, working inside the car. He quickly became aware that I had walked up, and he stood and turned toward me. Looking him in the eye, I discerned intelligence, and I spoke to him as a friend and said, "Brother, you're too good a person to be doing this—to be pouring this trash over yourself and everybody else. This is awful!"

Just like that, he turned off the throbbing noise and replied, "You're right." His voice and face were pleasant. I thought to myself, all right, the Spirit has it!

The next words just tumbled out of my mouth. "What would your grandmother do if she caught you out here doing this?"

He immediately blurted out, with a look of startled fear. "She'd kill me—that's what she would do!"

I came right back. "You're right, she'd kill you. She didn't raise you to act like this!"

He seemed rather stunned and nodded his head, saying, "Yes, sir, yes, sir. She sure didn't."

Now the Spirit really honed in on him, and I asked in a lower voice, "How do you think Jesus feels about what you're doing?"

The man knew he was nailed. He dropped his head, looking at the ground, and all he could say was, "Oh, man," with his voice trailing off like that of a young teenager.

I said, "This stuff is Satanic."

He sadly replied, "I know." His voice and his face showed true remorse. He was realizing he had been giving Satan a chance to use him as a platform.

I continued, "You can't let Satan kidnap you away with this trash. You know better."

He responded, "No, sir, I can't. I do know better." He was recognizing he had fallen in with the wrong crowd, a crowd that was eating his lunch.

I added, "Look how blessed you are, with a good mind, strong body, nice car, everything you need."

"Yes, sir, I am really blessed," he agreed.

The Holy Spirit was totally in charge and supplying all the words, quickly. I mostly just had to deliver them. I asked him his name and gave him mine. His name was Denzell. I asked, "Denzell, can I lead you in a sinner's prayer? I don't know what we are going to say, but you just repeat after me, if you agree."

"Yes, sir," he nodded. He was ready.

Denzell repeated every word carefully and with feeling as the Holy Spirit led us through a prayer of repentance for the choice Denzell had made to stray from the Lord and cross the line into Satan's territory, and then we prayed for forgiveness and that Denzell would be given another chance and be reinstated under God's protection. We finished the prayer with Denzell recommitting his life to the Lord.

I asked him, "Do you want to give me that tape?"

He said, "I would, but it was just on my phone and I turned it off. But don't worry, I'm not listening to that stuff anymore."

Denzell was now seeing the big picture and told me, "I meant to come to the car wash yesterday but wasn't able to get here. I believe our meeting today is an act of God—that He had it planned all along, down to the exact time." It was obvious he was feeling God's presence with us.

By now we were feeling close to each other, like good friends in church— maybe even closer. Denzell said that he had a girlfriend named LaShanna and they were planning to marry soon. She had a little girl named Diamond. We agreed that he couldn't be subjecting LaShanna and Diamond to such vile garbage, and he promised that he wouldn't, saying, "This is finished! I'm not listening to that trash anymore."

As we stood in the center of the car wash parking lot, in front of God and everybody, we shared a big, manly embrace, like two athletes who had just won the Super Bowl. We were both winners in this encounter and Satan had clearly lost. I told him he had goodness in him and that I could see it in his eyes. He nodded with real gratitude.

Denzell said I was the second man in the past two days who had encouraged him and tried to point him in the right direction. (The other man was a dentist in North Carolina, also named Gary.) I said, "Denzell, that's two!"

"I know," he said. He promised that soon he would bring LaShanna and Diamond to my shop so that I could pray for all three of them.

Denzell had been given a good start in a very different setting by his grandmother, and he had received what she could teach him as a child, but like any other person, the child must grow spiritually or fall away. Satan sets traps for those who haven't grown in their faith. Faith not developed and used will dry up and disappear, and then evil gets a free pass to take over.

Much like pornographic pictures, evil rap music can reprogram a person's formerly clear mind and point him totally away from the Lord and toward Satan—and possibly a lifetime of captivity. Denzell was fortunate that the Holy Spirit called him out while his goodness was still strong enough in him that he could hear and say, "Yes, Lord, have your way with my life."

Do not be deceived: "Bad company corrupts good morals."
                                            —1 Corinthians 15:33 (NASB)

Come back to your senses as you ought, and stop sinning;
for there are some who are ignorant of God.
                                            —1 Corinthians 15:34 (NIV)

Start children off on the way they should go, and even when they are old they will not turn from it.
                                            —Proverbs 22:6 (NIV)

Chapter 7

Standing for Life

In 1985, as I walked onto the sidewalk in front of Planned Parenthood, the local abortuary on Broad Street in Augusta, I had no idea what to expect. I knew I wouldn't be welcome, really didn't want to be there, and didn't want to be seen there. I had never stood on the street for any cause, but the Holy Spirit and my conscience had sent me. Even then, I sensed that this was a bigger mission than any I had undertaken before.

Nancy and I had recently seen the chilling video, "The Silent Scream," which showed the in-progress abortion of a well-formed, midterm baby, looking very alone and trying to escape pain and death with no one to care, no one to help and nowhere to go. As we watched this baby writhing in fear and pain, it unquestionably and forever ended the "no pain, just tissue" myth we had been sold. For us, abortion would never again be an abstract, sterile procedure that involved removal of "tissue," but rather the willful extermination of a defenseless baby—as human and alive as you and I will ever be, but at its most dependent stage. That video also ended our not-my-problem mindset. This problem belonged to everyone. Surely I could stand up for the most defenseless babies, when Jesus had gone to the cross for me so that I could live.

Excuses and disclaimers were heard everywhere, such as these:

"I have nothing to do with this issue."

"It doesn't affect me; I'm not responsible."

"I would never say yes to an abortion, but I can't tell other people what to do or not do."

"A fetus isn't human yet and can't feel pain."

"A woman's rights are what really matters."

"Who will take care of these 'unwanted' children if they are born?"

"Nobody wants to adopt unwanted, troubled babies. "

These kinds of denials have contributed immeasurably to the general inaction. There has been an endless flow of words justifying people's decisions to do nothing to right this wrong.

After I began going to Planned Parenthood, I learned it was the number one killer of babies worldwide, a corporate giant of mass destruction. For over thirty-five years, I haven't been able to walk away and leave this death trap and the deadly deception pushed on vulnerable women. It is just too evil to walk away from. I feel certain one of the main reasons a woman goes through with an abortion is that it is the law of the land, and she believes the lie: "If it's legal, it has to be all right." Most of the "patients" (victims) come to an abortuary expecting a solution; many later become totally distraught. Since abortion is a direct violation of God's law, it can never be a solution. It becomes the problem.

Some of my memories of being at Planned Parenthood and seeing the people inside and outside are haunting, and that does not subside. But standing for life is not about how you feel; it's about being faithful to the call to stand for those without a voice. I have continued to stand, along with many, many committed others, six times or more each month, in season and out, in hot weather or cold, in rain or shine, as the battle with evil goes on. Through these experiences I have yet to see good come from the "women's healthcare" business, but rather deception, darkness, pain, guilt, suffering and death—and often a lifetime of heartbreak, not just for the parents of the aborted child. A family member "gone missing" is also a major loss for brothers and sisters to carry.

Half of those who enter an abortuary for "treatment" don't survive the visit, and the other half leave wounded. None get better. This is Satan's form of prime healthcare, and it is the fulfillment of a plan for genocide formed by Margaret Sanger, who founded Planned Parenthood in 1916 to put into motion her own plan to eliminate "unwanted babies," as she saw them. Her eugenics agenda influenced Hitler later in his effort to eliminate the "Jewish Problem."

Along with the multitude of senseless deaths among all races, it is shocking to encounter the documented figures showing that abortion takes more Black lives than all other causes of death combined. Many of the Black race have been blinded to this attempt at genocide. What a tragedy! Deception at its worst.

Over sixty-five thousand lives have been sent to execution in the downtown Augusta building that housed Planned Parenthood. How did a business license ever get granted for such? Seriously! After decades of continuous killing, the public concern for what happened in that building steadily diminished. Few who passed by in cars or on foot even raised an eyebrow. How very far we have fallen as a nation; we have been lulled into a complacent coma while choosing to do nothing. Many of us have heard the quote attributed to Edmond Burke, "All that is necessary for the triumph of evil is for good men to do nothing."

We really shouldn't be surprised at the news and video footage that reveal the sale of fetal organs and body parts by Planned Parenthood and the callous attitude toward this practice. Planned Parenthood executives even targeted the pro-life investigators who took videos in their clinics, trying to get the pro-lifers prosecuted for felony crimes while denying any wrongdoing themselves as their organization dissected and marketed baby parts. Only Satan can devise such atrocious activities and sell them to the public.

These defenseless, "worthless" babies with no human rights, "unwanted" by the world, become quite valuable once their lives have been terminated, not just for premium-priced body parts but also for women's cosmetics. It is all a grisly, high-dollar business, far worse than this description. It would have seemed unbelievable in the America of the past, where everyone was promised life, liberty and the pursuit of happiness. But of course, we don't live in that America anymore. No one does, and maybe no one will ever again. That America has long since gone, and no one knows if it will ever return. The rapid acceptance of birth control pills in 1962 and their easy accessibility for use by women and girls of all ages, married or unmarried, greatly reduced appreciation for new life and for the sanctity of life itself. The consciences of men and women across the nation were deeply challenged, but righteousness was pushed aside, thus setting the groundwork for the legalization of abortion. When the Supreme Court legalized abortion in 1973 (likely its worst ruling ever) and opened the floodgates to death for hire and abortion on demand for any reason, its justices demolished the dam protecting America's goodness and greatness. And then evil poured in headlong, flooding every area of weakness. It brings to mind the quote often attributed to Alexis de Tocqueville: "When

America ceases to be good, it will cease to be great." The origin of the quote is questionable, but certainly the statement is not!

As a nation, we haven't stood up to this evil, and the conscience of the majority of Americans has been seared over the last forty-seven years. The results are staggering. When moral values and personal responsibility are abdicated and replaced by deception, apathy, complacency, denial, situational ethics and short-term personal comfort, Satan takes the day unencumbered. Our national response to abortion probably grieves the Lord as much as abortion itself.

Do not grieve the Holy Spirit...

—Ephesians 4:30 (NIV)

After all, if it is acceptable to take one's own child to professional killers to be executed, and for his or her remains to be disposed of or marketed as those killers choose, then what is no longer acceptable? We now see frequent breaking news of extreme violence and man's inhumanity to man. What do we think spawned this upsurge? With the high court's decision to say yes to abortion, the world's valuation of human life plummeted to pennies on the dollar. Not only did abortion move to front and center in our culture, but human trafficking, euthanasia, assisted suicide and even the idea of a "duty to die" now loom ahead in our country. These are perils we have brought upon ourselves by rejecting the Lord and his plans for life, and together they have driven an enormous wedge into our culture that could split it all the way to eternity.

Finally, in 2016, after thirty-eight years of dealing exploitation and misery, Planned Parenthood permanently closed its doors in Augusta. Its executives claimed that the closing was a financial decision, but we believe it was because of the hundreds of thousands of prayers through the years asking the Lord to shut it down. In His time, He did.

Abortion didn't just leave town, since there is another clinic a few miles away. The abortions that Planned Parenthood would have performed are now done there, so that is where we now focus our pro-life efforts. The name of the clinic, Preferred Women's Health Center, is just as misleading as "Planned Parenthood," and the outside of the building looks like death itself. It is a ragged, unmaintained property set in a fashionable professional center of otherwise nice buildings. It is a Saturday morning killing field. The parking lot out front is loaded with guys and cars and must resemble a tailgate party from Hell—flippant irresponsibility at its worst. What a printout of the present condition of our culture without bounds. Of all the business owners in the complex, only one has given any assistance in the effort to shut down this atrocity.

Since 1973, America has been self-destructing. If that statement sounds extreme, ask yourself this: By God's standards, how must our country rate today compared to the time before legalized abortion?

The slaughter continues in America at the rate of approximately three thousand innocent lives per day, over sixty-two million since the Roe v. Wade ruling by the Supreme Court. Many states' legislative efforts to outlaw abortion have effectively increased, and there is fresh hope of clinics being closed by the heartbeat bill, which states that once a heartbeat is detected, usually around six weeks of pregnancy, abortion is no longer legal. During 2019, several states introduced this bill into their legislative process, and such bills passed that year in Ohio, Georgia, Louisiana, and Missouri. It is hoped that these laws will severely reduce the number of abortions and make it extremely difficult financially for clinics to continue operating. With Amy Coney Barrett's recent confirmation to the Supreme Court, perhaps the overturn of the Roe v. Wade ruling is possible. Let's pray and believe for that. And in 2020, President Donald Trump became the first sitting president to attend and speak at the March for Life in Washington, D.C., the enormous pro-life rally that is barely covered by the news agencies, but which occurs each year near the anniversary of the Roe v. Wade ruling. What an affirmation and boost for marchers from near and far, and for all who stand for life.

The act of abortion doesn't require a bad person. God doesn't make bad people; we all are made in His likeness and image. Because of our humanity, we all make mistakes. Any one of us can make bad choices, especially under stress. None of us is blameless, *"for all have sinned and fall short of the glory of God." (Romans 3:23)* If we turn to the Lord and ask forgiveness, He will forgive us and set us free. Some abortionists have even been redeemed and are now actively pro-life. The Lord can save any one of us. Let us always extend forgiveness ourselves and invite the Lord's love in.

Certainly, not everyone is called to stand in front of an abortion clinic. Many can't, and they support us with their prayers instead. But if the Lord sends you out in front of a clinic to stand for the sanctity of life and for the unborn, here are a few things to remember. The Lord never sends us out with anger, hatred, resentment or condemnation; these are not in His character. Our battle is not against flesh and blood but against powers/Satan. We will never argue people out of Satan's grip—only God's love can lead them to the truth and change their hearts.

Don't worry about what anyone may think or say about your going on the street for the unborn. You are sent by God. You don't need their approval.

> *Nevertheless, many, even among the authorities, believed in Him, but because of the Pharisees they did not acknowledge it openly in order not to be expelled from the synagogue. For they preferred human praise to the glory of God.*
>
> —*John 12:42-43(NASB)*

The truth in this Scripture above is very freeing and empowering.

When we think of innocent babies being killed, it is very easy to hate the sin, and not nearly so easy to love the sinner participating. We should not go in front of a clinic unless we can love the sinner while hating the sin. This attitude can change us as well as them.

> *"Neither do I condemn you; go and sin no more."*
>
> —*John 8:11 (NKJV)*

> *"Father, forgive them, they do not know what they are doing."*
>
> —*Luke 23:34 (NIV)*

Please, Lord, grant us your mercy.

Rejoicing in His Ways, Singing in the Rain

Each year, as January 22 approaches (the anniversary of the Roe v. Wade decision that legalized abortion), a sense of urgency comes with it. For well over four decades, our country has basically looked the other way while carnage has taken place, a holocaust of over sixty million human lives sacrificed at the altar of abortion on demand.

In Augusta, we hold a rally that usually draws over two hundred people. That same week we often attend a large rally at the state capitol building in downtown Atlanta. The much larger annual rally in Washington, D.C., draws hundreds of thousands, although that's rarely made known in the media.

The day of the Atlanta rally had arrived, and that morning we boarded the Alleluia bus for our two-and-a-half-hour ride to Atlanta. The ride would go quickly because we were with an interesting group, diverse but all passionately pro-life. Our biggest concern that day was the inclement weather. As we left Augusta, the sky was totally overcast, a light rain was falling, visibility was low, and more rain was forecast as the day went on. We all prayed that the weather in Atlanta would be better, at least during the march. But rather than improving, the weather continued to deteriorate as we got closer to Atlanta. We had all brought rain gear, just in case, so we weren't dismayed. For January, the temperature wasn't bad; it was near fifty degrees. Regardless, we knew that standing for the cause would be worth whatever the discomfort.

We approached the church where we would be gathering for the rally, our bus was parked, and we entered the church for a mass for the unborn and their families. The church was packed to overflowing, but everyone was considerate and gracious. We were all there for the same wonderful common cause: to celebrate and defend the sanctity of life. The service concluded, and everyone headed outside for the rally in front of the state capitol building. We had hoped to find that the rain had stopped or subsided some, but it hadn't—it was actually coming down harder than before.

Our group became part of the larger group of eight to ten thousand, many of whom had traveled a great distance to be there. A program followed with music and speakers that lasted about an hour, with everyone standing in the soaking rain, before we began the actual march.

The big city police presence had greatly increased during the rally, and officers were all around, on foot, on motorcycles and in cars. There were even mounted police, and a police helicopter hovered overhead. Officers, in larger numbers than in years past, were stationed at the intersection for the start of the walk, which would cover a mile and a half and take approximately forty-five minutes as we walked through the central part of downtown Atlanta.

The emcee brought us to silence, and then over the speaker system came the compelling sound of a beating heart at a volume that dominated our senses. Then, just as we had adjusted to that sound, it stopped. It went silent—silent as death. The silence was even more compelling.

The lead police motorcycle cranked up, and the crowd began to move forward. As if on cue, the heavens opened and the rain became a downpour. It was encouraging that no one seemed to be leaving or quitting. Everyone seemed to understand and accept that this was what God had for us that day, and we were grateful to be allowed to be there and be part of such a group.

As always, quite a number of individuals had brought their trumpets to play taps and were stationed along the route. Hearing that mournful salute is very moving as we walk along silently. The most notable musician playing taps was a woman, surrounded by her children and her husband, huddled under an umbrella that he was holding over them. Year after year, they have attended the march as their family has grown in number.

As we walked the streets between the tall buildings of Atlanta, we were mindful of the onlookers. Most years, they are on the sidewalks at lunchtime, some there to look at our group but most trying not to look. On this day many people were inside, looking out from windows and doorways to avoid the relentless downpour over the city. We saw the faces of perplexed diners in the windows, comfortable in their setting but uncomfortable with ours. What could cause this many peaceful-looking people to walk together and get drenched in such horrific weather? And to look more joyful that the diners themselves?

The deluge had long soaked all of us and had even soaked through our rain gear. As we walked through one major intersection, the water rushing in a stream down the middle of the street was so deep it was coming over our shoe tops and filling our shoes. It didn't matter—we were all on a mission. (Thank you, Lord, for Your grace; Your grace is sufficient.) Throughout the walk, the deluge never abated. The crowd stayed constant to the end, and the participants appeared to all be greatly blessed, and to know it. The longer we walked, the more the joy level seemed to increase. We had given away our comfort early on and were enjoying our acceptance.

We slogged to our bus with our big crosses and banners and pulled our bodies with their heavy, soaked clothes on board. Our appreciation for each other escalated considerably as we looked around at everyone's "drowned rat" condition and saw endurance and accomplishment and jubilation.

Our long, wet bus trip back was filled with quiet satisfaction as we dripped big puddles onto the bus floor. We drank from the cup that was given us that day. We never heard any complaints from anyone about that day. Nor did we hear of anyone getting sick from the hours spent in the rain and wet clothes. We all treasure the memories of that trip and God's grace upon it that day. And we rejoice that we got to suffer discomfort for His glory.

> *...Choosing rather to share ill-treatment with the people of God than to enjoy the fleeting pleasures of sin.*
> —*Hebrews 11:25 (RSV)*

We had prayed for nice weather before going on that Atlanta trip. The Lord could have given us any kind of weather that He chose. The weather He gave us brought forth His grace, and His people under that grace, more than any beautiful, sunshiny day could have. Since that day, I've tried to pray that He will send the weather that will give Him the most glory. His grace will always be sufficient! And He seems to pour it over His rain-or-shine people.

Seventeen and Normal

Our pro-life presence in front of abortuaries has been greatly strengthened by a group of young high school and college students from the Alleluia Community. One especially Spirit-filled and committed group of young people turned out twenty or more strong to stand for life each Wednesday morning during the school year for three years. In subsequent years, smaller groups would sporadically come, and they have all been appreciated. I always think of them as "young stalwarts."

There is a powerful interplay between the forces of good and evil outside an abortion mill like Planned Parenthood, so we never know who or what is coming next, but we're open to whatever the Lord sends our way. If someone walks up with the intention of being a disruption, which is very rare, we try to deal with the person in a discerning and righteous way. More often, people are drawn by the crosses and approach us in the hope of receiving something good. To be on the street for Jesus is to be where things are most real—the front lines, in the midst of the battle. I don't know of anything that develops faith more quickly or powerfully.

One morning Cathryn and Annie were the last two students to leave downtown Augusta and head for school. They had both been in front of the abortuary regularly over the past couple of years and had experienced a variety of unexpected events. This morning we were in the center of Broad Street on a low concrete median about eight feet wide. My friend John and I, along with the girls, were concluding prayers, each of us preparing to head off to our agendas for the day. Then we saw a slim, middle-aged man some distance away step into the street and walk quickly toward us. His body language and stride struck us as purposeful, so we waited with anticipation for him to reach us. He walked right up, reverently took off his cap, and told us his name was Joe. He said that he had responded to an altar call at church the previous Sunday and given his life to Jesus. Joe appeared to be running on empty, struggling a bit, but maybe that had brought him to us. He wanted us to lay hands on him and pray over him that he could be faithful and live out what he had promised to the Lord. This all developed so quickly that it felt almost preplanned or scripted.

The two girls were right in step, and without delay, we all laid hands on him, leading him through a sinner's prayer, and we prayed for God's grace in his new life. This was a spontaneous, personal prayer of commitment, and Joe repeated every word, line by line. It may well have been more thorough and penetrating than what he had experienced during his altar call. Having received what he came for, Joe thanked each of us, put his cap back on and briskly walked away with blessed assurance and resolve.

We stood there in the center of Broad Street for a few moments quietly watching Joe depart and savoring the experience.

Then Cathryn spoke up, saying, "I'm seventeen years old, and I think this is normal."

And so it was, and continues to be, for so many of our young people. The seeds of living faith are planted in them at a very young age and grow as they do! What is normal for some would be radical for most. As believers, we are called to live radically for the Lord, and that can be life giving or even life changing for others.

> *"I am the vine; you are the branches. If you remain in Me and I in you, you will bear much fruit; apart from Me you can do nothing."*
> *—John 15:5 (NIV)*

King of Glory

Only two of us had arrived when we began setting up for our stand for life one Friday afternoon in front of Planned Parenthood. This event, a prayerful time with crosses, singing and banners, occurred twice a month, in addition to a similar gathering we held every Wednesday morning. The weather forecast had called for a strong chance of a thundershower, but in Augusta during midsummer, that could go either way. Usually the storms passed us by or held off for a bit, allowing us to take our stand as planned.

Just as we got everything out of my van and began setting up banners, the moderate wind turned to strong gusts. A loud clap of thunder pierced the quiet, and large scattered drops began to pelt down. Not a good sign. We quickly reversed course, putting everything except two crosses back into my van, just as a second thunderclap sounded nearby. Because my business had been located just a mile up the street for three years, I had learned how quickly rain can blow up on Broad Street, which runs parallel to the Savannah River a short block away. The rain "runs the river" and can be upon you in a moment, and so it was this day.

Of course, Planned Parenthood's entry porch is totally off limits to us, so Griggs and I grabbed the crosses and ran for the building next door, which was vacant and locked up but had a five-foot-wide awning running the length of the front. We had stood under this awning a few times before when the rain had been heavy, and we were grateful to have it that day as the summer shower came upon us. As we headed toward the awning, a husband and wife and another young woman—Jerry, Cathy and Barbara, from the Alleluia Community—joined us. They all lived on our Farm (a more rural area outside of Augusta where part of the community lives) and were quite at home in the outdoors and dealing with weather challenges. Right away, the big scattered raindrops became a driving rainstorm with strong, gusting winds and very close lightning strikes, punctuated by immediate and loud thunderclaps. As this raw display of nature was nearing a crescendo, an eerie sound could be heard. It was a sizzling "zzt-zzt-zzt... zzt-zzt-zzt" sound right in our ears, followed immediately by a thundering lightning strike. I had never "heard" lightning before. It seemed so directly overhead, we couldn't tell whether it was behind or in front of us.

This violent storm was coming from the northwest, moving southeastward. The five of us stood very still under the awning, somewhat sheltered from the strafing rain by the building behind us. But all of us were very mindful of the awning's metal framework and the large elm tree looming high above us.

By now the rain was hard and heavy and had been this way for about twenty minutes, so that the downspouts of the gutters on the city buildings were gushing water midair onto the sidewalk, like mini fire hydrants. We were locked into place, held motionless by this power display. The severe wind and electrical strikes were slowly moving over the center of town while the downpour remained in place all around us.

Then the greatest realization dawned on us. The King of Glory was passing over us—right then. The omnipresent God whom we pray to, the Creator God, the God of the Universe, was passing over us that very moment—and we felt He was mindful of us standing there. We had nothing to fear. We shared this sense with each other, and the five of us just relaxed and put our trust in Him. It was so peaceful and glorious. Even in the midst of this incredible storm, we just stood there unworried, basking in His awesome power and peace. It truly surpassed our understanding. It was like a power show that He had put on just for the five of us. After about fifty minutes of this spectacular outpouring, which probably delivered two inches of rain, we had to move on to our next commitments. The men ran through the downpour to get to the vehicles, then drove right up onto the sidewalk to pick up the women and the crosses.

We will never forget those sizzling zzt-zzt-zzt sounds and the lightning that escorted the King of Glory as He passed over that day.

So many Wednesday mornings our group had huddled in the dark in the dead of winter, bundled up to the max, enduring the biting cold air and the frigid sidewalk. On clear days, though (which were usually the coldest days), we had absolute assurance as we looked straight down Broad Street, through town toward the east, that the sun was about to make its appearance as a large orange fireball just above the buildings. As it did, we could almost instantly feel the warmth combating the cold. Soon, we would forget being so cold and begin to refocus on Him. We knew that the Lord had sent that great fireball for our good, and it was so like the King of Glory Himself. We would remind each other of the King of Glory coming and begin to praise Him. His presence changes everything for the better, no matter in which form he comes.

Who is this King of glory?
The Lord strong and mighty,
the Lord mighty in battle.
Lift up your heads, you gates;
lift them up, you ancient doors,
that the King of glory may come in.
Who is He, this King of glory?
The Lord Almighty—
He is the King of glory.

—Psalm 24:8-10 (NIV)

Near Miss

On an early fall Sunday in October of 2018, our pro-life group was holding our annual Life Chain to stand up for the unborn and the sanctity of life.

The size of the crowd was moderate, with adults, small children and babies numbering about one hundred. The sound equipment, musicians and speakers were set up in a business lot located directly across the street from the abortion clinic.

There was no public property to use, other than the street and a narrow right-of-way. Our police permit allowed us to use the street if we didn't block traffic. Since it was Sunday, the entire professional complex where we were gathered was closed, and there was no normal business traffic.

As we were nearing closing time for the rally, we turned our attention toward the clinic to pray. Everyone was gathered in a large semicircle that filled most of the street, and we began to say spiritual warfare prayers against Satan and the spirit of death. Just as the prayers began, a car abruptly entered the street, about sixty yards from our group. The driver began blaring the horn, and at the same time, pressed his foot on the gas, accelerating. I was standing at the back of the group, holding a large cross, and only by grace and urgent Holy Spirit help was able to jump out of his path, landing clear of the car. Others who were at the front edge of the lot were narrowly missed. A man and woman with a stroller and small children were only a few feet away from the speeding car.

Since the car flashed through so fast, never slowing down, we could tell only that it was white and a late model—a speeding metal blur. Because of its speed and the reckless driving, it would have been much more likely for this car to have hit and strewn multiple bodies than to have made it through without touching anyone. I doubt that the driver knew any of us. The event had the look of the terrorist attacks around the world that are reported on the news. It was difficult to contemplate the bodies, lives and futures that could have been mangled or taken that day—even the driver's own.

There surely must be no limit to the ways Satan can immediately inflame and activate people for his evil purposes. It's possible that many of those who are used have no previous thought of violence or violent intentions. As the car disappeared like a rocket out of the complex, with the horn continuously blowing, we turned and prayed fervently for the driver and for his salvation and deliverance.

"Father, forgive them, for they do not know what they are doing."
—Luke 23:34 (NIV)

We do know that the family is the prime target of abortion, and with any abortion, every family member is wounded. We also know that intimidation is one of Satan's favorite weapons, but, *"Greater is He who is in you than he who is in the world." (1 John 4:4)* Amen!

That driver needed lots of prayer, just as we did. For some unknown reason, he was singled out that day even more than we were. To be attacked by demonic forces is one thing, to be used by them is far worse. We pray for this driver and that what Satan intended for evil, God will turn for good.

For we do not wrestle against flesh and blood, but against principalities, against powers...
—Ephesians 6:12 (NKJV)

...Be on the alert. Your adversary, the devil, prowls about like a roaring lion, seeking someone to devour.
—1 Peter 5:8 (NASB 1977)

Chapter 8

Where Sin Abounds

The first time I stepped from my vehicle and walked in front of SHE Video, the notorious porno shop, I felt a little guilty all over. I had gone there for the right reasons, but this place represented some of the worst depravity the culture could dish out.

Two of us had knocked on the shop's front door the week before to alert them that our group would be coming there regularly with the intent of closing them down. Now, as I stood in front of this place, I remembered the few times I had crept into X-rated movies or had gone to a strip show in my "old man" life. I again felt the sense of guilt I had experienced as I left those places, hoping not to be seen or recognized, actually wishing for something I could put over my head to hide my identity. Even in those pre-Christian days, deep down, I knew that being there was not right. Now Satan was accusing me, trying to convince me that I had no right to come and stand at this place. This thought brought me back to why we were there, on such unholy ground.

SHE video was known for taking the vulgar to the extreme, mostly with private viewing cubicles. I had never been in a porno place, nor would I go. This was a subhuman den of iniquity, and many of the patrons were hopelessly addicted and in bondage to it, returning time after time, with no capacity to resist. Pornography is the gangrene of the soul, killing it a little bit at a time. It was incongruous that our group of men, who in the past had been intrigued by such voyeurism, were now dispatched by the Holy Spirit to stand staunchly against it. None in our group was unscathed by decisions of the past, but by His blood, we each had been washed clean, and we wanted to make up for some of our past errors. Such is the amazing, redemptive grace of Jesus!

Even though SHE Video was just outside North Augusta and Augusta, the setting was more like a stop along a highway, akin to those places with huge roadside billboards like Lion's Den or Pink Pony. The business was on a heavily traveled four-lane highway and was surrounded by a tall, wooden fence to hide all the parked cars from view. Most patrons appeared to be addicted, captivated; they stayed for lengthy periods of time. Although most of the voyeurs and their vehicles were thoroughly beaten down, we were surprised by the few well-dressed clients and those in expensive cars. They also were drawn in, as by a magnet. Many came with church bumper stickers on their cars, some had clergy stickers, and some women came there alone. Satan is the stalker of all humanity, and addiction is no respecter of persons, ever! Pornography also breeds many other crimes and can devastate an area as it attracts related evil.

SHE Video was family owned. Even the mother of the family and her daughter and daughter-in-law routinely worked in the sordid surroundings. Their shameless participation and angry demeanors compounded the sense of evil gone rampant in the culture. They seemed to see their work as normal work. For decades, their business had been "grandfathered in" by local zoning. Neither the city nor the county wanted it there, but the state couldn't legally deny them a business permit.

We often had twenty or more men (intentionally, no women) carrying a dozen or more tall crosses along the right-of-way. There were many U-turns made near the entrance by potential clients who had a sudden change of plans when they encountered the crosses. Others who continued into the lot were often distressed by the presence of the crosses, their dark spirits being suddenly challenged. Some would go inside and complain to the management. At times, an employee would come out and complain to us or threaten to call the police. We were encouraged by their threats and by any police visits, since the city had assured us of our rights and its support. We were on a mission to close down this evil. For sure, not all comments and gestures by passing motorists were favorable (no surprise—we never expected them to be), but most were encouraging. The frequent thumbs-up signs and blasts from truckers sounding their big horns were especially uplifting, since other truckers had been drawn into this Satanic trap.

There were some pleasant surprises. Once, while we were enduring a sweltering Friday afternoon in August as the sun, heat and humidity radiated off the broken-up asphalt and gravel lot, a minivan pulled up in front of the building. The unlikely occupants climbed out—a very nice-looking family, a mother and several young children we had never seen before. They had noticed us as they drove past and then stopped at a store, bought big, iced drinks for us and came back. Then the kids, at the mother's direction, respectfully served each of us. No doubt it was a special, teachable experience for this impressionable young family, who were doing a very good thing at a very bad place. They will likely not forget it. We were most appreciative and prayed a blessing over them.

One very cold winter morning in the dead of winter, just after daylight, we were there taking our regular Wednesday stand when a vehicle pulled up. A woman got out and brought over a bag of homemade sausage biscuits that she had made for us. She had noticed us as she had passed by on several other Wednesdays. As good as the hot sausage biscuits were as we stood out there in the cold, her heartfelt words meant even more. She was so grateful for our efforts against pornography because her marriage had been devastated by this abomination. Our prayers over her for restoration, new hope and trust in men lifted her spirits.

Our group went there regularly, six times per month for nearly three years, but we never got the business closed. We stood as repentant and redeemed brothers against this evil force that was hell-bent on defaming decency and purity. Even in the midst of such a vile backdrop, there were many exceptional experiences that happened at a moment's notice on that property.

The following are a few that come to mind.

One Wednesday morning shortly after 8 a.m., we were there, putting the crosses away in the van. A contingent of twelve young high school men from the Alleluia Community who had joined us for prayer had just left to head to school, and only three of us remained. Suddenly, an old jeep came bouncing over the gravel lot, right toward the front door. It came to a stop, and a muscular and very upset man about forty years old jumped out of the jeep and rushed toward the front door. That door was always kept locked; the patrons had to go around to the back. Near the door was a standing wood swing with two cutout plywood figures, a boy and a girl, sitting in the swing. This must have been intended to give the place a look of youthful innocence. The angry man spotted the cutouts, grabbed the figure of the wooden boy, and jerked down on it with all his strength, apparently expecting to rip it off the frame. Nothing gave. Quickly he went back to his jeep, grabbed a shotgun and came back. Without pausing, he fired at the figure, blowing a two-inch hole right through the face of the wooden boy. With that done, he turned on his heel, returned to his jeep and pitched the shotgun into the back. He now looked even angrier than he had when he first drove up. There was no way to guess what he would do next, but he definitely didn't look like he was finished. Since this place was "our field" of ministry, the Holy Spirit prompted us to walk toward him. He needed to be settled down before he did something worse. Of course, the Holy Spirit never abandons us. If He says, "Do it," then everything will be just fine. As we approached this irate man, we prayed for a calm demeanor to come over him (we were also working on our own calmness).

I said, "Hi, Brother, we're on the same side—but this is not the way to do it."

I hoped this wouldn't anger him more, but I couldn't tell. He just stood there looking at us as though disoriented.

We began to reason with the man to leave before the police came. He didn't want to. He felt his mission wasn't complete, but common sense was starting to return to him. Eventually, after a little more exhorting from us, he climbed into his jeep and drove quickly away, just as two anxious employees burst out the front door in reaction to the activity outside. As soon as they came out, they saw the hole through the boy's face. We assured them that none of our people had fired the shot, that a man we had never seen before had just driven up, jumped out of his vehicle, blown the hole through the sign and left.

We tried to get all the mileage we could out of the situation, bearing in on the porno employees and asking, "What if he had shot the door lock instead and had come inside with the gun looking for y'all? Surely whatever you've done to him has really upset him. He was out of control." We assured them that with all the evil they indulged in and the harm they did in people's lives, they were getting off light. Maybe this was some sort of sign given to them, a "shot across the bow."

We never saw that man again or heard any more about that outburst. For years, the plywood kids remained in the swing with the gunshot hole through the boy's face.

One Friday evening while we stood outside the place, a late model sports car slowly pulled off the highway and down to where the three of us were standing, quietly holding crosses. As the car got closer, we could see that the driver was well dressed and in his thirties. He had the look of a successful professional athlete. We introduced ourselves. His name was Lawrence.

Lawrence went on to tell us that he had been inside the building earlier viewing porno. When he drove past us, he noticed the crosses. He had pulled out of the lot, planning to drive home to Colombia, South Carolina, an hour away. But after he had driven some distance up the highway, he had been overcome by conviction from the Holy Spirit to come back, confess his sin and repent. Then he went quiet before shamefully admitting that for some time, he had been lying to his wife, telling her that he had to work late on Fridays. Instead, he was slipping over to SHE Video, driving the extra distance in hopes of not being recognized closer to home. He went on to say that he was a good Christian. He and his wife and two young daughters were regular churchgoers, very committed, and this was the only area in his life that was out of order. He then began to break and confessed to being addicted to pornography. As hard as he had tried, he hadn't been able to get free from the addiction.

The three of us reached into the car, laid hands on this crestfallen brother, and prayed a prayer of deliverance and grace to break the bondage of this debilitating sin. Tears ran down Lawrence's face, dripped on his clothes and splattered onto the floor of the car. He sat sobbing like a child, literally shaking. He was hurting down to his core over the misery caused by giving in to this degrading habit. He was so very embarrassed. We could feel both his shame and his goodness at one time. We hurt with him. ("There but for the grace of God go I.")

After prayers and after some time, he looked as if he had received some deliverance and had gotten himself together, and he thanked us over and over, telling us he was going straight home and would fully confess to his wife. He made a promise to us and himself that he would get whatever help was needed to stay free from the grip that this addiction had held on him. He could not, and would not, let this ever happen again! As Lawrence drove away, we could only marvel at what the Holy Spirit and the cross had done and how his family had been blessed. This could unlock a whole new life for the four of them. The liberating power of the Spirit and the cross over sin is amazing!

Those who belong to Christ Jesus have crucified the flesh with its passions and desires. Since we live by the Spirit, let us keep in step with the Spirit.
—*Galatians 5:24-25 (NIV)*

On several occasions while we were there, a SHE Video employee named Kyle had come out and talked to us. One of our men had worked with him in a retail store years earlier and had known both Kyle and his wife Cynthia. They had appeared to be an average young couple, but bad choices had hurt them and put them into a deep slide. Kyle was said to have been a clean-cut, nice-looking man, but his appearance had drastically changed since he had started working at the porno shop. He had shaved off his hair, started dressing like a heavy metal rock type, and had added tattoos, studs, piercings and earrings—each addition representing a progression toward darkness. We wondered if he thought this was the image he needed for porno work (his "game face"), or if he had really deteriorated that much due to the evil that was pulling him down.

Over time, he became arrogant and spiteful and would unlock the front door, stand there and scowl at us. Several times while we were out front praying, he had come out and poured a bucket of filthy mop water a few feet from us to let us know it was their property and we weren't welcome.

One day when we arrived for our prayer vigil, Kyle was waiting for us. He came right out, walked quickly to my van and told me he needed to talk to me, but somewhere else. He acknowledged that he had serious problems but couldn't talk then or there because he was working. I gave him my business card and strongly encouraged him to come or call anytime, day or night—I would meet him anywhere and hoped he would get in touch. He never called, and weeks later, our group moved our presence and prayers to Planned Parenthood.

Many months later, I looked out the window of my business and noticed a car approaching and stopping. Kyle slowly got out. He looked really wounded, beat down and ashamed as he warily entered my shop. Obviously, it was very hard for him to do. He told me that he had hurt his back, had gotten into serious trouble, his marriage was in trouble and he was fearful of being sent to prison. For over an hour and a half, Kyle told me of his troubles, choked as he talked and wiped away a lot of tears. I could personally relate to the aloneness Kyle was feeling right then—that sense of separation from God had almost killed me. I prayed over him, not accusing or condemning, just trying to be understanding in a tough time, offering him some hope and pointing him toward Jesus. That's what believers had done for me when I was so lost and broken. This would be a long, hard pull for him; he had given Satan far too much foothold. I tried to get him to come again, but he never did. That one time was special, though. I know he got touched. I could see Jesus' love for Kyle even in the midst of all that carnage.

"He [God] jealously desires the Spirit whom He has made to dwell in us."
—*James 4:5 (NASB)*

The number of people, male and female, viewing and addicted to pornography is at an all-time high, given its easy accessibility on personal computers and phones for private viewing. Even a reported one-third of the ordained clergy admit to frequent use. We should not be surprised, considering Satan's all-out attack on morals, marriage and the family. Pornography is an extreme violation of God's order and plan for sexuality, a tempting forbidden fruit that grows in toxic quicksand and can appear anywhere along the journey that we are traveling.

The world will never be rid of this evil until Jesus comes again, but we can and should try to help rescue the souls who will listen to the Lord's voice and be willing to amputate this gangrene of the soul while there is still time.

Where sin abounded, grace abounded much more.
—*Romans 5:20 (NKJV)*

Chapter 9

Checking Our Bearings

Therefore, since we are surrounded by such a great cloud of witnesses,
let us throw off everything that hinders and the sin that so easily entangles.
And let us run with perseverance the race marked out for us,
fixing our eyes on Jesus, the pioneer and perfecter of faith.
For the joy set before Him He endured the cross,
scorning its shame, and sat down at the right hand of the throne of God.
Consider Him who endured such opposition from sinners,
so that you will not grow weary and lose heart.
—Hebrews 12:1-3 (NIV)

Well, many of us have been on this journey of a lifetime for a long while now. How are we doing? We may already have come through some places that looked impassable. It is crucial that we stay on track. Free will could tempt us to venture off the path at any time and go where that takes us, but that's a likely way to get lost, and we may not get back on track. Completing this journey successfully requires using what we know, have been shown and have learned. This knowledge serves as our roadmap, and we must be willing to call upon roadside assistance (the Holy Spirit) as needed. None of us will guess our way in or stumble in to Glory.

As we look ahead, we can expect uncertain forks, intersections, junctions, bypasses, perhaps some toll roads, tunnels and bridges—and maybe even detours with the road out. We will get no AAA or GPS help from the world's system. Our destination can't be reached by means of worldly "wisdom."

What we have received is not the spirit of the world, but the Spirit who is
from God, so that we may understand what God has freely given us. This

is what we speak, not in words taught us by human wisdom but in words taught by the Spirit, explaining spiritual realities with Spirit-taught words. The person without the Spirit does not accept the things that come from the Spirit of God but considers them foolishness, and cannot understand them because they are discerned only through the Spirit. The person with the Spirit makes judgments about all things, but such a person is not subject to merely human judgments, for, "Who has known the mind of the Lord so as to instruct Him?" But we have the mind of Christ.

—1 Corinthians 2:12-16 (NIV)

There's a great crowd of travelers, and we know they are not all headed in the right direction. We have to be careful not to follow the crowd and be led astray. We are not approaching a stadium for a ball game or a rock concert, and choosing the right direction, the "road less traveled," is paramount.

"Enter through the narrow gate. For wide is the gate and broad is the road that leads to destruction, and many enter through it."

—Matthew 7:13 (NIV)

We may come across intentionally misdirecting road signs. We know that the world has them in abundance. We must be able to discern the signs of the times, stay close to those who know the way better than we do, and listen for any adjustments from the Holy Spirit.

Just to help verify that we are on the right route and to check our progress, let's come aside and look at this list of questions together. I invite you to consider yourself the "I" in each question. Let us see what this exercise tells us.

- Do I see myself called and placed in the position to help fellow travelers—even strangers on the road?
- Do I make God's love apparent and appealing, even to those traveling on the wrong road?
- Have I been able to reject the lure and glamour of the world on a continual basis, and not look back?

- Am I living my life and raising my family around my faith, with faith as the number one priority?
- Do I live as though I am a bona fide ambassador for Christ, reconciling others to God?
- How are my time management and schedule? Am I using my time well?
- Do I sense the Holy Spirit within me and know that I am equipped for any good work?
- Am I free from bondage to any sins of the past? Do I still repent for them?
- Am I giving freely of my time, talents and finances to build God's kingdom?
- Do I intentionally live my life to build His Kingdom here on earth?
- Am I faithful to my personal spiritual disciplines: prayer, study and sharing my faith?
- Am I as physically healthy as I should be, and could be?
- Do I stand up and defend truth and faith in the midst of this secular culture?
- Am I more captive to technology than is healthy, or than I want to admit?
- Do I frequently operate in the gifts that I have been given by the Holy Spirit?
- Do I act upon insights and direction that come to me through Scripture passages that feel alive and personal to me?
- Am I on duty to be used by the Holy Spirit, anytime, anyplace?
- Have I moved from sins of omission to acts of commission?
- Do I know the Lord has much more for me if I will use what He has already given?
- Do I expect and depend on revelations from the Holy Spirit?
- Do I expect signs, wonders and even miracles through prayer? Is that obvious to others?
- Do I really want God's will over my will—even when they seem opposite?
- Are my expectations sometimes too low for God, who has no limits?
- Am I working on living in the present moment?

- Do I live as though my life has been bought and paid for by Jesus on the cross? Do I live with ever increasing gratitude for that?
- Am I always mindful of the destination, even in the midst of major hindrances along the route?
- Am I traveling this journey in step with the Lord, not rushing ahead or lagging behind?
- Does my fire burn as brightly for the Lord today as it ever has?
- Do I see the Lord as enough for me? Is living my "yes" to the call truly my life's fulfillment? Is this life still exhilarating?
- Am I ready and willing to suffer loss to contend for the faith on this journey?

I believe these questions came from the Holy Spirit and are intended to be a brief scan of our hearts, minds and spirits. A number of them were hard for me—some identify areas yet to be dealt with seriously enough, or goals yet to be accomplished. But I was quite aware, as they came to me, that none of the questions was accusatory or condemning, but rather was meant to inspire introspection and soul searching, with a firm focus on the Kingdom and not the world. This kind of prayerful introspection really contrasts with worldly minded thinking of the past, before we made the clear choice to travel only the road to Glory. We need to be "all in" and closely following Jesus' example to reach our destination. I hope you did well with the questions, and I hope that each of us will try to do better.

Then Jesus was led by the Spirit into the wilderness to be tempted by the devil.

Again, the devil took Him to a very high mountain and showed Him all the kingdoms of the world and their splendor. "All this I will give you," he said, "if you will bow down and worship me." Jesus said to him, "Away from Me, Satan! For is written: Worship the Lord your God, and serve Him only.' Then the devil left Him, and angels came and attended Him.
—Matthew 4:1 and 8-11 (NIV)

There is abundant grace available to get us safely home. Let us press on with our journeys. It may be quite a way yet from here to Glory, and there could be some long hills ahead. Regardless of the distance for each of us, one of these days we'll meet Jesus face to face, waiting for us, and the reward will far surpass our greatest imaginings!

Through many dangers, toils, and snares,
I have already come;
'Tis grace hath brought me safe thus far,
And grace will lead me home.
                    —From "Amazing Grace" by John Newton

For our light and momentary troubles are achieving for us an eternal glory that far outweighs them all. So we fix our eyes not on what is seen, but on what is unseen, since what is seen is temporary, but what is unseen is eternal.
                    —2 Corinthians 4:17-18 (NIV)

Chapter 10

God's Favor

I was trying to take care of a repair project at home and needed one small, unusual screw. Surely it had to be in the collection of miscellaneous treasures that had accumulated in the drawer we had designated for the many worth-little-but-too-good-to-pitch items. (You may have a drawer like this yourself.)

As I rummaged around in the front half of the drawer, I came across every other kind of screw, drill bit and drive tip, along with decades' worth of "paperabelia"—cards, notes, names jotted on scraps of paper, etc., etc. They were all there, but not the screw that I needed.

Frustration was not far away when the Spirit said, "Take the drawer all the way out so you can really see." Sure, I said to myself, why hadn't I thought of that?

I took the drawer out, and there, standing on one edge in plain view, in the far back corner of the drawer, was a $100 bill! There was no accounting for how it got there or where it had come from—but, of course, I knew right away.

That $100 bill didn't make our financial day. It didn't even get spent that year. No, it was placed in the desk next to my neck cross as a reminder of God's favor on us, and to always be grateful. That surprise gift did us far more good in the desk than any purchase we might have made with it would have done.

A loose definition of "God's favor" might be "under the spout where the glory comes out" or under God's umbrella (His protection).

God's favor could be considered the extreme swing of the pendulum away from Murphy's Law, which is the outcome that the world tries to convince us to expect. We know our minds are capable of dwelling on either the expectation that everything will always go wrong, or that everything will always go *right*, or the way that God wills for us. Sometimes we get what we expect because of our attitude and the direction we are looking. Amen?

For some people, God's favor turns up in very quiet ways: finding just the right parking spot at the exact moment needed, locating a missing item in a place you wouldn't have looked, being led to an exact place in a store for a necessary, hard-to-find item, or travel assistance that ranges from unexpected, helpful directions in an unfamiliar location to unforeseen help that arrives to lift your car out of a ditch (even by hand) or up a steep embankment and puts you on the road again. No problem is too big for God's roadside assistance.

Sometimes, we are spared serious injury from dangerous accidents, or tumors that had seemed daunting can no longer be found, or a person whose life was hanging by a thread and prayers survives to live an exuberant life filled with praise and gratitude for what God has done.

At times His favor manifests in the ideal job provided at just the right time. Or a house that you need to sell, which hardly anyone has looked at, suddenly sells. Or the house in just the right location becomes available to purchase—or perhaps houses for you and your closest friends, who also need houses, become available right next to each other. Intercessory prayers (prayers for another person's needs) often result in God showing His love and favor as He meets those needs.

Sometimes His favor is intangible, but so timely and powerful. It might come in the form of a word He delivers or sends someone to deliver. Sometimes it's in the shape of something important revealed to you, an encouraging touch that expresses approval, or in one of the many other ways that the Holy Spirit affirms us to renew and restore our belief in ourselves and in Him. Sometimes His favor is manifested in a gift of vision, vitality or endurance—just what is needed to move us beyond a rough patch, a section of the journey that had looked nearly impassable, enabling us to keep on keeping on.

These things happen and we have witnessed them time and again. God shows His favor and good things happen; lives are even changed. We could come up with endless examples. There is no limit to what God can provide, and so much of His favor seems to result from our seeking Him. *"Draw near to God and He will draw near to you." (James 4:8)* It also helps to remember that He owns every cow on a thousand hills *(Psalm 50:10)*, and He can place some on your doorstep anytime. You can always call and ask Him. If you don't have His phone number at hand, the prophet Jeremiah has told us how to reach Him:

> *"Call to Me and I will answer you and tell you great and unsearchable things you do not know."*
>
> —*Jeremiah 33:3 (NIV)*

It is essential to realize that grace is God's unmerited, undeserved favor. If we live under His grace continuously, we will not only be equipped for all good works, but we will have inexpressible joy living life under the spout where the glory comes out !

> *Surely, Lord, You bless the righteous; You surround them with Your favor as with a shield.*
>
> —*Psalm 5:12 (NIV)*

We Smile, Too!

Certainly tornadoes, severe thunderstorms, rainbows, sunrises and sunsets remind us of God's hand on our lives as we move through this world, and these happenings can be awe inspiring. From the first time that I witnessed someone being "slain in the spirit," "rested in the spirit," or "laid out," I've been somewhat amazed by this phenomenon as well. The realization that God's unseen power and touch is so close to us and that we're sometimes allowed to participate in its action is rather mind-boggling.

Being slain or rested in the Spirit has occurred in Pentecostalism for over a hundred years and in the mainline denominations for half that long. For a more in-depth description, please see the chapter, "Slain in the Spirit," in my first book, *Swept Up by the Spirit: Journey of Transformation*.

This kind of Holy Spirit touch is not uncommon among people who are open to the Spirit's contact, and sometimes happens to those who are not. Such a touch can bring about healing, peace, revelation or a spiritual breakthrough in a person's life. The manifestation of being slain in the Spirit is usually initiated by the Spirit Himself, not by a person, although at times the Spirit may alert the person praying before the action takes place.

We won't know just how or when the Spirit will choose to move in this way, but being slain in the Spirit is very real and meaningful. It can sometimes be the turning point in a person's life.

Occasionally, the location, the setting or the manner in which someone is slain or rested takes us totally by surprise. Just what the Spirit is doing through these experiences, only He knows. I have witnessed and participated in numerous slain in the Spirit experiences in a broad range of settings, and I have never seen or heard of anyone getting hurt. The following are just a few examples that make us smile, partly because they're spirit lifting and partly because we can't understand nearly all that the Spirit does. Since these events are beyond us, it is better to smile and trust Him than to be perplexed and question them.

First Impressions

Nancy and I were on our first visit to an Alleluia General Community Gathering (GCG), and the program was drawing to a close. The three elders, Dennis, Dale and Kevin, had been on a raised platform in the center of the room throughout the meeting. Dennis had been leading and now stood at the mike as he prepared to close the meeting. Led by the Spirit, Dale rose from his chair and without a word, placed his hand on Dennis' head. In one motion, Dennis fell backward and went down like a tree. Kevin, being alert, caught him and laid him down where he fell, right off the low platform. Only his feet remained on the platform, pointing upward.

Bob stepped up and led us in a closing song. Then he looked down at Dennis, who hadn't moved, and led us in a second closing song. Dennis still hadn't moved a muscle. Dale came up to close the meeting, and those near the platform stepped around or over Dennis to leave. No one seemed concerned. They knew Dennis was in the Lord's hands and He would rouse Dennis when it was time.

Nancy and I had expected to find Spirit-led people when we came to visit Alleluia, and we were not disappointed!

Tom's Adjustment

One night as our prayer meeting concluded, Tom, a tall young man in his mid-twenties, came over to me, asking to be prayed over. He was in need of personal direction and was wondering if he should pursue work or school, and where. That was his only prayer request. As I prepared to pray over Tom, I sensed that he might go down (get slain), and I was mindful of the tile-covered concrete floor where we were standing. I motioned to Herb, a large, athletic man, to be prepared to catch him (a standard practice) if he went down. Now, with Herb in place and his hands on Tom's shoulders, I put my hand on Tom's head, closed my eyes, and began to pray for direction for Tom.

After a minute, I felt Tom falling away from my hand and I opened my eyes, expecting to see Herb catching and lowering him to the floor. Instead, Herb had walked away and had his back to us, while Tom was "out," hurtling fast toward the concrete floor. His body landed like a felled tree with a bounce, but I didn't see his head touch the floor. My first concern was a concussion or worse, and he was my responsibility. I knelt beside him and instantly shifted into prayers for his safety and well-being as he lay motionless. "Lord, don't let Tom be hurt," I prayed.

After a few minutes, Tom opened his eyes and got right to his feet. Standing with his hands on his lower back, stretching to the left and right and with a big smile on his face, he said, "This feels great! I've been having back pain the last few days—almost went to the chiropractor. I feel like I just got an adjustment." Tom walked away smiling and thankful. I was even more thankful.

Who Wants to Preach Pentecost?

It was Friday night of Pentecost weekend, and the regular GCG had begun. Dennis was leading and issued a Holy Spirit challenge: "Does anyone other than Fr. Lou want to come up and preach Pentecost?"

That was a daunting challenge that no one wanted to touch, and everyone turned, looking around the room for Fr. Lou, the firebrand and Holy Ghost preacher extraordinaire. Seated high up in the bleachers, Fr. Lou stood up and began to work his way down as everyone in the crowd extended hands toward him, praying in the Spirit. As soon as he reached the center of the platform, he was straightaway knocked flat on his back by the Holy Spirit. We sang two songs and were into a third one before we saw any movement in Fr. Lou's laid-out body. Slowly, he began to show signs of life, like one emerging from a coma. He regained awareness, struggled to his feet, brushed his hair into place, and then preached Pentecost like a flaming torch. The whole crowd ignited with him. We all "did" Pentecost—the Holy Spirit's way! And when *He* thought we were ready!

Fresh Air and a Fresh Touch

One Sunday morning, I was assisting Nancy at the soup kitchen, The Master's Table, and it was time for the guests to arrive. Among the mixture of street people and others in the group who entered was a big, strong-looking man I didn't remember having seen before. I spoke with him, just trying to reach out to him. He told me his name was George and that, the day before, after a long incarceration, he had been released from prison. He told me a few details and seemed starved for some fellowship with anyone he could trust. He also looked repentant for mistakes in his life.

George ate his lunch and began preparing to leave (with no place to go). Then he asked if I would pray over him for a good start in the next chapter of his life. Since the soup kitchen was jammed with people, I suggested that we go outside, away from the crowd. He was fine with that. We found a spot just behind a parked car. This was about as private a place as we could manage, since we were out on the street.

Shortly after I laid hands on him and began to pray, George started going down, like all the strength had left his legs. He just crumpled under the touch of the Spirit and slid down the back of the parked car into a heap on the street. Almost simultaneously, an oncoming pickup truck driven by a nervous man came to a sudden stop alongside us. The man had seen George going down and very excitedly called out, "Is he okay? Is he okay? Should I call 911?" I assured the man that George was fine and told him, "We're just getting rid of some demons." The driver rushed off in his truck, dismayed about the whole event.

Then, with considerable help, George was able to struggle to his feet, quite dazed but thankful for the Lord's special touch, likely a first for him, and His care. No doubt he will always remember the Lord's "drop-in" on him that day.

On the Road

We were on a music ministry trip to Nashville. Our van, loaded with the ministry team, had been traveling through the night. We were nearing our destination and planning to stop for breakfast around daylight.

Three of us had been having an impromptu counseling discussion with Doug, a very charismatic man who had barely escaped the world's grasp through a radical conversion. He was a master sheetrock finisher and also the drummer for our group. (He is now an ordained minister.) As we pulled into the Cracker Barrel restaurant, Doug wanted prayers before going in to eat. I told him that Jack and I would stay back and pray over him.

As I looked for Jack, who had mentioned his need for a restroom, I realized that he had already gone into the restaurant, so it would just be me praying over Doug. That would be fine—I wasn't concerned. Just after starting to pray, I felt Doug falling backward toward the asphalt parking lot. With no one there to catch him, my reflex action was to lunge and grab him around the back of his neck and try to catch him, which I was able to do. He outweighed me by some seventy-five pounds, and since he was falling fast, I was catapulted straight upward, feet far above my head, and then fell flat on top of him in the parking lot. The restaurant had just opened, and we were right outside the windows. We hoped that no one had been shocked by the sight of us—but we know that when we're following the Spirit, we don't have to worry about such things. It's all the Lord's doing.

As we looked back on the situation, we both believed this conclusion was quite fitting for Doug, a big, solid, hands-on, hard-driving guy. For a construction worker and a drummer, a strong physical touch seemed normal. Maybe that sudden touch from the Holy Spirit just punctuated what he had already been told in the van.

Good Friday

To me, Good Friday, Easter and Pentecost are simply awesome! They are the ultimate holy days—each one as important as the others, but so very different. On Good Friday, I want to reflect on the price Jesus paid, feel some of His suffering and try to appreciate His sacrifice. We participate in a special public ceremony on Good Friday called the Way of the Cross, and just being "out there" and staying focused on the Lord is a large part of what makes the day so meaningful to me.

Even though it's so little in comparison to Calvary, the Way of the Cross that we walk together each year has been our effort to "flesh it out" and make the sacrifice of Calvary more real. It's my favorite two hours of the year. Joining 500 or more men, women and children, walking, singing and praying while carrying crosses, taking our faith to the world, is so exhilarating and spiritually fulfilling that most of us don't want it to end. Many people complete the walk and go right into the Catholic church (the final stop on the walk) to participate in Stations of the Cross. We provide a shuttle bus at the finish, but many participants walk the mile and a quarter back to where we started just to savor the experience.

One year, a few of the men involved wanted to add something extra to the day. Set-up at Burns Memorial United Methodist Church would not begin until 9:30 a.m., so we agreed to assemble at 8 a.m. outside Ascension Lutheran Church, the second stop on the walk. We had no agenda; we just wanted to be open to the Spirit and see where He would lead us. Pastor Mike of Ascension would be speaking later at this stop, but first he wanted to take part in this early gathering. Mike had joined us numerous times in front of an adult video store in the area and at Planned Parenthood to stand against evil. The purpose of our meeting was to pray for the fullness of the day and to help launch the activities. We wanted more of the Lord this day.

Any of us could invite whomever we felt led to, and out of the dozen who arrived, about five were real surprises, people who were not known to be walking in the Spirit. Pastor Mike invited one of the leading men in his church, who brought his wife, the only woman there. We considered her courageous to have come. She was quite welcome to be there, along with the rest. No one there knew every one of the others. A new man, Brad, came that morning. He would become a close friend who later joined our church and the Alleluia Community.

We had crosses, five- to seven-feet tall, one for each person, and we began walking around the church, praising the Lord and praying. This continued for about twenty minutes. The spiritual intensity was noticeably strong. Then a couple of the men stopped to pray over another man and he went right down, slain in the Spirit. The next man prayed over also quickly went down, and we knew the Holy Spirit had moved in and taken over.

Several of this group had never experienced or witnessed this wonderful phenomenon that happens at the touch of the Spirit. That didn't matter, though—the Lord continued to move right through the group. As we prayed and laid on hands, we had to move quickly to catch those being slain. Some were laid on the grass, some among the shrubs, some on the walkway by the entry of the church. After being down, then regaining their feet, these men would pray for others. There was no interruption throughout the ministry. All went down except one man who had been brought by another man, and unfortunately, fear kept him well away and resistant to any touch. That was all right. The Lord never pushes or forces Himself on any of us. His blessings are freely offered.

Our little gathering was concluded in about forty-five minutes. It was a Spirit happening for sure, and we won't ever know exactly why. We guessed that maybe the Spirit just wanted to glorify the Son on this day, and put His "Amen" on our intentions and efforts. We were humbled and amazed. We had received far more than we could have hoped for, and after that, we were well prepared to embark on the Way of the Cross with the large group of people who would soon gather.

Come, Holy Spirit, on Good Friday!

The wind blows wherever it pleases. You hear its sound, but you cannot tell where it comes from or where it is going. So it is with everyone born of the Spirit.

—John 3:8 (NIV)

Possibly these strange and sudden encounters between man and God also bring forth smiles in Heaven. They must help alleviate some of the tensions the Lord has with mankind.

Tex

Tex was a tall, lanky Black man in his fifties or older who was part of the concrete crew that poured and finished the slabs and driveways of my houses. He likely had little, if any, money or education, but I knew him to be a physically hard worker. I had watched him using wheelbarrows and shovels, pushing one heavy load after another, shoveling concrete until every corner was filled, and working down on his knees at the end, putting on the final smoothing touches, sometimes after dark. The years of backbreaking work had long since taken a heavy toll on his body, and he now pulled his weight alongside much younger and stronger men, not nearly as much through strength as through necessity and determination. I sometimes wondered what he went home to at the end of the day.

One day when the crew was working for me, they took a break for some ice water. The temperature was in the nineties, and Tex downed his glass of ice water and went for seconds. As he was draining the second glass, turning it up toward the sky, Tex suddenly fell back, horizontal, like a tree cut down. He bounced on the ground, face up, still holding his glass to his mouth, with his eyes rolled back in his head. I was shocked, but the other men there who knew him paid little attention and left him lying there unattended. When I became concerned and asked Bill, the lead man, about it, he replied, "Oh that's just Tex—its ole alcohol—DTs—he be alright." In a few minutes they stepped over him and went back to work. Tex lay there shaking a few minutes more, and then his eyes regained their focus. Still dazed, like he didn't know what had happened, he shook it off and got up, going back to work. Drink was obviously a big weakness in Tex's life, and his friends and coworkers were all aware of it. They seemed to accept that weakness as just part of who he was.

A couple of years later, the same group was set to pour the basement slab in a house I had under construction. The lot was a downhill slope, all red clay, and it was slick as glass when it was wet. We all arrived that morning to find an orange quagmire. It had rained heavily all night, and the recently graded terrain was covered with countless standing puddles all across the lot, as far as you could see. It looked like any possibility of pouring concrete this day was out of the question. But I tried to be optimistic and hold out hope, especially since the concrete men didn't look concerned. Six of them were standing together talking near the newly poured basement walls. Tex stood way off to the right, by himself, very still, looking very focused. I began to watch him. After another minute or so, he took the shovel he'd been propped up against, scooped one shovelful of soupy red mud, pitched it behind him, and propped himself back up against the shovel, motionless. Then it happened. Muddy water ran out of that small hole and down the hill, and then a stream of water ran toward and through it. Suddenly, water across the entire property began to come alive and was moving toward and past Tex, picking up speed. Within minutes, with one exacting scoop, he had drained the entire property! Wow! I was amazed!

We lost no time. The concrete mixers arrived on schedule, and even with their massive weight, they had no difficulty driving on or off the property, and the slab was finished that evening. Tex had the gift that enabled us all to be successful with our work that day, and the other men knew it. I sure couldn't have done what he did.

That morning I had asked the Holy Spirit to help us get the slab poured and finished, and He supplied all the help we needed—not as I expected, but better!

None of us are blessed with the same talents or afflicted in the same ways, but we all have value and special gifts if we just look for them and recognize them, and each of us has our part to play for the higher good. It's just the way God set it up.

Indeed, the body does not consist of one member but of many. If the foot would say, "Because I am not a hand, I do not belong to the body," that would not make it any less a part of the body. And if the ear would say,

"Because I am not an eye, I do not belong to the body," that would not make it any less a part of the body. If the whole body were an eye, where would the hearing be? If the whole body were hearing, where would the sense of smell be? But as it is, God arranged the members in the body, each one of them, as He chose. If all were a single member, where would the body be? As it is, there are many members, yet one body. The eye cannot say to the hand, "I have no need of you," nor again the head to the feet, "I have no need of you." On the contrary, the members of the body that seem to be weaker are indispensable.

—1 Corinthians 12:14-22 (NRSV)

Topsoil

Our son Brad had his car in the garage for service, and I was dropping him off at his place of employment. His car would be out of commission all week. The first day, as we pulled up to his place of work, located on the back side of a defunct shopping center, I noticed a front-end loader, a track hoe, and a big, dark pile of topsoil on the land just beyond the huge parking lot. Since I had been a builder, the topsoil caught my attention.

The construction crew was on site, so I pulled up to speak with the project manager and ask what plans his company had for the dirt. Some contractors will give you common fill dirt just for the cost of handling it, since they have to get rid of it anyway and would rather avoid paying for the handling themselves. But the dirt I could see was definitely not common dirt. It was highly desirable topsoil, worth a lot of money. I told the man that the Alleluia Community, a Christian group just a few miles away, was ready to begin building a courtyard at its school and we had need of topsoil—lots of it.

He told me they were building a multiplex movie theater and would be grading for several days. He was uncertain about the plans for the dirt, but he would talk with the bosses, and I could check back with him once they neared completion of the grading. The project manager spoke clearly and to the point and seemed responsible, and I was hopeful that we would be able to get the topsoil. Each morning that week, as I dropped Brad off to work, I saw that the pile of dirt had grown larger and was still all dark, good-quality soil. When I checked on Thursday morning, the project manager explained that they would be wrapping up the grading that day and would decide by that evening if Alleluia could have some of the soil. He said, "Come back early tomorrow morning because the dirt will have to be moved then."

The next morning when I arrived, the manager said the company officials had agreed to let us have all the dirt, just for the cost of the time it would take for their track hoe to load it and for three tandem dump trucks to haul it to our school. Wow! They were going to give us quality topsoil for about $35 for every truckload delivered.

After he had agreed to send the dirt, the project manager told me that he had just been diagnosed with a serious illness and asked for prayer. As the track hoe began to load the dirt into the first truck, the two of us stood in the middle of that construction site praying to Jesus for his healing. I also offered thanks to the Lord for the manager, his company, and the gift of the topsoil.

That company delivered twenty-two truckloads of rich topsoil to our school campus that day for $770. The cost was several thousand dollars less than any landscape supplier would have charged for that amount of topsoil, given its market value (a price we could not have even considered).

The construction company likely had to purchase more topsoil to complete the landscaping for its project, since they had given us what they had. Unfortunately, the theaters soon went the way of the old shopping center—defunct. Our topsoil, however, became the foundation for the Alleluia School courtyard, which for three decades now has been referred to as "Holy Ground," where life is abundant.

I came that they may have life, and have it abundantly.
—John 10:10 (NASB)

Every good and perfect gift is from above, coming down from the Father of the heavenly lights, who does not change like shifting shadows.
—James 1:17 (NIV)

"Ask and it will be given to you; seek and you will find; knock and the door will be opened to you. For everyone who asks receives; the one who seeks finds; and to the one who knocks, the door will be opened."
—Matthew 7:7-8 (NIV)

The Markings

One afternoon we got a phone call from Ellen, who lived in a small town in South Carolina, a two-hour drive from Augusta. She was a personable single woman in her thirties whom Nancy and I had come to know over a period of several years. Ellen was in town visiting friends for the afternoon and was in need of a neck cross to wear while serving as an acolyte at her church. She had called hoping that we might have a suitable one available.

A small cross did come to my mind. It was made of olivewood, with a narrow rosewood cross inlaid on the front. I had made it a few years earlier and had put it away in a drawer, almost forgetting about it.

After I described it to Ellen, she came right over, and at first sight, she thought it was just what she needed. Maybe it had been "hidden away" just for her. She quickly claimed it, ready to wear it.

Ellen's schedule and distance from Augusta had prevented her from attending our recent prayer meetings, so we didn't see her for a time. Then one day, she called, and with a perplexed tone in her voice, she told us that something strange seemed to be happening with the cross. Red stripes had developed down the back side, along with a solitary red spot on the front. A friend of hers who knew about finishes had told her that all of the red marks appeared to be under the finish, while the finish itself was unaffected. I encouraged her to come to Augusta soon and bring the cross with her so that I could inspect it thoroughly.

Soon afterwards, Ellen came to a prayer meeting and brought the cross. Sure enough, the red marks were all underneath the finish, just as her friend had said. They were bright red, like fresh blood, and the finish was slick and unblemished. The pattern on the back was symmetrical, from one side to the other, symbolic of the scourging at the pillar, and the single spot on the front was midway down the right side. Ellen had put the clean and polished cross in an envelope to bring to the prayer meeting. Now the envelope was heavily marked all over with dark splotches, as of dried blood from fresh bleeding. Several of our friends at the prayer meeting who were in the medical profession—doctors, nurses and medical technicians— studied and checked out the cross and envelope at length. Each was virtually certain the stains were blood.

Ellen gave me the envelop to keep in case I wanted to have the stains analyzed. For whatever reason, it was quite a few years before it was tested. By then, the stains had faded in intensity, and the tests didn't prove that they were blood—but the tests didn't prove that they weren't blood, either.

Ellen said that her sister, who had been physically ill for some time and had not been close to the Lord, had become quite taken with the cross and its markings. They were having a strong effect on her.

Over the next few months, Ellen called twice more to report on the cross. In the first call she said, "The marks are all fading." In the second call, she told us, "The marks are totally gone—not a trace left." The inlaid rosewood cross on the front remained as vibrant as ever.

The Lord's ways are higher than our ways, and are sometimes very mysterious.

> *The Lord gave, and the Lord hath taken away; blessed be the name of the Lord.*
>
> *—Job 1:21(KJV)*

Just Looking

Our business, Images of the Cross, is located on a main traffic artery, Lumpkin Road, which is heavily traveled and fast moving, not the most conducive to retail traffic. This is not necessarily a problem for us, though, given that our business is primarily in manufacturing liturgical furnishings for churches and we don't rely on walk-in traffic. Our building is divided, with approximately three-fourths set up for production and one-fourth devoted to a gallery, or showroom. We have scores of crosses hanging in our showroom, and we sell them mostly to people who have already seen and appreciate our work and know where to find us.

One morning, as I was working in the shop, the front doorbell rang. I opened the door to a puzzled-looking woman I'd never seen before. She said she had been driving down the street as she regularly did when, for the first time, she had noticed our building and sign. She went on to say that something she couldn't explain caused her to turn around and come right back to check us out. Right off the bat, she said, "I am not here to buy anything." I wasn't surprised, but was taken by the fact that "something caused her to turn around and come right back," which had a Holy Spirit feel about it. Her name was Ms. Ramsey, and she was probably in her sixties and dressed in business clothing. She said she worked for the city but wasn't at the shop on city business, only to see what kind of business was in this building. I invited her to come in and look around.

As she walked across the floor, a standing crucifix on the counter caught her eye. She picked it up and turned it over to check the price, which was $235. Without a pause, she said, "I'd like to buy this, but I'm driving a city car and I'm not allowed to carry anything personal in it. Would you hold it until 5:30 this afternoon and I'll come pick it up in my own car?"

I assured her that would be fine. She asked if she needed to pay for it right then or when she picked it up. I told her, "Later will be fine."

With that settled, she departed for work, telling me as she left, "I'll be back at 5:30."

As she drove away, I thought she likely would be back, unless she had let impulse determine her decision and later buyer's remorse would override it. Still, I felt pretty certain that her decision was for real. A little after 5 p.m., I took the crucifix off the counter, polished it with lemon oil to make it nice and sparkling, and put it on my desk with an invoice for the amount. It was ready for her.

At 5:30, Ms. Ramsey rang my doorbell. I was encouraged that I had judged her correctly and she had done what she said she would do. As she entered the building, I told her I had her crucifix ready to go, but she walked past me toward the showroom wall hung with crosses. Again, with little pause, she pointed toward a cross, saying, "I'd like that one, also." (This was becoming enjoyable for me.) Then she noticed two ebony spike crosses hanging almost side by side.

Entering into my role as salesman, I took both off the wall, held them up, and asked, "Which one do you like?"

She replied, "Oh, I want them both." Then, apparently having finished her shopping, she turned on her heel toward the front door. I was blown away by the surprise and speed of it all. I fumbled around getting her package ready to go and totaling her bill—well over $600, which she paid with a check.

Ms. Ramsey smiled, thanked me and said, "Well, that's my Christmas shopping. I will be flying to New York this Friday to spend Christmas with my four adult children. This is their Christmas!"

Ms. Ramsey spent less than a half hour in our showroom and had her Christmas blessings for her family. Our family was also blessed by her visit. I absolutely knew the Holy Spirit had brought her ! He not only knows what each of us needs but also how to put it into our hands!

A man's heart plans his way, but the Lord directs his steps.
                                        —Proverbs 16:9 (NKJV)

The Casket in Waiting

In 1985, a dying friend requested that I build her casket. I thought of it as an one-time event. That notion turned out to be far off the mark, as the number I've now built has exceeded sixty-five. Each casket is special because of the life associated with it, but I want to share the story of one casket with a course that was very different from all of the others.

Charlie and Jeannie were members of our prayer and share groups in Marietta during the early 1980s. They had seven children, some already adults at that time and the others in their teens. Over a period of a few years, we shared our faith at many gatherings. In 1984, our family relocated to Augusta to join the Alleluia Community, and we lost contact with Charlie and Jeannie. They reappeared when their oldest son, Dave, relocated to Augusta, and we would see them at our local church during holidays from time to time. Dave later moved to Denver and we didn't see Charlie or Jeannie anymore.

One day in the spring of 2001, Dave called to inform me that his mother had pancreatic cancer and wasn't expected to live very long. We were jolted by the news—Jeannie was still very active and dynamic, although Charlie had died a few years earlier. Dave went on to tell me that his mother had instructed him to ask me to build her casket. I was honored to be asked and quickly committed to having it ready and delivering it to Marietta when it was needed.

Nancy and I delivered the finished casket as planned to the funeral home. Jeannie was special to us, almost like an Alleluia Community member, so of course we were there for her funeral, which was glorious, well attended, and had eleven Catholic priests in attendance. Jeannie and Charlie had been quite active in a variety of church ministries for a long time.

At the conclusion of the funeral service, Dave told me that the family had bought the casket to use just for the funeral service. Jeannie's body was going to be cremated and buried later in upstate New York next to Charlie's remains. I was surprised but realized that this was what the family had chosen to do, so I didn't think much more about the casket.

Eleven years later, in November 2012, I got an e-mail from Dave telling me that he had just learned about something that had happened the previous year, and he thought I would find it interesting. He told me that at the conclusion of his mother's funeral, the family offered the barely used, now empty cherry casket to a family friend, Fr. Tom, to be given to anyone he chose who might need a casket. Fr. Tom graciously accepted the gift, took it and stored it where he served.

Years later, Fr. Tom was caring for a dying clergyman and offered him the casket. In November 2011, the casket-in-waiting received for burial the mortal remains of former Atlanta Archbishop John Donoghue. It just happened that the Archbishop died on November 11, which had been the birth date of Jeannie's husband, Charlie. Archbishop Donoghue's remains were buried in the casket in Arlington Cemetery in Sandy Springs, Georgia, within a few blocks of some of the contract houses that I had built over twenty years earlier.

***

Some might ask, what's the big deal about this? When we see with the eyes of faith, God's fingerprints are all over this chain of events. Archbishop Donoghue was the most pro-life bishop ever to serve in Atlanta. For many years, he frequently stood on the streets in front of abortion clinics, alongside other defenders of life, standing for the unborn and for the sanctity of life. Nancy and I never met him but had heard him speak in Atlanta at Roe v. Wade gatherings. Not only was 1985 the year I built my first casket, it was also the beginning of our personal call to stand for life at Planned Parenthood in Augusta.

Upon receiving this news about the casket last year, it instantly brought tears to my eyes. It was as though God, in revealing this information, was leaving His calling card to be found by Jeannie's family, myself and others, just so that we could feel His omnipotence and perhaps receive a nod of encouragement. Nothing happens by chance or goes unnoticed in the Heavenlies—and the Lord is always far ahead of us!

O Lord, You have searched me and known me. You know when I sit down and when I rise up; You understand my thought from afar. You scrutinize my path and my lying down, and are intimately acquainted with all my ways. Even before there is a word on my tongue, behold, O Lord, You know it all. You have enclosed me behind and before, and laid Your hand upon me. Such knowledge is too wonderful for me; it is too high, I cannot attain to it.

—Psalm 139:1-6 (NASB)

No Complaining, Just Ask

Keith, a friend of mine and a very fine liturgical artist, dropped by my shop one day with a suggestion. He and his wife Martha were planning a trip to Mystic Island, Connecticut, to attend a liturgical art show. "Why don't you and Nancy join us there and show some of your stuff?" he asked. The drive would be long, and the timing was not great, but the idea intrigued me.

Nancy and I decided to go for it. We borrowed some special pieces that I had built for churches, filled our van with crosses, photos and samples, and headed north. The show's waterside location was gorgeous, but I soon tired of the artsy people with their art-related talk. I wondered if some of them were truly professional working artists, or only playing the part.

By the end of the show, I was very ready to pack up and head for home. We had made some contacts and our work had found favor, but it was unclear how much benefit the show had really been to us. I had the feeling I had probably lost a week's worth of work and the cost of the trip. We were facing over a thousand miles of road, jammed with Labor Day traffic, to get home. We hoped and prayed we'd have fewer potholes heading south than on the drive north, and that we would see no signs saying, "Expect delays, next 37 exits," like we'd seen on the way to Mystic Island.

We seemed to have gained nothing from the experience, but two years after the show, I got a call from an architectural designer named Sean who was located in Arizona. We had met him at the Mystic show and he was calling to see if I would be interested in building the sanctuary furnishings for a large Catholic church in Florida that was just breaking ground. Sean had designed the interior of the sanctuary, and he was designing the altar pieces as well.

The job would require dealing with more red tape, paperwork, codes and insurance than I was accustomed to, but it was a big contract that would ultimately be awarded to someone. I was capable of handling the work, but would I get the contract, or would pursuing it turn out to be an expensive rabbit trail? Just the procedural logistics would be a major challenge.

After a few weeks, we learned that we had been granted the contract. As we had foreseen, this job was going to be demanding. The church would have very high ceilings, a large amount of cubic space, and would seat over a thousand people. The altar pieces that I would be building would be larger than usual, heavy and difficult to handle physically. Their sizes would challenge my shop space rather seriously.

I almost always do my own designing, and then scale drawings for each piece. This time Sean sent AutoCAD perspective drawings that were not scaled at all. I would have to convert his CAD drawings and dimensions to be able to work from them. This was time consuming and required extra communication, which tested the patience of us both. Sean was not really knowledgeable about structure, but was instead focused on design and the finished look. It would fall to me to engineer the pieces to ensure they had adequate strength, while still achieving the look Sean had conceived.

All of the pieces were to be built of Honduras mahogany with maple accents and included expensive bronze screening from Germany. The church was quite showy, with work commissioned from a larger number of artists than I had encountered on any other job. The church was not a basilica or cathedral, but it was larger than many of them.

Building the furnishings demanded a large amount of material and lots of heavy handling. Mahogany trees yield some of the largest boards of any tree; some of those four-inch-thick boards weighed approximately two hundred pounds each when they arrived at my shop from the lumber yard. Transforming them from their rough, dirty condition to the right dimensions and shapes, with joints, detail and fine polish, consumed many long hours. There were no real glitches—we just had to stay with the job at hand and keep working until it was finished. It required nine months of full-time work to complete the various pieces.

As we approached completion and the last few weeks of this intense, consuming job, it dominated not only my time but a large portion of the space in my shop and showroom as well. And then I got a call from Sean, the designer.

He informed me that the building completion was running behind schedule by at least a month, and maybe more. This wasn't all good news, since I had been pushing very hard to meet the original schedule and now would also have to think about providing storage for the pieces.

About that time, I noticed myself silently complaining—and I know better than to complain. This complaint was in the form of, "Lord, I could use your help. This is becoming more than I bargained for." I knew without a doubt that I would keep giving the work my best effort, all the way through until completion, but I felt the need for some relief.

The Spirit, having heard my complaint, quietly but quickly responded, "Ask them if they can help." I definitely wasn't intending to do that. I just wanted to complain to myself a little. In all my years of business, I had never asked for more than the agreed-upon price, regardless of how hard the job became or what unexpected circumstances arose. I had never gone back and asked for more money, and at first it seemed unthinkable.

After I had mulled all those thoughts over for a day or two, the Spirit quietly repeated, "Ask them if they can help." By that time I knew that this was not a mere suggestion from the Lord, nor something under discussion, but a directive. After about three days, I had to act. My deep-rooted pride would give way to obedience and trust, even though it felt like pulling a wisdom tooth. I would obey the Voice and I would ask—that was my part. I deeply disliked the task, but asking was what the Lord was telling me to do.

There were three individuals involved: Sean, the designer who had initially contacted me, the pastor, and the church administrator, John. I started with Sean. I filled him in on the situation, and then said, "If I had it to do over, I would price the job $20,000 higher. Is there any way you can help?"

Sean quickly responded, "That would be up to the pastor or John. I'm not involved with the money."

One down. I then called the pastor, explaining in the same way. The pastor said, "John is in charge of the finances. You might try calling him."

Two down, one to go, and my last chance. I called John and explained my request to him. John is a very nice person, good to work with, realistic, with solid common sense. I felt if he could help, he would. John listened patiently and then carefully said, "I will see what we can do."

Okay. That was it. I had done what I believed the Spirit had told me to do, and then I turned it loose. Since the question was anointed by the Lord, I didn't really feel like a beggar... at least, not much.

Weeks later, with all of the furnishings completed and ready to deliver, I called John to advise him of our expected arrival. Just before we concluded our discussion, John added, "After you get to the church, we'll talk about the additional compensation."

Wow! What a nice new phrase. At least John had heard me.

We arrived at the church with the truckload of furnishings, and the new building wasn't even close to being ready for us to install the pieces. Scaffolding and workmen were everywhere. The church did, however, have a safe, empty room, air conditioned and protected, where we could store everything until the sanctuary was completed.

After we had placed all of the new pieces in the storage room, I sat down with John to go over the remaining invoices. With that accomplished, John spoke up. "Now, tell me again about the additional compensation."

I recounted some of the many challenges of the project and told him again, "If I had it to do over, I would price the job $20,000 higher."

John leaned forward and in an understanding tone said, "Well, we can't do twenty thousand." Then, after a short pause, he said, "But our people here have been generous and good to us, and we want to pay you an additional fifteen thousand."

I could literally have fallen out of my chair. Not two or three thousand, or even five thousand, but fifteen thousand. It was all I could do to hold it together. I knew I had worked for and deserved this money, but I was still shocked to have it granted to me! I told John I would wait to bill that amount until we had completed the last installation.

It was two more months before the building was completed and we could return to install the pieces. John told me to invoice the church the additional $15,000 and we would receive the check within a week. The amount had already been approved by the diocese.

The following week, the check for the additional compensation arrived. The Holy Spirit and John had delivered. This check clearly had the Holy Spirit's fingerprints. Three weeks after the check arrived, news broke of the 2008 financial crash in New York with Goldman Sachs, Lehman Brothers, and all the others. Immediately, the diocese in Florida, like most across the country, put a moratorium on all new spending—shut it all down. The financial crash slowed or stopped most church spending for capital improvements, and this greatly affected our larger church jobs. The good news was that the "additional compensation" provided the cushion needed, financially and mentally, for me to begin devoting one day a week, and then more, to writing my first book, *Swept Up by the Spirit: Journey of Transformation*. For years, writing the book had seemed a "stretch too far," but suddenly it was becoming a reality. Four years later, after the book was published, John ordered a box of twenty-eight copies for a men's study group at the church.

I learned through all of this that sometimes it's not enough to just ask God—He may show us that our role is to ask a key person for help, as well! The sequence of events in this story unfolded over seven years. I was focused on dealing with one thing at a time, but obviously the Lord was seeing the entire picture and orchestrating each event. As we follow His leadings and say yes to each one as it comes along, this seems to please Him and He opens the doors ahead of us. And that story is unending!

What a God we serve and get to work alongside!

"Ask, and it will be given to you; seek, and you will find; knock, and it will be opened to you. For everyone who asks receives, and he who seeks finds, and to him who knocks it will be opened."

—Matthew 7:7-8 (NASB)

But just as it is written, "Things which eye has not seen and ear has not heard, and which have not entered the heart of man, all that God has prepared for those who love Him."

—1 Corinthians 2:9 (NASB)

Why Committed Relationships?

When the Lord called many of us men and women to come and join the Alleluia Community, we already had the desire to know and serve Him and the heart to put Him first in our lives. The "yes, Lord, send me" response had started each one of us on a lifetime journey. Many of us had our faith awakened through participation in a charismatic prayer group, one of thousands of different prayer groups across the country. Each of these groups served as a valuable path to an exhilarating new life in the Lord, moving us away from the worldly way of life we had known and followed before. These prayer groups showed many of us the first step that was needed and lit within us the fire and the desire to grow our faith.

Unfortunately, most prayer groups could only take their members so far on the faith journey because these groups didn't develop committed relationships, the commitment to other members that is necessary to build and nourish the full Christian life. The help that such groups provided was limited to prayer meetings or similar gatherings and what could be delivered in and through those settings. One or two family members might participate in a prayer group, but rarely were entire families, including children, involved; children frequently were overlooked or left out entirely. Christianity without full commitment becomes hard to sustain and a prime target for weakness of the flesh and for burnout.

The kind of relationships that I am talking about involve, through grace, a lifetime commitment to do the following:

- Share life together with trust, love, loyalty and faithfulness.
- Undertake important and often hard work together.
- Be there for each other in good times and bad.

- Act out of concern for community members and their families, responding immediately when needed.
- Truly belong to the faith family, the community brothers and sisters, as with a blood family.
- Be there for each other in the late or difficult stages of life.
- Graciously help bury one another.
- Be honored to be buried by and near each other.

With this level of commitment in place, the journey not only takes on greater meaning but is fulfilling to travel, even when the path is uphill.

In 1984, Nancy and I brought our family to Augusta, Georgia, to join the Alleluia Community. To leave the Atlanta area, where our business was taking hold, seemed like a huge stretch to us but a necessary response of obedience. We definitely felt the call to Alleluia and the community's lifestyle, a way of life similar to that described in Acts 2, where we see the model response to the Holy Spirit's call to put into action our "yes, Lord, Your will, not mine." Scripture tells us that this response by the disciples actually began the Christian church. This lifestyle would have been downright unimaginable for Nancy and me (and all of our friends) when we married. But for many of the second- and third-generation community members, the lifestyle is absolutely normal. They have grown up immersed in this lifestyle and watched those around them act out of concern for others, depend on others and focus on following the Lord's plan. As adults, they have the opportunity to choose, and many make the choice to continue this special life.

Life in Alleluia would turn out to be a totally new experience for us. Not only were we able to share and grow in good, deeply spiritual meetings with Spirit-led friends, but our whole family would begin to live 24/7 with scores of other like-minded families and singles. This group of several hundred people was certainly diverse in terms of personalities, backgrounds, training, education, life experiences, financial status, gifts and abilities, and were from many different areas of the country. Some challenging personality differences might have seemed to exist among us. (My own personality surely challenged others!) Some Alleluia members would look like polar opposites in the world's eyes, but we learned that when you live alongside each other in the Spirit, these differences can become nonfactors or even positive elements in the bigger picture of God's call and mission.

We found the community mindset to be totally different from that of our former prayer groups. The spirituality was somewhat similar, but the way it was lived out was not. The covenant community mentality is not about sharing a meeting and an experience with friends, but rather about being lifetime residents who "share a life." The level of ownership and responsibility goes much beyond the prayer group experience, encompassing all aspects of life and family members of all ages. There is a sense of being in this together, a faith family called together by the Holy Spirit and totally ecumenical—the united body of Christ.

As we soon learned, there is no expectation in the community that we will come to be like each other. We are to be fully ourselves. Working and living together, we respect and come to appreciate our differences. We begin to learn to defer to each other—community is not a place for competition. (What a difference from the world's mindset!) Through the Alleluia covenant that we sign after a lengthy period of discernment, we agree to be there for each other, in good times and bad, and help each other arrive in Glory. We have our own individual homes, but we share our lives as much as is practical. Since the secular culture has moved so far away from the Lord's plan for communal living, this approach may at first seem extreme or even cultlike to many. We heard critical comments along those lines more often thirty years ago, after the badly deceived Jim Jones and David Karesh led the people who followed them into disaster.

To give up our own ambitions, wishes, and plans to be open to the "higher" and "better" for all is quite a goal. To renounce our independent plans and lives and yield ourselves so that we can be reshaped and molded to become the person God wants each of us to become—this is a very tall order indeed.

Spirit of the living God, fall afresh on me.
Melt me, mold me, fill me, use me.
Spirit of the living God, fall afresh on me.
    —*From the hymn, "Spirit of the Living God," by Daniel Iverson*

To become this new person we all need help, not just from the Lord, but from our brothers and sisters. They are the horizontal arm of the cross that we promised to take up daily. Without the body of Christ we will remain incomplete. Realizing and accepting this can take time for some of us.

> *On one occasion an expert in the law stood up to test Jesus.*
> *"Teacher," he asked, "what must I do to inherit eternal life?"*
> *"What is written in the Law?" He replied. "How do you read it?"*
> *He answered, "'Love the Lord your God with all your heart and with*
> *all your soul and with all your strength and with all your mind'; and,*
> *'Love your neighbor as yourself.'"*
>
> —*Luke 10:25-27 (NIV)*

We have all read and quoted these two commandments often, but that is far from putting them into practice. Scripture tells us many times that the spiritual journey is not intended to be solitary, but to be carried out with others. Isolation is a quiet, deadly spirit, like the dead sea with nothing flowing in or out, and many fall victim to it. We need accountability and other mature voices speaking into our lives—it's not enough just to listen to ourselves. We all need the kind of growth and change that only comes through trust and relationships with our brothers and sisters, and a willingness to climb on the potter's wheel and ask Him to change and mold us.

Living in community has the effect of ironing out the wrinkles from everyday life. We are able to observe and learn better ways to live, share marriage in a more harmonious way, raise children with less hassle, drama and trauma, become disciplined to look for ways to give more or serve more, and achieve a balance that can't be attained alone. Most of this is not taught but is "caught" through the good example of others. Being around people who routinely exhibit acts of kindness, generosity, gentleness and goodness rubs off some of the burrs of our old nature. Most of us came to community with plenty of those burrs. Working at dying to self is a major undertaking. Inner healing is often needed for us to grow as we should, and in community, anyone can request and receive inner healing ministry as needed at any time. We have grace to confess our weaknesses to each other and even use those weaknesses as well as our strengths to work to improve ourselves. Not one of us is fully healed yet; our humanity is being dealt with in stages by the Spirit.

The community as a whole is loaded with talents, gifts and abilities in the natural and in the Spirit, but without knowing the players, it would be hard to tell who is who. There are no stars or celebrities, no need for name plates, ribbons, plaques, awards, bells or whistles. We are all equal in the Lord's eyes and we try to live that way, giving one another due respect, as deserved.

On our first visit to Alleluia, I was surprised by how the community mixed faith and work together, with no separation between the two. It was definitely new but appealing to me to join the community work parties and see men in work clothes gather to pray for everything, and then go out to work on the community property, some with their sons in tow to teach them to love work. Right away, I pegged the community as having a blue collar mindset or approach. There was an abundance of physical work to be done, and all of the members were the workers, committed to do that work together. I had no idea at the time that these work parties would become one of my favorite activities. In our community life, we are never far away from hands-on work. Good work practices serve as a great melting pot.

The founders realized the importance of living in close proximity for fellowship, support, to share responsibilities and for schooling. There is strength in numbers, especially if you are going to live an alternate (really Christian) lifestyle in this day and culture, not for protection but for accessibility to like-minded people, growth and momentum. It has become known among Spirit-filled believers that Alleluia is one of the best examples of intentional Christian clustering in the world. The complex that most of us live in was built in 1951 as a duplex housing project and has been regenerated since 1973 into Faith Village. The village encompasses several blocks, and community members live side by side, just across the street, or across backyards from one another. There are backyard areas treated as common areas, with no fences. There is a sharing of resources on many levels, and members are there for one another, ready to extend assistance when needed. Houses, vehicles and household equipment are not owned in common but are often shared to meet a need.

Frequently, on Sunday afternoons, we will look out the back windows of our home to see a spirited pickup soccer game in progress, played by both men and boys (and sometimes a girl or two) ranging in age from ten to sixty. Called Center Circle, the field is our common backyard, longer than a soccer field, with a few large pecan trees. The same big yard may be filled with six hundred to eight hundred people—community members, family members and friends—on the 4th of July. Families and support groups (small faith-sharing groups to which all community members belong) use the space for potluck dinners and picnics, and many other events happen there. Center Circle is surrounded by the homes of older community members and can be used by any one of us. The next block over, called "K Block," is filled with homes of younger families with lots of young children. K Block's big, shared yard is loaded with play equipment and is used for learning or growth opportunities for kids, and also is host to many of our outdoor celebrations.

Alleluia also has three groups of members located at a distance from Faith Village. These groups are moderate to small in size, but the members' homes are also clustered near each other, and these community brothers and sisters have the same committed purpose, mindset, lifestyle and sharing of their lives. They are "all in" together.

The community always has plenty of service needs: setting up or taking down equipment used for group activities, helping with house moves, repairs, improvements, or maintenance of buildings or property, food service, counseling, child care, tutoring, elder care, care for those with disabilities, medical care, transportation to doctors' appointments, financial help. Whatever is needed, we collectively and individually are the servants; we each get to serve, and service is both assigned and voluntary. Some of our retired brothers and sisters offer "no-charge help"—their new avocation. The Lord surely must have designed service to help us decrease in self-concern and increase in humility and helpfulness.

> *"For even the Son of Man did not come to be served, but to serve, and to give His life as a ransom for many."*
>
> —*Mark 10:45 (NIV)*

In addition to all the work that gets done within and for the community, we have abundant outreach opportunities. We provide music and sometimes speakers for conferences, host international conferences, and hold prayer services in other cities as well as regular prayer gatherings on our property. The wide-reaching Golden Harvest Food Bank employs some community members, while other members serve there as volunteers and help with food distribution. A sizable number of community men regularly work in the Kairos prison ministry, spending three days and nights at a time, twice a year, in the prison. For forty years, our community has been very involved in pro-life efforts, both on the street in front of the abortion clinics and behind the scenes. In addition to all of this, many of our members are engaged in individual evangelistic efforts.

Our Alleluia school, with grades K-12, is quite a community work. All of the students and teachers are from community families, and all parents of students are invested in teaching their kids at home. The development of their characters and faith ranks above academics. The highest awards given by the school are the two Christian Character Awards, given to one young man and one young woman. The battle with Satan for the hearts and minds of all our people, including our young people, never ceases, but the strong Christian peer-pressure among the students and graduates helps lead them to make good personal choices.

The school program offers many balanced opportunities for students to grow in body, mind and spirit, to participate competitively in sports, and to grow up enjoying the life and each other tremendously. They have opportunities to help and serve frequently in community and to go on mission trips to serve the less privileged. On their senior trip, they travel to New York City to be awed by the sights and sounds, but come back realizing how good they have it at home. Surely, it is "good to be here." We have our share of graduates who have wandered away from the fold, but an increasing number come back later. Those who do are ready to live for the Lord.

Teachers in our school often give up the opportunity to work in public schools for much higher pay in order to teach for a higher good and contribute to the development of faith and character in our students. We also have a number of members who teach in public schools or universities. Many first- or second-generation members serve in the medical field as doctors, nurse practitioners, physician assistants, nurses and technicians. We have a number of second-generation members who take on social work to help the disabled or poor. A sizable number of members have committed their life work, their vocation, to the Lord—among them, eleven Catholic priests, four protestant ministers, and several nuns. This has not gone unnoticed in our various churches. Living a life centered around faith as they grew up was probably a primary reason for their decisions. Of course, we have lots of other members who work in a variety of industries and careers; covenant members almost never relocate for a better job. This really develops an exceptional sense of permanence and trust in each other.

As we watch the third generation coming up and exhibiting the traits, personalities, and fire of their parents or grandparents, sometimes at a level that exceeds what we saw in those who went before them, it gives us a lot to look forward to and warmly remember. Life is so much more fulfilling when we know the players all around us. Living our life among multiple generations, all with a holy goal to make Jesus the Lord of our entire lives and arrive in Glory, gives us a healthy understanding of life, removes most of the fear of death, and encourages us all.

Because relationships become so strong between families, and since so many of our young people have known each other throughout their entire school lives, when it comes time to select a partner for life, many don't look seriously outside of the community. Their hearts are captured by longstanding, trusted, special friends. The only "arranged" marriages among our people are those clearly arranged by the Holy Spirit. The young married couples have many good examples to follow, since Alleluia has a large number of couples whose marriages have lasted forty and fifty years or more. After four decades of this "clustering" life, we are seeing a number of families with three generations under one large roof—not by necessity so much as by choice, for practical reasons and because of their desire to share with and care for one another. As the families have developed, it is not unusual for our kids to grow up with both sets of grandparents only a few houses apart. The Lord's ways work, even in today's disintegrating world!

Over the years, we have had many "households" in community. This term usually applies either to a group of young men living together under the leadership of an older man, or young women living together with an older woman leading them. These households are for the purpose of formation as young Christian adults and so that participants can learn to live out community in new roles of responsibility. Some single adults are invited to live in a household with a married couple and their children, usually as preparation for marriage or to discern the Lord's will for the single's future. We have many great stories of household victories—some quite surprising. Alleluia has two different couples who, as young men and women, went into households as singles, with strong aversions to each other. The Lord had a different plan, and both couples have had long-term, exemplary marriages!

Hospitality is a very important part of community life. It is not unusual to have guests arrive anytime, from anywhere in the world, for a quick visit en route to somewhere else or to check out life in the community as a possibility for themselves. International conferences held here can last for several days, and sometimes faith leaders arrive here on "Kingdom" business. We have had twenty to thirty guests at a time from Brazil and Australia, staying and living community for a couple of weeks or longer. Two young Alleluia women have married men from an Australian community. All of the guests need dinner and housing, and we try to place them in community homes where they will fit in well and receive the most benefit. When we have a large group for a conference, maybe eighty or more will need meals and housing, and this can stretch us a bit, but it always works out fine. (We even seem to do better when stretched. We frequently hear more about the hospitality than about the conference!) We make little effort to impress our guests with our resources or facilities—for the most part, these aren't very impressive by the worlds' standards. We just try to be real, share what we have, keep on living our normal lives (with adjustments as needed) and add the guests to our lives. We want them to get a true picture of the life we share together, not a "walk in the park" idea. We are not out to sell anyone on community life; if that happens, it is a work of the Spirit. We do want guests to be greatly blessed and encouraged, and we enjoy them as much as they enjoy us. Sometimes their visits help them make important decisions, and some who come to discern whether Alleluia is for them may decide it is not, at least, for now.

Alleluia has numerous men, women and kids who have developed strong disciplines, especially in their spiritual practices. This is obvious through their prayer life, handling of Scripture and strong faith. We have quite a number of small groups that gather across the community. They are all different, all optional to participate in and all worthwhile for growth. To become an impact player, usable by the Spirit in this perverse culture and these perilous times, requires a great deal of development. This development is a major work, and it requires faithfulness, knowledge, discipline and perseverance—qualities hard to come by alone. The men's group I am part of meets three mornings a week, from 5:30 to 7 a.m. I have been a regular there for over thirty years and never miss it, if that can be avoided. Our group is led by the Spirit, is very practical, and helps us to put the gospel into practice in all kinds of situations. I credit our morning group along with street ministry as the two best opportunities I have had for spiritual growth and whole-life balance. We all need others to give us their perspectives, broaden our vision and help us to stay real, locked in and grounded.

> *"Iron sharpens iron, so one man sharpens another."*
> —*Proverbs 27:17 (NASB 1995)*

I have come to see Alleluia as the *pearl of great price* in a blue collar setting. Just recently, while reflecting, I saw Christianity itself as blue collar, a hard work when really lived out, whether by blue collar workers or white collar professionals (in community we have plenty of both). To live out our faith, to walk the talk, is a continuous work, without a doubt.

I also saw Jesus as the blue collar Savior and began reflecting on that. This term might sound irreverent to some until we reflect on the life He lived on earth, from His birth to His ascension. Jesus came to save everyone, from the lowest to the highest. But He Himself lived a blue collar life, working long, hands-on hours in the grit and grime, doing acts that ranged from healing lepers to raising the dead. I wish I had been open to realize this at a young age and not been shackled by deception for two decades. Jesus is definitely the man's man's blue collar Savior.

> *"Take My yoke upon you and learn from Me, for I am gentle and humble in heart, and you will find rest for your souls.*
>
> *For My yoke is easy and My burden is light."*
> —*Matthew 11:29-30 (NIV)*

We share together a very rich and full life in community. Most of us who came here later in life never had it so good! Community offers a completely different kind of living. If there is a sorrow to mourn, we all grieve; if there is a victory to celebrate, we all rejoice. We just gradually grow into this level of empathy with one another. We are truly on this journey together, very much marvelous comrades to each other, friends and neighbors who have learned how to love and be loved.

> ...*So that there should be no division in the body, but that its parts should have equal concern for each other. If one part suffers, every part suffers with it; if one part is honored, every part rejoices with it.*
> —*1 Corinthians 12:25-26 (NIV)*

Alleluia is far from being all work and no fun. We have much to celebrate and frequent celebrations: birthdays, anniversaries, weddings, births, graduations, Lord's Day meals, personal successes and other special personal days or milestones. When we join together to sing, "We love you with the love of the Lord... We can see in you the glory of our King, yes, we love you with the love of the Lord," the words bring many to tears. (Our version of the hymn is based on a similar one by Jim Gilbert.)

Even with all of our community celebrations of life, none is more moving or meaningful than those that take place when a member passes into Glory. Our wakes, funerals and burials are nearly indescribable as we celebrate a life lived unto the Lord and with the body of Christ.

Knowing that we will bury each other is very comforting and reassuring. Of course, the Lord holds all the timing in His hands. Certainly the concern, prayers and special care that lead up to anyone's departure are extremely important and anointed. The Alleluia brothers who dig the grave by hand put deep love, care and effort into action. Usually the sharings at the wake bless us so that even we go away with new insights into the life of the friend who has just passed. Our funerals are uplifting; we are brothers and sisters gathered to support and honor, with praise and worship music, the one who has been "promoted."

And then there is the sending out, the burial, probably the greatest spiritual group activity that Alleluia has—and that is saying quite a bit! Our burials have an unspoken order to them. Everyone works together patiently to close the grave, shovel by shovel, some shoveling while others wait to shovel. There is no hurry. First, the closest family members participate, then close friends and then others, including the children. Each person can shovel as little or as much as he or she wants. All participate respectfully, reverently and lovingly.

These are glorious good-byes, with soft praise and worship music played and sung at the graveside. What a wonderful way of dispelling any fear of death that one might have.

"O death, where is your sting?"

—*1 Corinthians 15:55 (NASB 1995)*

Burials are a priceless opportunity for children and young people and are deeply moving for family members who are not part of the community and for anyone who has never been present at such a happening. The process may take an hour to complete, and it is as though time stands still and those present are privileged to get a glimpse of Glory as it all unfolds. The burials provide peace and closure. We make the effort to treasure the life that this faithful traveler on the journey has given to the Lord and to us. Through it all, we are standing amongst the markers and tombstones of the valiant, the faithful departed who have gone before us. We are standing on holy ground.

Our covenant agreement calls us higher at times when we would rather not go higher, further when we are really tired, deeper when we thought we had bottomed out, and to press on together. For any who want to get to the Beautiful City, the journey is much richer when traveled together.

Through this shared life we become aware that:

- We can accomplish things together that would be impossible alone.
- We can allow others into our lives (and gradually, we discover that we really need them).
- We can admit our weaknesses and failures and will find that people love us more for sharing those truths.
- Life will get hard at times, and it helps to have uplifted spirits around us always.

- Each of us will get older, but young people help us retain our energy and fervor.
- Young people need older people around them for wisdom, understanding and discernment.

As we grow in these lifelong relationships, fear of all kinds loses its hold over us and we are freed to embrace the Lord's chosen ones and His will for our own lives, whatever that may be. Yes, it's unknown, but it is by far the best possible plan for anyone, and best lived with those you have come to love and who now love you!

Because we have willfully come under the Lordship of Jesus in our lives and asked Him to lead us as He will, we have come under God's favor, and it begins to show in every area of our lives, in all that we do, in our choices, in our families, in our work, and in our interactions with each other and people in general. The Lord shows us how life is intended to be lived at its highest and best and gives us plenty of opportunities to work toward that.

The combined result of living our faith, hope and love through our commitments to one another is so strong and omnipresent that we feel surrounded by this energy, whether in praise and worship with hundreds of our community members, when confronted by some unexpected trauma, on a ministry trip far from home, interceding for the needs of others, working through a work dilemma, and in so many other times and places. What a strength and assurance we experience as we are bolstered and undergirded by the prayers, yes—but also by the faith, hope and love of the committed body of believers behind those prayers, a body to which we all belong.

We realize as individuals and as a community that we are far short of having it all together, but we know that somehow, through answering the call and giving our best, we are part of an awesome Holy Spirit happening in process. We tend to take it for granted at times and need others " looking in our windows" to remind us how blessed we are. No group can make this happen apart from the call and anointing of the Holy Spirit. The community's age, forty-seven years and counting, is quite amazing, and truly shows His unmerited favor poured out.

Our journey to Glory is too good to travel alone, far too good!

Behold, how good and how pleasant it is for brothers to dwell together in unity!

—*Psalm 133:1 (NASB)*

They devoted themselves to the apostles' teaching and to fellowship, to the breaking of bread and to prayer. Everyone was filled with awe at the many wonders and signs performed by the apostles. All the believers were together and had everything in common...

Every day they continued to meet together in the temple courts. They broke bread in their homes and ate together with glad and sincere hearts, praising God and enjoying the favor of all the people. And the Lord added to their number daily those who were being saved.

—*Acts 2:42-44, 46-47 (NIV)*

I will close with a recounting of an experience that happened over fifty years ago.

I had just started working at a furniture manufacturing company in Nashville. The company had become dissatisfied with its glue supplier and the product itself. Our management had contacted several glue suppliers to come to the plant and demonstrate their glue.

A representative of Franklin Glue came to demonstrate its product, Titebond, to a number of our company executives and workers. The rep supplied the glue and had our workers use it to edge glue some hardwood panels by running them through a fast-set gluing machine. The boards were just straight-line ripped, not tongue and groove. Seconds later, when the glued panels emerged from the gluing machine, the rep grabbed them and threw them hard onto the concrete floor, then took his sledgehammer and smashed the panels to pieces. This violent destruction of the just-glued wood shocked us all!

The rep then invited us to gather up the shattered hunks of wood, look at them closely, and pass them around. He called our attention to the glue joints, which were all intact; not one was damaged. Then he simply said, "Titebond glue is stronger than the wood itself and is made to resist shock." No more demonstrations or explanations were needed. Franklin Titebond was the company's glue from that day forward (and in my own work for the rest of my life, also!).

Fifty years after witnessing that rep's sledgehammer decimate those panels into splintered chucks without damaging a joint, the memory is still vivid to me today. I worked for over three years at the furniture plant amidst tens of thousands of glued-up panels, and I don't recall one failed glue joint.

And so it is with fully committed relationships. They can stand up to anything. Just as Titebond glue is stronger than the wood itself and is shockproof, so are the committed relationships lived out through our covenant. The bond between us makes us stronger than we are ourselves. We have seen this time and time again when one of us gets hit with a sledgehammer event in life, especially the death and loss of a close (or closest) one, and the bonds of our relationships hold us together to carry us through, bonds that cannot be broken.

Even great glue holds nothing together while it's still in the bottle—it has to be spread around. So it is with relationships. They hold nothing together while bottled up. Let's all invest in these marvelous comrades the Lord has picked out and given to us, and develop our bonds ever stronger.

> *Bind us together, Lord, bind us together, with cords that cannot be broken.*
> *Bind us together, Lord, bind us together, Lord, bind us together in love.*
> *There is only one God, there is only one King, there is only one Body,*
> *That is why we sing...*
> *You are the family of God, You are the promise divine;*
> *You are God's chosen desire, You are the glorious new wine.*
> *—From the hymn, "Bind Us Together," by Bob Gillman*

A Cheerful Giver

Remember this: Whoever sows sparingly will also reap sparingly, and whoever sows generously will also reap generously. Each of you should give what you have decided in your heart to give, not reluctantly or under compulsion, for God loves a cheerful giver. And God is able to bless you abundantly, so that in all things at all times, having all that you need, you will abound in every good work. As it is written: "They have freely scattered their gifts to the poor; their righteousness endures forever."
—2 Corinthians 9:6-9 (NIV)

He was a salt-of-the-earth, hands-on working man. He wore work clothes and drove a pickup truck and worked in a profession that is dirty and sweaty by necessity, but so important to those who depend on it. He was "the man," often loud, boisterous, impulsive, joyful, engaging and approachable. In his efforts to push through everything he had to get done, he frequently became a bull in his own china shop. His employees gave him space. His size was considerable, but his heart of compassion and generosity was larger. He was a brother to some, a favorite uncle to many and a surrogate father to others. He was the go-to person in time of need to countless people—even people who seemed to have unfixable situations. His name was Rick Keller.

Rick didn't foresee what he would become. No one can who becomes such a willing, useful tool in the hands of the Lord.

Rick opened a Firestone tire dealership and auto repair shop in the early 1980s on busy Peach Orchard Road, in a moderate-income business district of South Augusta. In 1984, the Holy Spirit located Alleluia Community's new school and office about a mile up the street. At the time, only the Lord knew what the forthcoming relationship between Rick and the community would grow to be.

250

Shortly after moving to Alleluia in 1984, Nancy and I had a car repair need and asked friends if they could recommend a mechanic. Some Alleluia members had come to believe that Peach Orchard Tire and Auto Care (known as Rick's) was capable, trustworthy, and not inclined to take advantage of customers or overcharge for services. We decided to try Rick's shop.

Rick took care of a few minor repair jobs on our vehicles, and I got to know him. He was far more gracious and approachable than any other automotive services person I had met before, and I noticed his genuine concern for his customers—not just their cars. One day, I took my van to Rick to have some minor work done. When I returned at the end of the day to pick it up, Rick said, "I noticed your tires were getting pretty worn and could be going soon. I had a set leaning against the wall we had taken off and replaced on another vehicle. They still have a lot of life—lots better than yours—so we swapped them out. No charge. I hope that was okay."

That was the first of many "no charge" invoices from Rick over the years. I came to learn that he did these kinds of favors—including sets of free tires—for many others, too.

Over a three-decade period, I came to know Rick and his method of operating pretty well. Countless others did, too. He became the first option when cars didn't run or wouldn't work properly or when tires wore out. "Call Rick" or "take it to Rick" became bywords for scores of people, many of them from Alleluia. He became a de facto community member because of his service, kindness and care for us all. As Rick met the car needs, he revealed his heart to help people and get them up and going again, whether they could pay him then, or later, or much later.

As Alleluia members, we grew in our understanding of Christian unity through our relationships with Rick, and he also grew as he learned from us. He was a very active, evangelical Protestant and was at first perplexed by the mostly Catholic, Spirit-filled community customers who lived their born-again faith much like he did. Before community members began bringing their cars to Rick, he hadn't heard a lot of good things about Catholics. Alleluia members learned from Rick about a deep, prayerful, Bible-believing Protestant faith life full of good Samaritan actions—faith with lots of works.

As the years passed, we could see more clearly the Holy Spirit's work in the little jammed up, automotive prompt care rescue mission of a shop that ministered to cars, trucks, tires, dilemmas and disasters. That small shop had a magnetic power that drew people in. From the shop shone a beacon light of Christianity through broken-downness, worn-out tires, dirt, sweat, common sense and tough love. Outspoken faith in the Lord was just part of the interactions between customers and the staff. The name of Jesus was always welcome and proclaimed loud and clear by men and women, Black and White. "God is good, all the time. All the time, God is good," was a sentiment and a reality regularly manifest in this place.

Rick's shop was unlike any other place I've ever been. When fully staffed, there were nine or ten employees. The waiting room out front could accommodate about four seated people, plus those standing near the small counter and those waiting in line to reach the counter. It was a crowded space, with the mechanics passing in and out to return completed orders to the office and to pick up new ones.

This waiting room opened to the parking lot and the very busy street beyond. As the door was opened by each customer, coming or going, the traffic noises would come and go, too, as did the bursts of inclement weather: rain, wind, cold, or heat. It all added up to a very real slice of life. The shop often seemed like God's oasis, with all those who were thirsty drawn to drink from it, maybe like the multitudes were drawn to drink from the Living Water, Jesus.

One day I arrived at Rick's in a distressed state. When Rick asked what was wrong, I told him that I had just been approached by a Black man with a wife and family and no job, who was carrying a handicapped infant daughter in need of major medical care. I felt bad because I could not help the man and his family much. Without another word, Rick reached for his billfold, pulled out two $100 bills, and said, "Give him this." Neither of us knew it at the time, but Rick would become an ongoing benefactor for that family, giving them both automotive and financial help.

Rick's warehouse of gifts to others included an enormous number of acts of kindness. He never spoke of these, but the recipients did. One night, a group of community women went to a restaurant. Rick and his wife Betsy were eating at the same restaurant, and as they finished to leave, they spoke to the group of twelve women, most of whom knew Rick as their "car man." When the women went to the register to pay, they were told that their bill had been paid in full by the man who had stopped to speak to them. This was not a one-time occurrence; Rick did this kind of thing often, as the Spirit led. Of course, Rick was the number one go-to person for Alleluia members, young or old, who were raising funds for a cause—and they didn't have to be the first one to approach him to benefit from his generosity.

Rick was not a wealthy man; he lived on what he earned, but he drew from a deep well of generosity that he had put in with the Lord's help. There were times I wondered if he might put the bucket in one time too many and drain the well dry, or give away "the farm," but he never did. He had come to know and absolutely believed that you can't outgive God.

Rick did many other things that his customers never knew about, such as working on outreach mission trips to the islands, developing young Christian groups, facilitating and leading spiritual programs in his church, and working toward the building of his church's grand new building, all while being a loving and excellent patriarch to his often challenging family.

Rick had several family groupings: his blood family, his employee family, the family of people whose needs he took care of, and his family of friends, and each of us felt like part of his family. He epitomized the phrase "larger than life," and he became that through dying to self and dedicating his life to serving and helping others. That giving life became his life.

Then Jesus said to His disciples, "Whoever wishes to come after Me must deny himself, take up his cross, and follow Me. For whoever wishes to save his life will lose it, but whoever loses his life for My sake will find it. What profit would there be for one to gain the whole world and forfeit his life? Or what can one give in exchange for his life? For the Son of Man will come with His angels in his Father's glory, and then He will repay everyone according to his conduct."
—Matthew 16:24-27 (NASB)

Rick had a mission from God to take care of people. And his commitment to delivering repaired cars by closing time put daily pressure on him. All of this took a toll on his health, mostly affecting his heart and his back, and he sometimes had difficulty sleeping. He was a man of prayer and a strong, faithful prayer intercessor for others' needs. He seldom mentioned his own health problems, only bringing them up when he would ask to be prayed over. Several times I came to his shop and he said right away, "Come on outside, I need you to pray over me." We would walk through the crowd of customers out to the parking lot and take it to the Lord.

One Monday morning in 2018, just days before Christmas, Rick got up early and went downstairs. When Betsy awoke and went downstairs and saw him, she realized he wasn't well and tried to convince him to stay home that day. He reasoned that the business, customers and employees needed him at work.

After a hectic, demanding morning, with people packed into the storefront, Rick was feeling worse and decided to take his lunch out to his truck to eat and get a break for a few minutes. After about a half hour, his employees sensed something was wrong and went out to check on him. When they reached him, they were shaken to the core. A massive heart attack had taken him out, and efforts to revive him were to no avail. He was gone at the age of seventy—with his boots on. He had been called up. Rick was already in Glory, and no doubt receiving a hero's welcome. Surely they must have been overjoyed to be able to add Rick to their great team up there.

I was honored to be a member of Rick's family of friends, and I deeply felt (and still feel) his passing, and the loss of having him in his place at the shop. There won't be another like him. Rick was the most universally generous and caring person I've ever met, and I have known some really good ones. He walked the walk, carried the load, tried to meet every need, contended for the faith—and against Satan—and he gave the Lord all the glory.

After his passing, it became known through reports from young and old of some of the rescue efforts, as well as the gifts, love and kindness that Rick had given out; few were aware of how much he had done. Betsy had known for a long time that Rick felt responsible to the Lord first, to his family second, and then to meet any needs he was called on to meet. Even knowing that, Betsy was amazed by the number of glorious reports of Rick's generosity that found their way to her.

Those reports likely had a bearing on her decision to step up and keep the business going, both for Rick's employee family and his customer family.

The business was a blessing to too many people to close it down. (Running a business God's way works!)

By sharing life with Rick, our expectations of God, ourselves and others were all raised. He was a powerful example of living faith that inspired us all.

> *"Great is Thy faithfulness!*
> *Great is Thy faithfulness!*
> *Morning by morning new mercies I see:*
> *all I have needed Thy hand hath provided—*
> *Great is Thy faithfulness, Lord, unto me!"*
>   —*From the hymn, "Great Is Thy Faithfulness," by Thomas Chisholm*

Chapter 11

Life Comes at Us

It was a beautiful early Sunday morning in October. Nancy and I were standing outside on the sidewalk, preparing to go on a short day trip with our daughter and her family. Suddenly, about three houses away, a young girl about seven years old bolted out of her front door, screaming in anguish as she ran full speed down the sidewalk, heading across the street toward her aunt's house a block away. Immediately after, several other distraught kids rushed out the door. They were all members of the same family, a family with ten kids ranging in age from nineteen years to a few months old. The children had just discovered that their mother Theresa had died during the night in her sleep. Joe, the husband and father, was in Mississippi working with FEMA in the wake of Hurricane Katrina. When he received the news of Theresa's death he was overwhelmed—truly devastated. He could barely stand up when he arrived home.

Joe's mother, sister, brother and other family members lived just up the street, and Theresa's sister and her family also lived nearby. They all pulled together, along with many community members, and stepped up to help. Collectively, they propped Joe up, day by day, and helped him fill the roles of provider and both parents to his children.

Even though Joe is a very capable, energetic and resourceful man, there were times that it appeared he had almost lost his hope and peace. He was carrying on purely by grace and will.

Years later, Joe admitted it was hard to accept Theresa's passing and to not question God from time to time. But he had a strong faith and trust in the Lord, had been raised in faith, and his family members were all grounded in faith. They, too, were longtime members of the Alleluia Community and had witnessed the Lord deliver others from disaster. All of this kept the family together and moving forward, but they had a long hill ahead of them that at times must have looked almost too steep to climb.

Five years passed, during which time Joe gave no thought to dating anyone, and then he began to be prompted by the Holy Spirit to be open to remarrying, not only so that he would have a wife, but also so that his children might have a mother.

Joe devoted a lot of prayer to this matter over a few weeks' time, and then, by the leading of the Spirit, he made contact with a former Alleluia member, Kathleen, who at that time lived five hundred miles away. Joe had hardly known her when she was in the community, but many knew her to be an altogether good, strong, spiritual woman.

Kathleen was about Joe's age, very intelligent, personable and caring. She was quite attractive, single and had never married. She and Joe carefully began a long-distance relationship that developed over a couple of years. They both wanted to be sure about the relationship and not rush things, since so much was at stake. Over time, it became obvious to them that the Lord had marriage ahead for them. Kathleen would be getting eleven people with the marriage—Joe and ten children!

Certainly, Theresa is greatly missed by Joe, her family, and everyone who knew and loved her. It was later determined that she had died of an undetected heart defect. It was Theresa's time to be called up to be with the Lord, and nothing could change that.

The Lord had kept Kathleen for Joe and his family for all those years, and then brought them together. It lifts our spirits these days to see Joe, Kathleen and the growing kids filling one or two pews at church. The Lord not only handpicked Kathleen for her role of wife and mother, but He poured abundant grace over the entire family to be able to meet such a daunting challenge and embrace His solution. The family today looks like it was always meant to be this way.

"As the heavens are higher than the earth, so are My ways higher than your ways and My thoughts than your thoughts..."
—Isaiah 55:9 (NIV)

Be on the Alert

As we look back on unusual events, we may only be able to guess why they happened. Over the course of my adult life, I have experienced a number of road or highway incidents. After my own life-threatening wreck, and then my conversion experience, situations that happen along the road have caught my attention immediately, and when I come upon an accident or collision, I feel an urgent need to help those involved and to try to get to the driver—if there are no EMTs or police keeping everyone back. Sometimes, even when the emergency personnel are there, the Holy Spirit gets me past them so that I can lay hands on the victims and pray for them.

A few years ago, Nancy and I were heading home to Augusta from Atlanta. We were east of Atlanta on I-20 at about 3 p.m. The traffic was moderate and there was a light rain, so the road was wet. We were in our van traveling about sixty miles per hour in a left lane, one lane away from the median. Surprisingly, my eye caught sight of a car in the far right lane with front wheels that were wobbling. When I looked again, I saw the wheels wobbling more dramatically, and then the rear end of the car fishtailed. Suddenly, the car jackknifed out of control and began rotating full circle, heading toward the median.

We were directly in its path, with no apparent way to avoid being hit, and this car was definitely coming all the way. Since it was impossible to tell at what point of rotation the car was going to collide with us, and whether it would hit our front end, side or rear, we just hung on, maintained our speed and prayed.

The entire event seemed to be happening in slow motion, as accidents sometimes seem to do. We braced for the impact. The car now spun toward our rear end, sliding hard and fast. Anxiously watching in the rearview mirror, and out of the right windows, I saw the sliding car pass directly behind us.

There seemed to be no way it could avoid hitting us, but it just didn't. Instead, it crashed into a big Dodge Ram truck that had been driving just behind us in the lane to our left. The impact drove the truck into the concrete barricade, and the car careened back into the highway, grinding to a stop, with its front end demolished and steam and water pouring out of its radiator. I pulled off to the side as quickly as possible, and Nancy and I ran back to the crash site, fearing what we would find. As we ran, two young men ran past us down I-20 in the other direction. Apparently, they were the driver and passenger of the wrecked car, which was now disabled in the middle of the highway. It seemed they wanted to be gone before the emergency services arrived.

The truck had plowed into the concrete wall, but praise God, the driver was already out and walking around. Nancy and I rushed up, almost breathless, asked if he was all right, and then introduced ourselves. His said his name was Ralph, and he didn't think he was hurt. Ralph was a big man, around sixty years old; he looked like a hard-working, self-sufficient, salt-of-the-earth type. In the back of his truck were two big metal-working milling machines. Ralph told us that he had just bought them from the company he worked for, and he was taking them home to use in his own shop. Undoubtedly, the machines were extremely heavy, probably several hundred pounds each. When the truck slammed into the wall, one machine had lurched toward the cab and had stopped just inches short of the glass behind Ralph's head. There didn't seem to be any logical reason for the machine to have stopped. Had it kept going, or toppled forward, its massive weight could easily have crushed Ralph's skull.

Nancy and I had a time of thanksgiving with Ralph before the emergency teams arrived. We were able to tell him how fortunate he had been, how blessed he was, and what could have happened, especially with that massive weight right behind his head. My own experiences with car accidents gave me a voice that seemed to resonate with him and open him up to hear. Shaken, Ralph listened to both of us, but he gave no indication that he was a man of faith. We told him again that God had saved his life that day. Nancy and I had a sense that many prayers had been offered for this man and for his salvation. As we stood there on I-20 with cars going past, we got to lay hands on him (that may have been a first for him) and offer up a prayer of gratitude for the Lord's protection and for sparing Ralph's life.

Looking back, I believe Ralph and his truck were struck by a "missile" that was intended for Nancy and me. Whatever the target, it clearly appeared to be an overt work of the evil one—but the Holy Spirit intervened!

That near miss on I-20 didn't harm a hair on either of our heads, but it did give us cause for serious thought. In addition to my high-speed car wreck in 1969 (the second time in just a few years that my car was totaled on my side of the highway), Nancy and I have both been hit several times while driving. Four of those collisions happened within hours of standing in front of the abortion clinic. So our history on the roads does cause us to be careful and vigilant in our faith—but never to back off! The battle between good and evil rages all around us, and the best place to be is on the front lines, and all in!

Around the same time we experienced our adventure on I-20, our daughter Sherre had her own near miss. A large tree growing alongside a road in Augusta snapped off about four feet above the ground on a perfectly clear morning with no wind. It fell all the way across the road and crushed the car that Sherre and our granddaughter Mary Grace were riding in. The tree crashed through the roof of the car, right in front of Sherre's face, pinning her in. When the EMTs with their "jaws of life" freed Sherre from the car, she emerged roughed up and with a broken arm, but with little more damage and with far more gratitude to the Lord for His protection. The Lord even sent an unknown Black man to extend his arm through the open window, hold Sherre's hand, and keep her calm until the EMTs arrived. No one saw the man after that.

In addition to the risks when driving, especially on highways, I'm always aware of my regular exposure to high-speed, dangerous equipment. I have operated saws and cutting tools for most of my life, in my line of work, making hundreds of thousands of cuts of all kinds, in lumber of all sizes and in all conditions. My hands frequently need to be within a half inch or less of the saw blade or knives. I am extremely mindful of hands, fingers and eyes, much more now than when I was younger and took more risks. A workshop like mine is no place for lazy hands or a distracted mind.

The other day I was in the office at my shop, putting the finishing touches on this story, and then returned to the shop to do woodwork. I began machining cherry posts on the table saw and jointer. Everything was running better than textbook until I caught sight of the twenty-first post, after the cut was completed, touching the saw blade. A blur of wood rocketed by, grazing and thumping against my right side as it flew past and then creating a noisy commotion behind me. After finding that I wasn't really hurt, I began to look all around the floor for the post.

It was nowhere to be found. But then I looked higher, and there it was—four feet above the floor and protruding from the wall at an odd angle about eighteen feet from the saw. The end of the post had gone completely through the sheetrock wall, and there was a deep gash down the back side of the wood.

I can only imagine what the post would have done to my body if I had taken the impact that the wall took. I had not witnessed an industrial "missile" like this in decades, not since working in the furniture plant in my thirties. I was greatly protected by the Spirit, or an angel, that day. I am so grateful and glad that I got to experience that event. The warning may be of great help in days to come.

> *Consider it pure joy, my brothers and sisters, whenever you face trials of many kinds, because you know that the testing of your faith produces perseverance. Let perseverance finish its work so that you may be mature and complete, not lacking anything.*
> —James 1:2-4 (NIV)

When any one of us is walking in the Holy Spirit and expecting to be used in His service, we are equipped with every tool we need, but we must also be on high alert. The closer we draw to the Lord, the more we come under the scrutiny of the evil one with his fiery darts. If you live for the Lord anywhere on the "cutting edge" of life, be ever mindful of the moment and all of the conditions around you. Know that Satan is mindful of you. And for sure, keep on pushing through—in the Holy Spirit!

> *Be sober-minded; be watchful. Your adversary the devil prowls around like a roaring lion, seeking someone to devour. Resist him, firm in your faith...*
> —I Peter 5:8-9 (ESV)

Floyd

In late September of 1989, Hurricane Hugo was bearing down on the Southern Atlantic coast with an expected landfall near Charleston, South Carolina. Hugo did strike land, practically as forecast, on September 21 as a category four hurricane, with sustained winds of 135 miles per hour and gusts of over 160 miles per hour. Hugo killed twenty-seven people along the coast, left tens of thousands homeless and resulted in over $10 billion in damage overall. It was the most devastating storm on the Eastern coast since 1900. A mandatory evacuation of Charleston County, quickly put into effect, likely kept the death toll from climbing much higher.

Our city of Augusta, Georgia, is approximately 150 miles from the Atlantic Ocean and is not considered at high risk from hurricanes. Even with a storm of this magnitude, winds up to fifty miles per hour and sustained soaking rains are usually the worst to hit us. And so it was with Hugo.

Ten years after Hugo, Hurricane Floyd was approaching the Atlantic coast and was expected to make a direct hit on Savannah, Georgia, just south of Charleston. Augustans weren't boarding up windows or hunkering down or evacuating, just keeping an eye on the Weather Channel and Savannah and praying for people we didn't even know who were in the storm's path.

***

One evening in the middle of September of 1999, a call came to Bob, one of the community leaders, from a community member. The caller reported that cars "packed with people" were rolling into the Alleluia Community School parking lot. They had been directed there by a broadcast radio announcement that Alleluia's school was a shelter for Savannah-area residents who had been evacuated because of Hurricane Floyd, which was then bearing down on the city. This was the first we had heard that our school would be put to this use.

Calls quickly went out across the community to inform members of the urgent news. Since we are accustomed to helping those who are distressed and in need, community members began arriving at our school gym almost as fast as EMTs on call might. Scores of cars continued to stream into our quickly filling parking lot. As we greeted the people and welcomed them to "our house," it was clear to us that they were a weary, harried bunch. Although Savannah is less than three hours from Augusta by car, many of these beleaguered folks had been traveling for up to nine hours, due to the clogged highway traffic. It had been stop and go most of the way. They dragged their tired bodies and aching joints out of their vehicles as if being released from prison. This had been a grueling experience for them already.

The majority of the people were Black, of all ages, from very young to very old. Most had come in family groups. They had received short notice of the mandatory evacuation, with little time to prepare and limited space to bring anything other than themselves. For the most part, they had just left home as ordered, followed directions, and here they were. Some of the elderly people had never been outside of their home county. No one knew how long they might be in Augusta, but it was certain they could not return home until the evacuation order was lifted and the highways reopened. It was also unknown whether they would have homes to return to, and whether their possessions, left unattended, would be safe. Their faces reflected their worry and concern. Now they had arrived at an unknown place, uncertain about the facilities and the hospitality. Nothing about this ordeal was comfortable for anyone, but here we all were, and it was becoming obvious, at least to us, that the Holy Spirit had orchestrated their part and ours. Having some kind of shelter would surely be an improvement over being stranded on the road in their cars.

Our gym was quickly opened to them and was filled almost as quickly. Community members began assisting them as well as we could, directing them to the restrooms, telling them our names and asking theirs, helping with their small children, distributing snack food, mats and blankets, and trying to make them feel welcome and loved. We had never served as a shelter for an unexpected mass of people, but somehow it seemed natural and began to come together. Soon, the displaced folks were looking less stressed and more relaxed. As the news of this spontaneous happening spread, more helpers and supplies began to roll in from the fire department, fast food places, and other sources in our area.

Then the question of how to handle sleeping arrangements arose. It was soon decided that the Alleluia members who could provide housing and hospitality for families should volunteer to do so. Right away, we found that most families didn't want to split up and go to different homes. That made sense and was rapidly worked out. As housing options became known, host families and their guests were paired up and headed out to their sleeping destinations. Transportation was easily handled, as most of us live within a mile of our school. The evacuees remaining, primarily young singles or couples, were to stay in our gym along with some community members, who would supervise and give assistance. Everybody was being adequately cared for and their needs were being met. The whole event came together so easily, it was almost as though it had been planned that they were to arrive at just that time and be accommodated in just those homes.

Nancy and I have a house sufficient for four or five to live comfortably. We took a family of nine, who ranged from two young, six-foot-tall men to a wheelchair-bound man in his nineties. Since we had a ramp into our home, they became our group. We gave them the back half of our house, which has two bathrooms. The majority of them slept on the carpeted floor—it was what we had to offer, and they seemed relieved to be there. Our soup kitchen and night shelter experience, especially Nancy's, came in handy. Although our provisions were limited, they still far surpassed what would have been offered by a night shelter, and we had to be at peace with that.

Our guest family consisted of grandparents, a parent, an aunt and uncle, big kids, and two elderly great-grandparents. Being uprooted from their life-long home, dispatched into the unknown, and winding up in our house over the space of twelve hours was somewhat overwhelming to them, although the young people saw it as an adventure. We were very fortunate to have a matriarch figure, Hattie, leading our guest family and keeping everything in check.

The next morning we learned that most of our immediate neighbors in Faith Village had also taken families into their homes. Some had larger groups than ours. Our guests were able to reconnect with friends and fellow evacuees in the large common backyard. This greatly eased the stress on everyone, making them all feel more at home.

Back at the school gym, people were waking up and emerging outside, walking around the school grounds in the daylight, and adjusting to where they found themselves. Our impromptu rescue shelter was rising to its next big challenge—breakfast. The school kitchen and cafeteria were already a beehive of activity, with volunteers coming in to cook and serve breakfast and others bringing prepared food. Nearby businesses were sending food and drinks, too. Best of all, everyone seemed in good spirits, with surprisingly positive attitudes!

The host families were invited to bring their guests back to the school cafeteria for breakfast. This relieved a lot of potential stress. Most of the men and many of the women in the community work regular jobs and didn't feel they could leave their guests at home during the day. Most of the guests spent the day back at our school campus with those community volunteers who could spare the time to be with them. Some women took the day off to make that work. Pretty soon, even activities for the young people and little kids were being put into place. One community member, Celia, a doctor and a longtime missionary in Africa, was a godsend in all of this. It was a natural fit for her. The guests loved her. A strong sense of faith was surfacing among our guests, too, and that made everything go even better!

As it turned out, Savannah did not suffer a direct hit or any major damage. Floyd was a significant hurricane but turned northward and pummeled the Carolinas with high winds, heavy rains and damage. It would be a couple of days before the Savannah area was declared safe and reopened for the evacuated residents. With each passing day, our emergency rescue program worked better, and relationships were developing between the hosts and guests. Several families had much in common with their guests. Most of the meals became large group events at our school cafeteria.

On the day our family of nine was to leave, Nancy prepared a big going-away breakfast for them in our dining room. Most of them were surprised and a little overwhelmed—it was a "first" of sorts for most. Just as we were about to eat, we learned that it was the fiftieth birthday of Hattie, the matriarch. We sang "Happy Birthday" and "May the Good Lord Bless You." She wiped away tears of gratitude. We exchanged goodbyes and hugs as great-grandpa was rolled down the ramp. Everyone piled back into their vehicles and headed for the school to gather for the big departure.

We all came together in the school parking lot with our shared gratitude to the Lord for what He had planned and what He had empowered us to do. And then it began to dawn on us: Our material intervention was nearly completed and we would soon be back to ordinary life. But our guests were returning to the unknown, many facing setbacks and losses, and they couldn't afford many setbacks. Some of them were pretty worried. Their time with us had been a glimpse of a different life, not only for most of them, but for us as well.

We laid hands on them and prayed over them and for their vehicles, and then watched their long caravan head south toward Savannah. There was more than a touch of sadness, seeing them leave. We had all grown in dying to self and trusting in the Lord through their unexpected stay. We hoped that they had received as much as we had.

> *Above all, love each other deeply, because love covers over a multitude of sins. Offer hospitality to one another without grumbling. Each of you should use whatever gift you have received to serve others, as faithful stewards of God's grace in its various forms. If anyone speaks, they should do so as one who speaks the very words of God. If anyone serves, they should do so with the strength God provides, so that in all things God may be praised through Jesus Christ.*
>
> *To Him be the glory and the power for ever and ever. Amen.*
> — *1 Peter 4:8-11 (NIV)*

Storm Clouds Gathering

The experience of Hurricane Floyd, along with our outreach to the people, remains a major milestone for our community and has been revisited in our memories for nearly two decades. Clearly, all of us, by the Lord's grace, dodged a bullet. The outcome for both the evacuees and us could have been far less favorable. What if Hurricane Floyd had hit Savannah directly and our guests' stay had not been a couple of days, but rather a couple of weeks or months—or even longer? What if we had been called to send crews and help rebuild their storm-ravaged homes? How would we have done in those circumstances?

Many in the community believe our Floyd experience was a prelude to the "big one," a larger calamity yet to come. Will the "big one" be related to a natural disaster, such as a hurricane, tornado, flood, storm surge, tsunami or forest fire (or perhaps multiple disasters), requiring shelter, housing, food and provisions? Or could it be a spiritual crisis—people in need of salvation, the Holy Spirit and renewed hope? Will we need to be light bearers to people desperate to learn how to endure and live in a depraved and hostile culture that has been given over to darkness and evil? That would likely be a much longer and more challenging rescue effort. Our country and our culture are probably less prepared for that disaster than we have ever been. Will we be prepared for the Lord to send us people like those, with their needs?

We don't know the answer, or what's coming, but we do know we'll be called to step into the challenges when they come. Just like with Floyd, we'll be called to be rescuers. That's what we said yes to a long time ago, and He accepted our yes.

And this is the judgment: The light has come into the world, and people loved the darkness rather than the light because their works were evil. For everyone who does wicked things hates the light and does not come to the light, lest his works should be exposed.

—John 3:19-20 (ESV)

For He commanded and raised the stormy wind, which lifted up the waves of the sea.

They mounted up to heaven; they went down to the depths; their courage melted away in their evil plight; they reeled and staggered like drunken men and were at their wits' end.

Then they cried to the Lord in their trouble, and He delivered them from their distress.

He made the storm be still, and the waves of the sea were hushed. Then they were glad that the waters were quiet, and He brought them to their desired haven.

—*Psalm 107:25-32 (ESV)*

Radiance

Teresa was a vibrant wife and mother of four in her mid-forties; her children were teenaged or older. She and her husband Bill poured themselves into their faith, their family and serving their church. Teresa was also an artist, with an eye for capturing the beauty that surrounds us. She had written, illustrated and self-published a children's book. She was both creative and industrious.

One day, Teresa was diagnosed with cancer. She had long been in active pursuit of God's will for her life, so the discovery of cancer did not change her trust in the Lord in any way. She and Bill talked and prayed about their course of action for the disease, asking the Lord for His will. After extended prayer, Teresa felt she was to simply trust the Lord with the solution to the problem. She wanted His will, either to be healed through faith in Him and stay among us, or to go and be with Him in Heaven. She had reconciled herself to either outcome, and she didn't feel they were to intervene for her medically with radiation or chemotherapy treatments. Bill supported her in her faith walk, so a pray-and-wait approach was decided upon as their course of action.

Teresa dealt with the cancer by continuing her normal routine and remaining active and involved, and with lots of prayer, the cancer stayed in check with no treatments at all. Then her body began to weaken and deteriorate. As her time drew nearer, her spirit and resolve got stronger. One day, Nancy and I went by Bill and Teresa's home for a brief visit and to pray with them. When we arrived, Bill took us up to the bedroom where Teresa was sitting up in bed, radiating God's peace like I had never seen. Throughout our entire visit, she was just glowing. Then, as we were getting ready to leave, she asked if I would build her casket. Of course, I was honored by the request (and did agree), but I was shocked to be asked about her own casket by anyone looking that radiant.

The last time I saw Teresa was early one morning about two weeks later. We took our regular Wednesday morning prayer group, mostly high schoolers, more than thirty all together, and surrounded Bill and Teresa's house with love, crosses and songs. Bill helped Teresa to come outside and sit in a chair on the porch. Her radiance had increased. I have never seen anyone shining so brightly in the glow of the Lord. One of our men asked for a bowl of water and washed Teresa's feet as we all surrounded and prayed for her. Her countenance was glorious; she showed no fear and no doubt. We were all blessed just to experience this reverent time with a sister who was totally peaceful, fully given over to God's will.

Teresa's life here on earth ended a few days later as she went to be with Jesus and to the special place He had prepared for her. But the memory of her radiance and trust lives on.

Do not be anxious about anything, but in every situation, by prayer and petition, with thanksgiving, present your requests to God. And the peace of God, which transcends all understanding, will guard your hearts and your minds in Christ Jesus.

—Philippians 4:6-7 (NIV)

The C Words

Our family has been blessed over the years with good health, and we've been thankful for it. We have many close friends who have endured a whole host of serious health issues, and some have had chronic illnesses for years. We never braced for the day we would hear terrible news or attempted to talk through the "What if..." question. It's likely that we intentionally avoided that. Maybe most people do.

One night in 2006, Nancy was hit with a severe abdominal pain. She made an appointment with a gynecologist for a checkup, and he scheduled a scan that revealed a small tumor. It seemed to be about the size of a lemon. An operation was immediately scheduled for the following Monday, and to our surprise, an oncologist was to perform the surgery. Suddenly Nancy's surgery changed from necessary to potentially very serious. This was a new experience for us. I wondered if the faith we'd had when faced with the illnesses of others would carry us through this.

When we arrived at the hospital, Nancy's blood was taken and some tests were run. Her blood cell count was too low for surgery. She was given three units of blood and the surgery was scheduled for the next day, November 1. The Feast of All Saints!

The loss of blood seemed to be a major concern to the doctors, so the surgery was arranged to take place as soon as possible. During the surgery, the oncologist removed the tumor and all reproductive organs. The tumor was not lemon sized, as expected, but softball sized, and a half liter of blood was found in Nancy's abdominal cavity. Dr. Ghamande, the oncologist, diagnosed the tumor to be ovarian cancer, stage III, and thought Nancy had a twenty-five percent chance of living for five more years. He proclaimed the surgery successful and prescribed a course of chemotherapy to start soon.

Probably because I looked so downhearted, the assisting surgeon spoke to me right after the surgery, saying, "Don't worry, you'll have plenty of time together yet." I don't know that the doctor understood spiritual gifts, but I heard and received the message as a word of knowledge (a prophecy sent by the Holy Spirit), and my spirit was lifted.

Those C words—cancer and chemo—have to be two of the most feared words anywhere. They can dominate your mind and thoughts until you are finally able to put them into perspective. We soon learned that even though ovarian cancer is one of the most deadly types of cancer, it is not a death sentence. We would learn to live with cancer. This was not just Nancy's cancer to deal with, but our cancer. It was what we had on our plate as a couple, and there would be grace to go through it and deal with it together. I became Nancy's companion caregiver in the hospital, the treatment rooms, and in our support group of cancer patients and caregivers.

The chemo treatments started, and they totally surprised both of us. The heavy, gloom-and-doom spirit of death that we had expected just wasn't there. Instead, the nurses who administered the chemo were caring and showed joy, and most of the other patients we encountered expressed real hope and faith.

A treatment could take up to five hours, but each time, our spirits were bolstered. The upbeat, hopeful spirit was contagious. These women were learning to "fight like a girl" (they even had this printed on shirts) and "live with cancer" one treatment at a time. Nancy was saturated with prayers from many people. She had ample grace for the chemo.

The treatments continued every three weeks for seven months. Nancy was never disabled or really ill, mostly just uncomfortable and achy, and food didn't taste good to her. She basically lived in her recliner for two or three days and nights immediately after her treatments, and then she was back up and in the game. She lost all of her hair, but when it came back, it was very soft and curly.

During the years since her diagnosis and treatment, Nancy has developed many strong friendships with other patients going through the same ordeal. Being a part of a cancer support group has given all of them strength to press on through the unexpected challenges of such a serious illness.

About four years after her chemo treatments were completed, a small spot appeared on Nancy's scan. It was considered too small to need treatment. Dr.

Ghamande just watched it very closely with follow-up scans. By the beginning of 2013, it had grown considerably, and he wanted to remove it.

During the surgery, Dr. Ghamande found the cancer had spread to a three-inch-long lymph node attached to Nancy's aorta and bowel, making the surgery a higher risk. The lymph node needed to be removed. By his own admission, the operation was an extremely complex undertaking and one that few surgeons would have attempted. Through great grace, with skill and courage, he was able to remove the lymph node. After this surgery, the chemo treatments were given for a full year, as Dr. Ghamande wanted to be sure that none of the cancer would return. (He has always cared for Nancy the way he would have cared for his own wife. He couldn't possibly have been a more concerned and conscientious doctor.)

When she finished all of the treatments, Nancy was declared in remission and got to ring the "all-clear" bell, the bell in the treatment center that patients would ring at the end of successful treatment. What a nice celebration we had, with Dr. Ghamande and all the chemo nurses gathered around, along with several patients who were working their way toward their own opportunity to ring the bell. We all rejoiced and thanked the Lord.

Nancy has had clear scans every year since, and we are deeply thankful to the Lord for every one.

Trust in the Lord with all your heart and lean not on your own understanding; in all your ways submit to Him, and He will make your paths straight. This will bring health to your body and nourishment to your bones.

—Proverbs 3:5-6,8 (NIV)

Chapter 12

Looking Beyond, the Day May Come

A word to the young and to the not yet older: Please stay with this story, as it is meant for everyone, of any age. You may expect to never age, but if you live long enough, you will. Your parents may already have, and it's very likely your grandparents have. Whether we like it or not, aging goes with the journey.

***

Wouldn't it be great if, when we were young, we had known what we know now, and had the wisdom we've gained through years and life experience. And wouldn't it be wonderful if today, with this wisdom, we still had the energy and strength of youth to carry out our work tirelessly.

But such is not the case for most people; instead, we have seasons of life. As Christians, the Lord gives us grace to meet those different seasons, to accept the changes they bring, to be at peace in every season—and by His grace, to do well in each one.

When I started my first woodworking business as a teenager, some people undoubtedly wondered if I was old enough to handle their work successfully. But my business venture back then turned out very well and set my course. Now, sixty years later, when I talk with a client about a large job, I sometimes sense that they have confidence I can handle the work, but might be wondering if I will live long enough to finish it. I am still doing the same work I have done for many years, including some large recent projects, and by grace I have finished each job well, although not without more effort. Lessened strength and agility and less keen eyesight make excellence more challenging to attain.

While I was too busy to pay much attention, six decades have come and gone, first very slowly, but in more recent years, much faster. If you have lived many decades, you know this. It was never my expectation to get old—probably somewhat older, but not old. Many of us would likely agree with that. We expected to stay young through the years while other people aged. But time moves forward for everyone, like the hands of a clock. Certainly, when I was a young firebrand, there was no question of energy; it was just that the work days were often not long enough to accomplish the goals. The body would rush into whatever the mind proposed. Ambition was the sparkplug, and drive, determination and necessity carried the day.

There were so many projects to start and complete, and the more challenging, the better. I was driven. From the early years, I knew I had a special gift for woodworking and design, and I felt compelled to use it. Some of the seasons of my life, I felt that the talent owned me instead of the other way around, much like people who "belong to the land." For a long time, I have loved work to the degree that when I have been under pressing time constraints to complete a job, I have not always known when to call it a day. I remember two different times, once when I was working in homebuilding and once when I'd begun building church furnishings, when my "day" ran thirty-four hours long, and the work was still not finished—we were back at it, and under pressure, the very next morning. I've had many fourteen-hour work days and eighty-hour work weeks, while giving it little thought. But there comes a time when this catches up with us. The many years of high stress and daily grinding exacts its toll, whether we admit it or not. Long after the fact, I realized I had worked far more at my business than I could afford to work, and rather than my customers paying for that "more," my family had, and I had little to show for it.

Since we know neither the day nor the hour, perhaps as maturing adults, God would have us slow down, get our affairs and relationships in order, live in the present moment, reflect on the reality of death and leaving this earth, and be prepared to gracefully exit this life into eternal Glory.

Looking beyond today, I believe the day may come, for me, when:

- The big heavy wood is too much to handle.
- The high-speed equipment is too dangerous to operate.
- The eyes betray the hands in the effort for precision.
- Math and fraction calculations are no longer automatic.

- Enthusiasm for the next project finally isn't there.
- The smell of sprayed lacquer has long drifted away.
- No woodwork is in process and the shop stands still.
- Dust settles over everything and a lifetime of work is only a memory.
- The building stays locked and the lights turned off.

When these things happen, my professional work will have run its course.

At the time of this writing, none of these things have happened yet. I'm not ready to be separated from my lifetime friends, the tools and equipment, just yet. I sense there may yet be a crucifix or two to sculpt, new crosses still to build, some art pieces to fashion from glorious woods, or even a large contract or two that involve more designing and consulting. And who knows, maybe another book, too. But I know the day may come—the day when my work life will cease.

There may come a time for any of us, if we live long enough, when our health, gift or skill has waned and we have to lay it down or turn it loose. We each have our own challenges to face. It can happen in a variety of ways: A professional athlete may no longer be able to play at his level. A surgeon may begin to experience more stress while operating. An airline pilot might start to feel more concern about turbulence. A gifted singer might strain to retain her voice and stage presence. An experienced marathoner might start to struggle with the pace and the distance. A disciplined gymnast may begin to grope for strength and balance. A successful coach might start to feel troubled about recent losing seasons. A 10K runner may feel quite happy to stand and watch the race. Any skill that has held a special place in our hearts might, over time or with the changes brought on by aging, finally run its course.

There may come a day for any of us when we are no longer at the top of our fields, can no longer perform up to our own standards, don't think and react as quickly and clearly as before, or can't effectively stay with the program. We might lose sight of the real priorities and dwell on distractions, be unable to contribute as we always have, or be unable to hold our own. For the very first time, we might not make the cut. We might be unable to answer the bell that has always called us to action.

Certainly there is a sadness that comes with the fading of a long and passionate drive within us—we might have had a long, successful run that seemed almost to be life itself. Probably there was a gift, talent, skill, profession, career, vocation or position that was our identity of choice. This can be true for any one of us. Losing it or giving it up could even seem akin to the death of a spouse, a family member or a very close friend.

But the end of this treasured anointing is not the end of life—not mine, nor yours, and not the next person's. Each of our lives is much more than any work we have done. As Christians, we each belong to Him and have a *lifetime call* and assignment to build His Kingdom here on earth, using all the talents, gifts and abilities that are present to us at any moment, along with His Holy Spirit's help and grace. Our abilities will change and develop with time, discernment, insight, wisdom, knowledge, patience, trust and faith, and may even increase as we keep pressing on for the prize. And He will also modify the course and the hills ahead of us. Regardless of all else, our hearts and souls must be "all in," all our days. That's what He has always wanted, and it is all He has expected from each one of us.

> *Being confident of this, that He who began a good work in you will carry it on to completion until the day of Christ Jesus.*
> —*Philippians 1:6 (NIV)*

> *Not that I have already obtained all this, or have already arrived at my goal, but I press on to take hold of that for which Christ Jesus took hold of me. Brothers and sisters, I do not consider myself yet to have taken hold of it. But one thing I do: Forgetting what is behind and straining toward what is ahead, I press on toward the goal to win the prize for which God has called me heavenward in Christ Jesus.*
> —*Philippians 3:12-14 (NIV)*

> *"Not by might nor by power, but by My Spirit," says the Lord Almighty.*
> —*Zechariah 4:6 (NIV)*

> *Do you not know? Have you not heard? The Lord is the everlasting God, the Creator of the ends of the earth. He will not grow tired or weary, and His understanding no one can fathom. He gives strength to the weary and*

increases the power of the weak. Even youths grow tired and weary, and young men stumble and fall; but those who hope in the Lord will renew their strength. They will soar on wings like eagles; they will run and not grow weary, they will walk and not be faint.

—*Isaiah 40:28-31 (NIV)*

Dreaming of Being Called Up

I discovered the wonderful world of baseball at eleven years of age. It was 1947, the year that Jackie Robinson broke the color barrier, enabling great Black players for the first time to play in the major leagues. Larry Doby, Satchel Paige, Roy Campanella, Don Newcombe and others would soon follow him. Ted Williams, Joe DiMaggio, Bob Feller and Lou Boudreau became my instant heroes, and Mel Allen was the voice of ultimate knowledge. By means of our great companion, the radio, live broadcasts from major league games played in faraway cities were brought into our home. Wow! Baseball was like a world unto itself, filled with excitement and mystique—and a world that was totally foreign to me, because baseball wasn't part of our family life. Equally foreign to my family was the idea of chasing your dreams to such lofty heights or distant places as the world of major league baseball.

Soon I took up learning to play baseball. Since I lived next door to one of the world's great natural athletes, who was two years older than I was and saw everything as a competition, I began partly out of interest and partly not to be left in the dust. Mastering the skills of the sport, throwing, catching and hitting, became a consuming interest, the very first love of my young life. At every opportunity, a few of the guys would be in the street or yard throwing and catching baseballs, sometimes for hours at a time, until dark caught us. I just couldn't get enough. Many nights I would sleep with my glove tucked under my pillow with a ball inside—maybe it would help me play better!

When I was thirteen or fourteen years old, my friends and I formed our own team. We walked or rode our bikes to the local baseball field. There were no teams organized for kids younger than high school age—at least, not in the South. We took full responsibility for the logistics involved, including the equipment, the schedule and getting to games. Unlike today, no parents or family members came to watch us play, but we played good, exciting baseball. After playing in the streets while dodging the curbs and cars, getting to play on a real field with base bags, white foul lines and a backstop was an awesome experience. For a couple of hours, it was easy to imagine that this was our very own field.

It was also during this time that we became aware of professional baseball. My family lived a half hour north of Atlanta, in Marietta, and the Atlanta Crackers were "our team." Atlanta was not yet a major league city, and the Crackers played AA ball in the Southern League. A quaint old stadium named Ponce de Leon Park hosted their games. Jam packed, the stadium held twelve thousand people and reeked of cigar smoke, which it seemed you could smell before you were close enough to even see the light towers.

The Crackers were a unique team. They were a very successful franchise, independently owned, one of the last teams with no major league affiliation. This was both good and bad. Good because the Crackers controlled their players' contracts, but bad financially because they were competing with the big money of the major leagues. That was beyond my understanding. I just loved baseball and thought it was played for the love of the game, not for money.

Jack, one of my friends, had lived in Philadelphia and had attended major league games. When his family moved to Marietta they adopted the Crackers, the only professional team around. Occasionally, Jack's parents took some of us to see the Cracker games. To us, that was as good as it got. We loved to sit along the third base line, close to those professional players, and dream of someday playing professional ball ourselves. Maybe we would make it all the way to the big leagues and be featured on the radio, or maybe even on the new phenomenon, television. Wow, what a dream!

Eventually, the Crackers had to align themselves with the major league to survive and became a farm team. That changed everything. Suddenly "our" best players became hopeful or future major leaguers. One day they would just be called up—no apologies to the Cracker fans. The big team needed them. It was what minor league baseball was all about, getting prepared to be called up to the major league. I grieved a lot over the loss of one of "our" players, especially if he was one of my favorites. I followed the former Crackers in major league box scores and on the radio, but I really wished they were still Crackers. I had become attached to them, and I wasn't ready to give them up.

I remember a tall young guy named Eddie Mathews playing for "us" one year. He would misplay a pop-up by twenty feet (one we could have easily caught), but he hit home runs over the tree in center field, 450 feet away. Nobody else in the league could do that. He was only nineteen years old, barely five years older than we were. We knew they would teach him to catch pop-ups and he wouldn't be back next year. We knew we had better study his hitting because he was headed for the majors and would pack the stadiums.

Later that year we heard of another player who was burning it up in Class A. He was from Mobile, where he wasn't allowed to drink from the water fountains or use the "White" restrooms, but they said he could hammer a baseball. We never got to see him play as a Cracker because he bypassed class AA and went straight to the majors. He would become the legendary Hank Aaron. There were others who were called up, not as gifted or well known, but each living out his dream of making it to the big leagues. When called, they left behind some of their best friends, who played on in the minors, chasing their own dreams of becoming big leaguers.

I still love baseball and draw from those experiences. Through the years, I've revisited my high school baseball park, with its thick concrete walls and not a blade of grass, even in the outfield. I go to my old position in center field and remember how it felt—it was like playing on top of a huge brown pool table, hard as a rock and fast as lightning! When I listen hard, I can still hear the ball cracking off the bat, sounding like a rifle shot—and the adrenaline flows, and my whole body tightens!

Dreams have a way of being replaced by reality. Not one of our group of aspiring young athletes played beyond high school, but it wasn't for lack of love of the game. Our shortage of natural ability and skill kept us all at home, and other pursuits would later claim us.

I've come to realize that life is a lot like professional baseball. We try to play our best here in the minors, playing as if this is really "it," while knowing all the while that we're in the big farm system and our higher goal is to make the Real Majors. It's important to understand this in order to play here with success and not get overwhelmed or disillusioned. But we still get jolted when one of our family members or friends gets "called up." We try to be happy for them, but we sure miss them. Sometimes they are some of our very best players. And sometimes they are surprisingly young.

Surely that's the way it's supposed to work, because there are no mistakes in the Real Major League. Some of this we won't understand until we get there ourselves. But even now, it's so gratifying to know that the "big team" needed our loved ones. Isn't that about the best it can get—knowing that the "big team" needs us?

My major league career in this world has involved building crosses and sanctuary furnishings to glorify Him, the Great Master who does the "calling up." My call to this work has all the peace and fulfillment that only reality and God's plan can bring. I've even been like an occasional equipment manager, having the privilege to build caskets for many who have been promoted to the Big League. Each time, I'm helping to check someone out of the old minor league locker and into the luxurious major league clubhouse, with all the best of everything.

Even though it is a great opportunity for a friend to be called up, there's usually a sadness. That's part of being human and still playing here. Perhaps the sorrow comes from the separation, or from momentarily losing sight of what the farm system is all about.

In all my years of following baseball, though, I've never heard of a major leaguer wishing he could be sent back down, and I'm certain that with life, that is even more true. Surely once we've experienced the highest and best, nothing less will ever do.

Congratulations to our friends and loved ones who have been called up. We are happy for you and so very proud of you. Yes, we really miss you. But enjoy it. We too are striving to play well enough to get called up and be in the same lineup again with you. We believe that our best games together are ahead of us. Forever! In the Real Major League!

> *For the Lord Himself, with a cry of command, with the archangel's call and with the sound of God's trumpet, will descend from heaven, and the dead in Christ will rise first. Then we who are alive, who are left, will be caught up in the clouds together with them to meet the Lord in the air; and so we will be with the Lord forever. Therefore encourage one another with these words.*
>
> —*Thessalonians 4:16-18 (NRSV)*

Walking by Faith

We each have a personal rendezvous awaiting us with the One who went to the cross and paid the price so that we might live forever in Glory. We don't know when, but that meeting will happen. Some of us have great expectations of it that call us on; for others, it might loom ahead as downright terrifying. Some doubt or deny that meeting ahead, and they are the ones to be most pitied.

> *Behold, He is coming with the clouds, and every eye will see Him, even those who pierced Him, and all tribes of the earth will wail on account of Him. Even so. Amen.*
>
> *—Revelation 1:7 (ESV)*

At forty years of age, I received the greatest gift I had ever been given in my entire life—the gift of faith, living faith. From the very first day of its activation, this mysterious, wonderful gift began a domino effect of awakening and transformation that has flowed through my whole family, bringing each member through his or her own transformation. The gift of faith brought about the same kind of personal transformation in the finest group of people I could have hoped to call friends.

Each person ever created has been given a gift of faith, a measure of faith, that mysteriously connects us with the Creator God. Because we are made in His likeness and image, we have Him in our DNA. He has known each of us since the moment of our conception, and He also wants us to know Him, personally, with a closeness beyond that found in the closest human relationship that we have. That might sound like a stretch, but that's His plan. Jesus extends to each person an invitation to, "Come and see," or "Come, follow Me," and this invitation is the key to life itself. Knowing Him comes about only by faith, and it all starts by first believing that He Is. Here and now, He is alive and present. It helps us tremendously to recognize and admit our need for Him. Faith is defined in Hebrews:

Now faith is the assurance of things hoped for, the conviction of things not seen.

—Hebrews 11:1 (NASB)

And without faith it is impossible to please Him, for he who comes to God must believe that He is and that He is a rewarder of those who seek Him.

—Hebrews 11:6 NASB (1995)

"He jealously desires the Spirit whom He has made to dwell in us..."
Come close to God and He will come close to you.

—James 4:5, 8 (NASB)

How we invest and use that gift of faith is the question. Jesus tells us that *faith moves mountains*, but He also tells us that He could do *few miracles in His hometown because of the people's lack of faith*. Man's faith is the activator that moves God's hand. Do we live as though we fully believe that?

As I said earlier, I tried for two decades to live in my own kingdom, with me in control. I had been in such pursuit of the "good life" that I had shut out the God life from which all good comes. Nancy carried the torch of church faith for our family through the long period of our kids' formative years, with no help from me. The golf course and football field were my churches. My self-centered mindset cost my family and me more than I know, and if left unchecked, it likely would have wrought destruction in our family for generations to come. What a terrible mistake and burden to put on any family.

Conversely, the greatest gift any of us can give our spouse and family is living faith, bringing the Father, the Son and the Holy Spirit into our home and our entire life. I have known of countless numbers of women who pray for their unbelieving husbands to open up to faith for the sake of the marriage and the family; I've also known strong, solid men who carry their deepest pain because their wives have chosen not to join them in the fullness of faith. There is nothing more bonding and life-giving than deep, shared faith. Then we can walk life out, one step at a time, on the promises of God, all the way to Glory!

To walk by faith is quite a serious undertaking. Since we can't have it both ways, we must decide which is most important to us: the glamour and glitter, comforts, opportunities, temptations and penalties of this passing world, or the genuine riches, goodness and blessing, now and forever, promised by the unseen, triune God. If we won't yield our self-will to God's will, we can't expect to be able to turn away from the allure and pleasures of the world and contend with the accusations and assaults of Satan, which seek to deceive and destroy us. We won't have the fortitude to avoid and withstand the near occasions of sin.

The famous old World War I song, "How Ya Gonna Keep 'Em Down on the Farm (After They've Seen Paree?)" raises what may sound like an impossible issue. But in fact, it is not at all. The answer is to show them something better, *the pearl of great price.* Show them God's plan being lived out by those who made a clear choice; show them what it looks like to *taste and see the goodness of the Lord,* and to *live in the joy of the Lord.* There are plenty of "Parees" and Vegases and Hollywoods and New Yorks, and there is no doubt that the worldly lifestyles enjoyed by some would be exciting and appealing to others for a while, but the deception, disillusionment and destruction for those who choose them is a mighty high price to pay.

Do not love the world nor the things in the world. If anyone loves the world, the love of the Father is not in him. For all that is in the world, the lust of the flesh and the lust of the eyes and the boastful pride of life, is not from the Father, but is from the world. The world is passing away and also its lusts; but the one who does the will of God continues to live forever.
—1 John 2:15-17 (NASB)

The goodness of the Lord is beyond description, but experiencing it does not result from a partway, part-of-the-time decision. We each need major transformation. That transformation is waiting for anyone who will choose it and follow through. Good morals and good intentions alone fall far short of what it really means to walk with Jesus, to walk in His footsteps.

And do not be conformed to this world, but be transformed by the renewing of your mind, so that you may prove what the will of God is, that which is good and acceptable and perfect.

—*Romans 12:2 (NASB)*

We learn that deep, abiding faith doesn't just "happen" for anyone. The development of faith must be very intentional and requires commitment, diligence, work and discipline. To realize that *I must decrease and He must increase* and to make Him Lord of my life are "where it's at." This critical work is the work most likely to get overlooked, cut short or neglected. Satan pushes those bad practices of "omission" far more than we realize. Luring us to busy ourselves with "too much" must be one of his favorite tools. Growth in faith is not always about adding more to our days or our lives—sometimes it's about taking things out.

Impact Christians often invest in their spiritual lives like Olympians would invest in their training and performance, and they make time and invest energy to build their faith lives alongside their regular full-time work. They see it as that essential! Every person will make time for what they consider most important.

There are countless ways to develop faith, but here are some examples. Certainly, regular, active church participation is important, as is a consistent, solid prayer life, with time spent personally with the Lord, either during a special time set aside or through ongoing prayer throughout the day (*praying without ceasing*). Prayer should involve intercessory prayer (time spent praying for others and their needs) and reading and searching Scripture for the deeper meanings and for revelation and wisdom for the day or the need. Other spiritual reading strengthens and enhances our faith by teaching us about the faith lives of saints or martyrs, those both recognized and lesser known, throughout the ages. Participating in prayer and praise gatherings (what a foreign word *praise* was in the old life) and spending time with others of faith to listen, learn and share, as in an accountability group, develops our faith to be more balanced, practical, usable and unshakeable. Being on duty for the Lord, battle ready, and contending against the world, the flesh and the devil for the faith, our family, our culture and our country are absolutely essential. The use of our spiritual gifts through spontaneous evangelistic efforts, time spent counseling others, praying over people at various times and places, acting on prophetic words or words of knowledge, and all types of works of kindness and service add immeasurably to our store of unwavering faith and trust. The healings and changed lives along the way are a great encouragement to go farther, to press on, to use our spiritual gifts. Humility and gratitude—such important characteristics—develop in our transformed selves. Last, but not least, is fasting, denying ourselves of food or other comforts or pleasures as the Spirit leads us individually. Fasting is a choice that gives us back more than we give up.

This may sound like a lot to undertake, and it certainly is. *Our God is a consuming fire.* But this full faith life develops over time, and the Lord has made sure that *anyone* can live it. Each person's movement toward good or evil starts with a step in that direction, and then the next step and the next. Even the saints started with a first step, as did those who are lost forever.

I look back on the beginning of Nancy's and my transformed life, and to simply say grace before every meal at home with the family was such a change after nineteen years of living as a family with no thought of prayers. Neither of our families of origin had prayed before meals, either. This new addition to our daily life shocked our kids. They sensed they were in for a very different new ride. When we started praying before meals at restaurants, regardless of who was with us, that seemed a big step up and shocked others. Now it would be totally unacceptable for us to omit prayers because of the setting or the group.

I wouldn't think of starting a business meeting or a new project without calling on the Holy Spirit for help. I need His help! He is the best player on the team or worker on the site, the most talented, most experienced, most perceptive, has the coolest head, and is the best team player ever. I need Him working with me every day, and He is always available. Just knowing that as a young man would have changed my life.

To say the Lord's Prayer (Our Father) each day at home as a couple or with the family and at each spiritual gathering may seem basic, but it grounds us and helps us to keep on course more than we know, especially if we really reflect on the words. Faith never stands still, and we are always moving toward God or sliding away. We must be intentional with our faith and with our heart, or desire, for faith, in order for faith to become the top priority in our lives. The disciple

John warns us over and over, *"Guard yourselves against idols."* There were plenty of false gods in his day, and there might be even more in our day. *Anything* placed above the Lord in our life is an idol. To live free of idols requires a lot of soul searching and work so that we can correct disordered priorities. Regardless of our varied individual priorities, faith and family should top the list—in that order.

> *Anyone who loves their father or mother more than Me is not worthy of Me;*
> *anyone who loves their son or daughter more than Me is not worthy of Me.*
> —*Matthew 10:37 (NIV)*

People who are best at walking by faith are "all-in" for the Lord—one hundred percent. That level of commitment destroys any ambivalence within us that Satan might try to use. As in football, the best defense is a good offense, and our best efforts and self-discipline 24/7 take the battle to Satan. To keep Satan off our field and out of the game is the best plan; to exercise spiritual warfare daily against Satan and his demons is powerful and helps to keep evil at bay. Eviction of demonic spirits that are already in can be much more challenging than keeping them out in the first place. If you have done both, you know that is true.

There is nothing passive about walking by faith. It is the route of courage. Jesus' twelve disciples took on His disciplines. Over time, this cost them everything on earth but earned them far greater rewards that would last forever. They were spirit-driven, fearless men of faith, giving it all for the Lord and for their call. They had walked for three years alongside Jesus. Their "yes" response to His invitation to, "Come, follow Me," required them to leave their old lives behind, but this put them on the journey to Glory. They were "called." Eleven of the twelve were able to live out that call, and of those who did, all except John would be martyred. He had been placed in a cauldron of boiling oil, but it proved harmless to him, so he was exiled to Patmos. Those eleven saw the Kingdom of God break forth in a multitude of ways daily, wherever they were. They saw the Kingdom on earth interacting with the Kingdom in Heaven. They saw Satan's lies and deceptions unmasked as they saw God's promises fulfilled. They shared those firsthand reports with countless others who came to believe and then lived their own Holy Spirit experiences. What does the world have to compare with that? Nothing! Jesus is still inviting us to come and see, and saying to us, "Come, follow Me."

I believe that walking by faith is the most important subject in this book, since without faith we totally miss the fullness of life itself. This certainly has been the most challenging section of the book for me to write. So I am taking a different approach, hopefully by the leading of the Holy Spirit. I will write only part of the section, and we will trust Him to reveal and make known what "walking by faith" means through a collection of passages from His Word, included at the end of the book as an epilogue to be read through. We ask the Spirit to make personal connections as only He can. The passages are from many books in the Bible, but it seemed that the Spirit wanted them placed in the particular order in which they have been arranged.

This focus on Scripture might seem ironic, since over the course of my first forty years of life, I had no interest in reading the Bible. And so I didn't open it, not even in my darkest and most desperate times, when I had a crucial need for answers and direction. Like many people, I thought the Bible was outdated, not relevant to today, had nothing to tell me, and was a whole lot of pages and words with no life. I was dealing with today's "real problems" that needed "real solutions."

When I had my great awakening to the Lord and to truth and made my first move away from self-centered bondage, everything changed on a dime.

For this reason it says,
"Awake, sleeper,
And arise from the dead,
And Christ will shine on you."

—Ephesians 5:14 (NASB)

With that awakening, that epiphany, I realized for the first time in my life that the Kingdom of God that surrounds us here on earth is just as real and present as this passing twenty-first century world—the Kingdom of God is bursting forth everywhere, and it will never pass away. I had missed this completely and had never even ventured to open and look at the owner's manual, the handbook of life, to learn the way everything is made to work. When I did seek to know and understand the Scripture passages, they became so personal and life-giving to me that they literally leapt off the pages and were made crystal clear by the Holy Spirit. I couldn't get enough. They surely must have been written for me—for right then! That has been the story of millions of other Spirit-filled believers as well. Some of their stories would amaze us.

I remember the testimony of a nineteen-year-old woman who lived in the huge dump in Juarez, Mexico (mentioned in the next section, Walking Out the Call). This young woman went missing. She was totally illiterate, but she had found a paperback Bible in the dump, holed herself up, and did nothing except read Scripture for three days until she was found—a totally different person.

> *For this reason we also constantly thank God that when you received the word of God which you heard from us, you accepted it not as the word of mere men, but as what it really is, the word of God, which also is at work in you who believe.*
>
> —*1 Thessalonians 2:13 (NASB)*

> *And then their eyes were opened and they recognized Him; and He vanished from their sight. They said to one another, "Were our hearts not burning within us when He was speaking to us on the road, while He was explaining the Scriptures to us?"*
>
> —*Luke 24:31-32 (NASB)*

Since first awakening to Scripture, I have used and depended on many particular passages like specialized tools or equipment that meet every need or problem, anytime, anyplace. Scripture is God's wisdom for any occasion. How could I have missed that for so long? Sometimes we are not allowed to see beyond what we choose to see.

> *For the word of God is living and active, and sharper than any two-edged sword, even penetrating as far as the division of soul and spirit, of both joints and marrow, and able to judge the thoughts and intentions of the heart.*
>
> —*Hebrews 4:12 (NASB)*

Scripture is an ever-present help in so many different ways: a lamp unto our feet, a walkway of nonslip stepping stones, a light unto our path, a handrail in precarious areas, a grab bar to hang on to, an encouragement to press on when we had rather not. The Word is a lifter of our spirits when we are heavy laden, an energizer when our bodies tire, the herald of a bright new morning after a dark night. The inspired Word is a welcome messenger of peace, hope and truth, a deliverer from demons if they show up on our path—and of course the Lord's personal "just because" note to each of us. We are never alone on our journey. The Word is always near us, in our hearts.

When we walk by faith, not by sight, we are by no means walking blind. We are walking with spirit eyes, and our thoughts, our steps and our course are led, guided and directed. The Holy Spirit is the greatest of guides through the toughest and tightest of places, and He uses the living Word to put us, and help keep us, on the path. No one walked with more faith in the Father than Jesus when He walked from the garden, to Pilate, to the scourging, to the cross. He totally trusted the love and the plan of the Father. *Perfect love casts out all fear.* We must be fearless and surefooted in our faith walk, trusting that all we have heard, seen and experienced through the Spirit will lead us to place our next step in the right spot, without regard for what surrounds us or what lies ahead. For each person, there surely will be trials or troubles ahead. James tells us it is not a question of if, but when. Certainly, when that time comes, we want to be walking by faith already.

> *Consider it all joy, my brothers and sisters, when you encounter various trials, knowing that the testing of your faith produces endurance. And let endurance have its perfect result, so that you may be perfect and complete, lacking in nothing.*

> *But if any of you lacks wisdom, let him ask of God, who gives to all generously and without reproach, and it will be given to him. But he must ask in faith without any doubting, for the one who doubts is like the surf of the sea, driven and tossed by the wind. For that person ought not to expect that he will receive anything from the Lord, being a double-minded man, unstable in all his ways.*
> —*James 1:2-8 (NASB)*

As I have worked on this "Walking by Faith" section, my mind and memory have returned time and again to a spectacular event in 1970 that got the world's attention. It was both memorable and phenomenal.

Karl Wallenda, the most accomplished and famous high-wire walker in the world, was contracted to come to Tallulah Falls Gorge in North Georgia to put on a truly death-defying performance. It would mean life or death, for certain. Through the years, he had lost three family members; they had fallen to their deaths while performing high-wire pyramid acts with him. Still, the call to use his great gift and talent remained upon him.

Now, at sixty-five years of age, as the sole remaining aerialist of his family, he had come to Tallulah Falls to walk a cable stretched across the rock gorge 750 feet below. His faithfulness to his call wouldn't allow him to permit any net or other safety devices to be placed between himself and certain death from a fall. The cable spanned twelve hundred feet from tower to tower on each side. Great numbers of people, in person and on TV, watched to see if he would make it across, believing he would not fall to his death and that such courage should not be allowed to die.

Wallenda stepped off the tower onto the cable with only a balance beam, his trust in all he had learned throughout his life, his thousands of hours of disciplined work to develop control of his mind, body and steps, and his absolute faith and belief that he would get across safely.

He stepped off the tower onto the cable, each step well measured and patient, and with quiet confidence, he made his way over the gorge to the center, did a headstand on the cable, returned to his standing position and proceeded to walk to the far side.

Having completed his walk across the gorge, he then turned and began to walk back across the gorge, did a second headstand in the center and completed his walk to the tower where he had begun. Wallenda arrived quite safe and victorious. He had used what he had been given, lived out his call, exceeded all hopes and blessed and encouraged many to take up and complete their own walk.

Every place on which the sole of your foot steps, I have given it to you, just as I spoke to Moses.

—Joshua 1:3 (NASB)

Wallenda's walk was impeccable. He was not bothered by the jagged rocks on each side, nor the hard ground far below, nor by other circumstances of life.

He was focused solely on each step and on the goal ahead. As he prepared for the walk, his life experiences told him that he could do it, his great discipline told him that he should, and his faithfulness to his call told him he would.

Maybe not with Karl Wallenda's spirit of risk-taking, but with blessed assurance, we can and should walk by faith and not by sight, focused solely on each step, on the goal, the prize, on Glory. Saying no to the world, no to the flesh, no to Satan, and no to doubt and fear, we walk by faith and trust.

Walking Out the Call

As we walk this walk and use our faith time and again, a trust develops in us that God hears us, cares about us, meets our needs and is drawing us close to Himself. Over time, this ongoing interaction with the Lord develops the fruit of faithfulness, and we discover that the Lord also has come to trust us. This is only because of the Lord's awesome favor, a gift we don't deserve but which He desires to pour out over each of us. As the Lord comes to trust us and our faithfulness to carry out all that He asks of us, a "call" may be placed on our lives: a call to a particular work or service, or a life change that He has anointed us to embrace. Sometimes that call is clear as a bell. Other times, it may not be certain at all, but the drawing, the pull toward the call, is there and does not go away. We may need help from other believers to discern God's will.

When a call is placed on us, the grace is already on us to say "yes" and to take on this new venture, even though the call may seem entirely unusual or foreign to us. It may relate to something for which we have no training. The Lord often sees aptitude in us that we don't know exists. When we begin to walk by faith in His Spirit, we start to walk toward God's will, in which all things are possible. If the desire of our hearts is to walk in His will, then we can leave the hows and wherefores, times and places up to Him. If we embrace and put ourselves into the call He has placed upon us, He may well call us to works that are greater than the first. Availability is the key. He has warehouses full of ability to pass out.

For consider your calling, brothers and sisters, that there were not many wise according to the flesh, not many mighty, not many noble; but God

has chosen the foolish things of the world to shame the wise, and God has chosen the weak things of the world to shame the things which are strong...
—*1Corinthians 1:26-27 (NASB)*

"Also the one who had received the two talents came up and said, 'Master, you entrusted two talents to me. See, I have earned two more talents.'

His master said to him, 'Well done, good and faithful slave. You were faithful with a few things, I will put you in charge of many things; enter the joy of your master.'"
—*Matthew 25:22-23 (NASB)*

I can do all things through Him who strengthens me.
—*Philippians 4:13 (NASB)*

The Spirit has moved us through faith, trust and faithfulness into the call, and I believe we are supposed to look at the word "call" more closely.

When I was a teenager attending a Baptist church, the word came up in two ways, but only two, as I remember. One family had two sons whom they said were "called" to the ministry to become pastors, and they did. Two couples in the church were "called" and became missionaries in foreign countries. To me, these sounded like clear calls from Heaven in the middle of the night. I thought of them as being as dramatic as the Lord's spoken voice, and a done deal—irresistible and irrefutable. I didn't hear anything about ordinary people who worked regular jobs receiving calls to take on a mission from God as part of their everyday lives.

Through the years, I've come to believe that a call comes forth once we begin living a life of faith immersed in the Holy Spirit and gradually take on the mind of Christ, the heart of Christ, and then the work of Christ. When we are open, the Holy Spirit shows us where and how He wants to use us and He puts a call on us. If we accept the call and say, "Yes, Lord, use me" (however we say this), the call literally gives us a responsibility. If the Lord has entrusted us with a work, it is ours to carry out, no matter how we feel about the results. He may provide helpers, but the call is ours, as well as the grace to follow through on it.

You may be living out several calls from the Lord simultaneously, and He may yet have more to give you. That is awesome! May He anoint your handling of each of these calls, and may your response to each one help prepare you to respond to others.

I'd like to walk through some of our own experiences of calls placed on us.

About three years after being baptized in the Spirit, Nancy received a radical call to serve the homeless, first the street people in Atlanta and then those in Augusta. These were the marginalized people she had always been most uncomfortable being around and had avoided whenever possible, but the Spirit changed all that and gave her eyes and a heart to really see them as individuals in need of help and to reach out to them. This started with a strong call (which persisted for several years) to work frequently in soup kitchens and feed the hungry, and eventually to bring home three of the homeless people from the soup kitchen to live with us. I helped her with both works, but Nancy was the one who had the call.

Not long after she received this call to serve the homeless, as she was reading Scriptures from Acts, chapters 2 and 4, Nancy heard the call to come join the Alleluia Community. The Holy Spirit personalized those Scriptures for her —they leapt off the pages and instilled a desire in her that never let up and wouldn't go away. She heard community life as described in the book of Acts as the way Christianity was to be lived. Due to my resistance, it took two visits and two years before I heard the call and we as a couple could say, "Yes, Lord," and as a family relocate to Augusta and the community.

We have a friend, Rodger Gardner, who as a younger man was filled with anger and rebellion. He was wasting his life and creating havoc, riding his motorcycle as a member of the Hell's Angels gang. He was bad news coming! But then Rodger met Jesus, who saw goodness in him, saved him from his "old man" mindset and began transforming his life. The Spirit burned the Great Commission into his heart, stirred compassion in him and put a call on him to serve the homeless, the lost, the street people—both their bodies and their souls. Rodger was called to give them a hand and help them rediscover hope and purpose.

Rodger began ministering to street people who were living under a downtown Augusta bridge, bringing them the saving good news of Jesus and whatever material help he could muster. Over many years, Rodger's response to the call grew into the huge Under the Bridge Ministry, which regularly delivers the Word, hope, an abundance of food, clothes, shoes and coats, direction and opportunity. Several churches in the area have joined Rodger to help him meet the great physical needs, but it was Rodger who said yes to the call and took responsibility. God's grace filled in all the blanks.

The great stories of the saints remind us how powerful grace is. It seems that when someone is called by the Lord to a dangerous mission, possibly life changing or even life risking, when they say, "Yes, Lord, send me," and move into the mission, their perspective changes. The fear of danger or hardship is replaced with a deep fulfillment as a result of saying yes to the Lord's call and walking it out in faith. Their Kingdom-mindedness lifts them above worldly restraints and bondage of the mind or heart to this world. Hardly any saints were born saints; they just chose God over themselves and invited Him in to be the center of their lives.

Fight the good fight of faith; take hold of the eternal life to which you were called, and for which you made the good confession in the presence of many witnesses... Instruct those who are rich in this present world not to be conceited or to set their hope on the uncertainty of riches, but on God, who richly supplies us with all things to enjoy. Instruct them to do good, to be rich in good works, to be generous and ready to share, storing up for themselves the treasure of a good foundation for the future, so that they may take hold of that which is truly life.
—1 Timothy 6:12,17-19 (NASB)

The martyrs and saints were awakened to the truth and began living for the Lord with total faithfulness, doing whatever He told them, however He led them. Their single-mindedness moved them to the next level of response. Many of them were born into great wealth, some into abject poverty, others led promiscuous or deviant lifestyles, but when they were awakened by the Great Light they became determined to conform to God's will at all costs and to make the greatest difference they could as they passed through this earth. They were passionate contenders for the faith and ranged from grizzled old men to fragile young girls. Many suffered the most inhumane treatment and deaths that Satan could throw at them, but they found God's utmost favor forever.

He chose to be mistreated along with the people of God rather than to enjoy the fleeting pleasures of sin.

—*Hebrews 11:25 (NIV)*

Paul tells us that he didn't know whether it was better to stay here in this world and spread the good news, or go on to be with the Lord. He likely had developed a martyr's mindset. Given all of the attacks on his life, surely he knew this world was not his home—he was living in an alien land.

Hebrews 11:6-40 contains a long list of Biblical stalwarts and saints who came to know that this world was not worthy of their lives, and they invested everything in their eternal homeland, holding back nothing, knowing they would take nothing out of this world. They realized that passing through this world is just the test. Real life begins after the Lord decides that the test is over and it's "time to come home."

Instead, they were longing for a better country—a heavenly one. Therefore God is not ashamed to be called their God, for He has prepared a city for them.

—*Hebrews 11:16 (NIV)*

Certainly not every Christian is called to be a martyr, accepting death as part of contending for the faith. We may never get that close to the epicenter of the life-or-death battle, but if we are "all in" for God's will and single-minded in our efforts to live that out, we may well stand in the presence of saints. There is both an outward and inward martyrdom. Some refer to inward martyrdom as white martyrdom, a total dying to self for the cause, but without mortal death. Surely there must be martyr's grace or "departure grace" to override the brutality that the suffering saints and martyrs endure. As Stephen was about to be stoned to death, he paid no attention to the imminent end of his earthly life, but rather was ecstatic at seeing Jesus at the right hand of the Father and his own glorious departure.

But Stephen, full of the Holy Spirit, looked up to heaven and saw the glory of God, and Jesus standing at the right hand of God. "Look," he said, "I see heaven open and the Son of Man standing at the right hand of God." At this they covered their ears and, yelling at the top of their voices, they all rushed at him, dragged him out of the city and began to stone him. Meanwhile, the witnesses laid their coats at the feet of a young man named Saul. While they were stoning him, Stephen prayed, "Lord Jesus, receive my spirit." Then he fell on his knees and cried out, "Lord, do not hold this sin against them." When he had said this, he fell asleep.
—Acts 7:55-60 (NIV)

Some of the horrific (but at the same time, encouraging) stories of saints and martyrs throughout history cause us to want to step up, man up and be all that we can be for the One who gave His all for each of us. It can jolt us to learn that there were more people martyred in the twentieth century than any century before. There can be great costs to walking by faith and standing for the faith, but each of these people knew that their citizenship was not of this earth. They were expending their lives for a higher reward.

We look forward to meeting Jesus face to face, along with many of the saints and martyrs who showed us how to take the high road on this journey to Glory. Wow!

Brothers and sisters, join in following my example, and observe those who walk according to the pattern you have in us. For many walk, of whom I often told you, and now tell you even as I weep, that they are the enemies of the cross of Christ, whose end is destruction, whose god is their appetite, and whose glory is in their shame, who have their minds on earthly things. For our citizenship is in heaven, from which we also eagerly wait for a Savior, the Lord Jesus Christ; who will transform the body of our lowly condition into conformity with His glorious body, by the exertion of the power that He has even to subject all things to Himself.
—Philippians 3:17-21 (NASB)

I could not complete this story without thinking of some of our contemporary spiritual stalwarts who have said, " Yes, Lord, send me," while having limited understanding of where that yes might lead. Here are some of their incredible experiences and results—so many others have been blessed by their, "Yes, Lord, Your will, not mine."

A list like this could fill a book of its own, but I want to mention these faithful here so that we might reflect on their responses and how they turned loose all that this world had to offer. Many of them you might recognize; others you might not.

Mother Teresa responded to a clear call from the Lord to leave behind any comforts that she had as a well-placed nun teaching in a school for girls in Calcutta, India, and relocated to a poor part of the city near the second largest garbage dump in the world. There, thousands and thousands of the most helpless, homeless people are left to die on the streets of an uncaring world. Mother Teresa founded the Missionaries of Charity, which has spread around the world to care for the poorest of the poor, the next dying person in front of them, without regard to any person's faith or origin.

The sisters bring hope, life, dignity and respect to those the world has counted as worthless and discarded, and they find Jesus in each one of them. Mother Teresa showed us that we are not called to be successful—we are called to be faithful.

Billy Graham, the famous evangelist, stood as a beacon of hope and light, calling people to repent of their sins and be born again. In large stadiums packed to the highest seats, his beseeching altar calls lifted people to their feet to make the long walk down to the stage to give their lives to Jesus as the old song, "Just As I Am," played on. Its lyrics, "Just as I am, without one plea," tugged on every heart. Billy, along with his wife and family, fully lived what he preached until he went to Glory.

His son, Franklin Graham, carries on the ministry globally through a number of good works that provide for the most devastated and needy people in the world. This ministry, Samaritan's Purse, responds to disasters ranging from acts of nature to acts of inhumanity—and of course, Franklin continues to plead for souls to turn away from sin and be saved. He has a real heart for our devastated American culture.

Martin Luther King, Jr., answered the call to lay down his life to help free Black Americans and other minorities from the bondage of social slavery, inequity, injustices and unfair treatment. Through long, hard and costly efforts, coupled with his inspired dreams and exhortations, he helped the oppressed believe they could and would succeed. He showed people how to refrain from retaliating, accept abuse for the higher good, do the right thing and trust the Lord to bring good results. He himself would not live to experience the victory with them. Others, like Medgar Evers, joined him in the work and also died for the cause. They became larger in death than in life and brought about changes that few would have believed possible.

Pope John Paul II transformed millions of people's understanding of faith across the world by leading the Catholic Church for over twenty-five years, flying untold miles to bring real faith to areas that no other Christian leader had ever been. He grew up in Poland, endured the Nazi occupation and oppression there, and lost some of his Jewish friends during World War II. He became recognized all over the world as a hands-on faith leader. Along with President Ronald Reagan, he was instrumental in the ultimate downfall of the Soviet Union and other communist governments in Eastern Europe. He became the beloved people's pope, known as "JPII" to millions, showing people how to live by faith and to suffer and die with grace.

Joni Erickson Tada broke her neck in a diving accident in 1967 at the age of eighteen; she was paralyzed from the shoulders down and thought her life was destroyed. After two years of grief, anger and rehab, she opened up to the Lord and began seeking His plan for her life. She then started a ministry, Joni and Friends, to aid the disabled. This ministry has grown for over fifty years and has supplied thousands of wheelchairs to the disabled around the world, vacations for families of the disabled, and encouragement and hope through Joni's talks, music, books, and radio spots. She is one of the brightest, most uplifting voices of faith ever to be on the radio. Using her teeth, Joni is able to drive a van and to paint with great artistry. She acknowledges that she could never have made such a difference in the lives of others if she had had a fully functional body. Joni praises the Lord for her accident, the call on her life, and the deep fulfillment it has brought.

Fr. Damien De Veuster was the lone priest who heard the call to serve on the island of Moloki, a remote island in Hawaii that had been designated a leper colony for the "unclean," the most ostracized, "sent away" people in the world.

It was very difficult to find a volunteer priest to serve there for even a short time, since leprosy was considered so contagious and such a devastating disease. But Fr. Damien volunteered to go, and he never left. The lepers became his people, and he treated them like everyone else. He showed them how to become productive, to live and work together, and to respect themselves and each other, and he served as their caregiver, coffin builder, and grave digger. With the help of the Holy Spirit, Fr. Damien helped them develop a strong spiritual life and a vibrant community life. After sharing life with them for eleven years, Fr. Damien contracted leprosy himself. He continued to work hard for five more years before going to Glory. He is known as the Apostle of the Lepers.

After acquiring a prestigious Ivy League education and achieving considerable success in business, Chuck Colson was named head counsel to President Richard Nixon. Chuck used his position and influence with abandon in the highest places, but he was convicted for his part in the Watergate scandal. While serving his prison sentence, he met Jesus, and a total transformation began. Upon his release, he received his call and founded Prison Fellowship, which has grown globally. Chuck spent the rest of his life speaking and writing of the good news of Jesus and traveling around the world to the worst prisons, those with the most inhumane conditions. Even though most of the prisoners he encountered remained behind bars, many with life sentences, Jesus freed their souls indeed.

Fr. Rick Thomas, a Jesuit priest, was stationed in El Paso, Texas, across the Rio Grande River from the impoverished and homeless people of Juarez, Mexico. After months of observing these destitute people, Fr. Rick became troubled and moved to action by the hopeless plight of these "least of the least." These people lived in and off a huge garbage dump, scavenging for anything they could eat or sell. With members of his church, Fr. Rick went across the river and provided a Thanksgiving meal for the hundreds in the dump. The food never ran out— the legendary wonder of food multiplication took place. This call on Fr. Rick launched a whole new life and culture for these impoverished, nearly illiterate people. The Spirit showed them that they were not "garbage" people or throwaways, but children of God and Heirs of the Kingdom. Fr. Rick spent the rest of his life showing the people there how to live and be the good news of Jesus.

The Spirit called Rolland and Heidi Baker to leave the pleasures of oceanfront California to be missionaries in a third world country. After many years of faithfulness to seemingly unending work and a challenging lifestyle, with limited results, they received a new call. The Lord was giving them Mozambique (as a ministry)—a land with a tremendous number of people, great needs and often deplorable living conditions. Today the Lord is using them in one of the most powerful, dynamic , "love of God" ministries in the world. Whenever and wherever they are, the love and presence of the Lord is manifested by healings, miracles and changed lives. Missing body parts and limbs are created anew in front of their eyes. Even the African kids who travel with them on mission trips, "Mama Heidi's kids," become frequent ministers of healing. Heidi and Rolland tell everyone that they aren't anything special; they give all the credit and glory to the Lord. They say they are only doing what the Spirit leads them to do, and trying to pour out Jesus' love over His people.

Thousands and thousands of saints and martyrs have laid down their lives, answered the call and lived in difficult, dangerous, unimaginable conditions for the higher good.

Faith is the doorway to our "real life," and nothing else can be. Unlimited numbers of lives depend on what we will do. Jesus asked, *"When the Son of Man comes, will He find faith on the earth?" (Luke 18:8)* Are we spreading the Good News and increasing faith on the earth? Will it be recorded in the Book of Life that I used what was given me to contend for the faith?

> *But you, keep your head in all situations, endure hardship, do the work of an evangelist, discharge all the duties of your ministry.*
> —2 Timothy 4:5 (NIV)

> *I have fought the good fight, I have finished the race, I have kept the faith. Now there is in store for me the crown of righteousness, which the Lord, the righteous Judge, will award to me on that day—and not only to me, but also to all who have longed for His appearing.*
> —2 Timothy 4:7-8 (NIV)

Chapter 13

And Then, 2020

Somehow I had expected 2020 to be a year to remember, and many others did, as well. I also had hoped to publish this book before the year came to a close. That seemed important, and I had worked toward that goal for some years.

The year rolled in, and many people had good reasons for high expectations. The national economy was booming, employment levels were setting records and the rate of unemployment was radically dropping, people of all backgrounds and colors were experiencing opportunities and prosperity like never before. The nation was riding a wave of three years of continued improvements, and many had high hopes that the next four or more years would be even better. America looked like the land of plenty, finally coming back into the light. With a clearer purpose in mind, we were starting to make America great again.

Many Americans had been completely surprised by the results of the 2016 election, when a President was chosen who was totally patriotic, understood what needed to be done and had the courage and seemingly the ability to do it, whether others agreed or not. A number of President Trump's egocentric and abrasive traits were hard for many good people, especially believers, to tolerate and accept. His past life of loose morals and sinful behavior forced us to reevaluate the meaning of redemption but also deepened our understanding of it. Strong confidence in the character of Mike Pence, the vice presidential candidate, had won the votes of many; his faith shone like a bright light anytime he was seen or heard.

Scripture tells us, *"You will know them by their fruits,"* and we saw good fruit through strong leadership for over three years. A willingness to stand up for God's laws and for the sanctity of life were brought back into the open.

In the Alleluia Community, we devote the first prayer meeting of the year to prophetic words or words of knowledge that are given to and delivered by community members to the whole body. These prophetic words have been key tools over the years by which the Holy Spirit sets a tone, direction or theme for the new year. I expected a string of hopeful, prophetic words from a number of people as the new year began with its seemingly important date. As I listened to the Spirit, I received a word, one that I thought right away was unusual, even ominous. I kept it to myself for the next week as the prayer meeting approached.

I went up early in the meeting to deliver the word. It was the hardest word of the evening, and not the kind of word that we expect to hear as we embark on a new year. The following is that word.

> **"My people: Fear not! This year could be a rocky road of tests and trials for many of you. Do not be dismayed. You are on the right course. Keep your eyes on Me—and your trust in Me. Do not let the world and its happenings cause you to turn to the left or to the right. Your faith and the Spirit will get you safely through every hard place and obstacle. Trust Me with your whole heart, soul and being. You have been bought and paid for by My Blood. My People, <u>fear not, and joyfully finish what you have put your life into.</u> I will be with you through it all. I have promised and I will do it!" says the Lord.**

Three weeks later, at the end of January, the news broke about a fast-moving, deadly virus attacking the people of China and spreading into other parts of the world. President Trump quickly blocked all air travel into America from China. The virus had already surfaced on the West Coast in America, and the greatest lockdown/shutdown in our history began, not just in America but across the entire world.

The synchronized global system of reciprocal trade and travel that had developed over decades quickly ground to a near halt. Other than businesses or facilities providing medical care or essential goods and services, little remained open and operational. The sky, eerily quiet without commercial airliners, was reminiscent of the days immediately following September 11, 2001, but the grounding went on for weeks. All healthcare facilities and workers moved into highest gear in their efforts to care for those who were sick or dying due to the virus. Even refrigerated storage trucks were parked outside nursing homes to hold the overflow of dead bodies. Frantic efforts were made to fully equip healthcare workers to save lives, and an executive order was issued to prioritize and greatly increase our manufacture and distribution of masks, sanitizers, ventilators, and other much needed medical equipment and supplies. An emergency plan was initiated to develop a vaccine for the virus, and several pharmaceutical manufacturers and research teams joined forces in an all-out effort to develop and quickly produce a vaccine in huge volumes for the American population. This was a monumental task; normally it would take well over a year before the first shots of such a vaccine could be made available.

Suddenly our consumer-driven, supply-dependent, high-tech, same-day-shipping mindset was indefinitely replaced. Words and phrases like *unprecedented, social distancing, thorough hand washing, sanitizers, masks, ventilators, vaccine, testing, quarantine* and *sheltering in place* became the new everyday vernacular, around the clock, across the globe. Nothing, not even the two great World Wars, had ever before stopped this much of humanity in its tracks. The world had been turned upside down.

The events that have taken place since the end of January 2020 are nearly unbelievable, like nothing ever experienced, either in recent history or long ago. Surely there will be countless reports, videos, books and personal accounts that will eventually come out and describe it all in great detail. I am just giving a simple overview of the scope of this silent killer that quickly crisscrossed the earth and brought about an extreme reset of the culture, putting on pause a society that had been moving at breakneck speed.

Mandates were put in place that forced businesses to close, and off-and-on, crippling periods of closure dragged on for month after month, affecting businesses large and small. Airlines and small businesses began to suffer losses of business and revenue. Ultimately, countless small businesses had no choice but to permanently close. Financial assistance from the government helped individuals and multitudes of businesses stay afloat, but that kind of help is inadequate and unsustainable; businesses have to be operational to carry our economy. Schools of every type were subject to mandatory closings, many of which were unwarranted, affecting students of all ages. Some students were kept at home for the majority of the school year. (As of this writing, at the start of 2021, some students in various parts of the country still have not returned to school.)

As devastating as this killer virus is to physical health, it may take a greater toll on other parts of life as we know it. The fallout and financial upheaval, along with the extreme mental anguish, distress and depression, and even the number of suicides, will be enormous. Isolation is a far greater enemy to most people than we may realize. We have likely seen only the early results, but we know that much of life as we've known it will never be the same. Significant adapting and adjusting will be needed for an indefinite period of time, but the Lord is out ahead of us and He will show us what is needed as we ask Him.

Soon after the pandemic first hit, the Alleluia leaders heard a word that we were to pray the 91st Psalm daily for personal and group protection. We have all tried to faithfully do this, and we have felt a great peace as we've gone through this challenging season of unknowns.

Whoever dwells in the shelter of the Most High will rest in the shadow of the Almighty. I will say of the Lord, "He is my refuge and my fortress, my God, in whom I trust." Surely He will save you from the fowler's snare and from the deadly pestilence. He will cover you with His feathers, and under His wings you will find refuge; His faithfulness will be your shield and rampart. You will not fear the terror of night, nor the arrow that flies by day, nor the pestilence that stalks in the darkness, nor the plague that destroys at midday.

A thousand may fall at your side, ten thousand at your right hand, but it will not come near you. You will only observe with your eyes and see the punishment of the wicked. If you say, "The Lord is my refuge," and you make the Most High your dwelling, no harm will overtake you, no disaster will come near your tent.

—Psalm 91:1-10 (NIV)

Standing on the promises of God may be unfamiliar, even to many Christians, but is in fact very comforting and brings about peace and powerful results. When we read one phrase at a time, this great psalm just clothes us with blessed assurance. *Dwell in the shelter of the Most High. Rest in the shadow of the almighty.* Take *refuge* in His *fortress. No harm will overtake you, no disaster will come near you.* Amen!

This book is about faith and living it out, not about political conditions. Having said that, I feel that the state of our country has to be discussed, that we might understand our present circumstances in America. Denial of this reality is the very thing that has gotten our country into the condition in which we find ourselves today, a condition most of us find hard to believe.

Since the legalization of abortion in 1973, deception and denial have been two of America's greatest enemies. We know that our battle is not against flesh and blood but against powers and principalities; we must be able to know and recognize them. There is an old warning for Christians to stay clear of politics, that the two don't mix. There's a more practical warning for Christians to not get so heavenly minded that we are of no earthly good. If we are to be useful to the Lord, we must be aware of those things that pertain to us and those that war against us. We are still very much in this world, while not "of it." We are "in it" because that is the test put before and all around us, but to not be "of it" means that we do not belong to it and are not dependent on it or its ways. That is our choice, the choice that we make of our own will. As believers, our goal is to think with and act with the mind of Christ, to influence and lead this alien world toward the Lord.

Most Americans took the easier, wider road of destruction, while Satan took over our values, trashed them and pitched them. Do we want those values back enough to contend for them? Only time will tell. Changed hearts, minds and actions are required. Will we step up or stand down? The clock is running and we are on borrowed time even now. The Lord is waiting for our response. We know He is merciful—just look at how well He has treated us for so long. He is also **just**; that's His nature. The greatest generation, those who fought in World War II, knew they were in the battle of their lives for the survival of America and the free world. They were willing and ready to put their lives on the line, holding nothing back. Today, would most Americans even acknowledge that there is a life or death battle with evil raging for the future of our country?

Just twenty years after that great global victory, we as a nation turned off our consciences and tuned in to our desires and privileges. We were deceived into believing that our great freedom is free for the taking and enjoying, with no maintenance or defense required. The church has ceased to call sin what it is, **sin**, to call sinners to account, to impact the runaway culture and show us the way. For a long time, that process has been reversed, with the culture changing the church and the church seemingly trying hard to stay in step with the culture and not be left behind. The moral free fall among churches and churchgoers is one of the worst examples of sin being tolerated and running loose. This is apparent in churches of many denominations and even at high levels of leadership.

Then the 2020 election was upon us. Like no previous election, this one came down to a battle between good and evil. That is clearly borne out in the two expressed platforms the parties ran on, one a pro-life platform that included God, the other a pro-abortion platform that openly rejected God. Satan makes sure that the choices don't seem that clear or defined to most people; he blurs and obscures the lines whenever possible. The strongholds of deception and denial that have grown up in our culture have allowed apathy, complacency and irresponsibility to take over. Evil can be the hardest of all enemies to spot, identify and contend against, but contend we must if we want our country and culture back.

We find ourselves at a great crossroads. We can either contend for our faith, our family, our country, our culture and for all our descendants, or we can continue on the path that our culture has conceded to, accepted and adopted. That path, if not redirected toward the Lord and His ways, will lead to destruction and punishment beyond belief. Surely none of us want to experience the Lord's vengeance.

When the year 2020 began, uneasiness began to grow among Americans. We saw that street disorder was likely to erupt across the country throughout the summer leading up to the November elections. Many expected riots and fires like we had seen in Watts, Detroit and other racial hot spots years earlier. A severe split between political parties with no common ground in sight was leading up to a major confrontation.

But the unrest, protests and riots we had expected in the summer broke out even sooner, in the spring, and instantly were called racial riots. They turned into all-out anarchy and an effort to shut down America, drive goodness and God out of our country and replace them with socialism, Marxism and godless ideals.

Recruited and paid anarchists were shuttled from state to state and allowed for months by city and state governments to occupy and destroy entire sections of major cities in an effort to undermine Trump, conservatism and Christianity.

Satan had never been given so much room for destruction in America, but this was the result of decades of widespread preparation. Corruption increased by leaps and bounds, to the extent that we saw an untold number of fraudulent election returns in November that likely cost President Trump reelection. Massive amounts of money were thrown at efforts to buy the election results at many levels, especially in the last two senatorial races that would lead to control of the U.S. Senate.

Along with many millions of other Americans, I believe Donald Trump was one of the most productive presidents in our nation's history. Together, Trump and Vice President Mike Pence were responsible for monumental positive accomplishments and changes for the good. Their tireless, round-the-clock efforts to battle the pandemic and avoid financial disasters were remarkable, while their endless work to move the country toward patriotism and godliness and welcome God back into our country were reminiscent of the Ronald Reagan era.

Nevertheless, when it came to the election, multiple millions of votes were cast in the name of change. People voted for change just for the sake of change, with no idea what that change would mean or what might be the cost, or the result. This was in part a blind reaction to an unprecedented pandemic and its enormous fallout, as if any individual could have stopped or reversed those events. And, of course, it was an effort to remove the God-fearing administration from power and replace it with a more worldly system of government. Setting aside the fraudulent election results, the change that so many voted in will likely bring more unprecedented disaster than the pandemic itself, and could take many years to rectify, but these changes have been many years in the works.

"Father, forgive them, for they do not know what they are doing."
—*Luke 23:34 (NIV)*

So, to what is this all leading?

Throughout the ages, the Lord has seen this scenario repeated over and over, and He knows how to bring His people back to Himself.

Observe the commands of the Lord your God, walking in obedience to Him and revering Him. For the Lord your God is bringing you into a good land—a land with brooks, streams, and deep springs gushing out into the valleys and hills; a land with wheat and barley, vines and fig trees, pomegranates, olive oil and honey; a land where bread will not be scarce and you will lack nothing; a land where the rocks are iron and you can dig copper out of the hills.

When you have eaten and are satisfied, praise the Lord your God for the good land He has given you. Be careful that you do not forget the Lord your God, failing to observe His commands, His laws and His decrees that I am giving you this day. Otherwise, when you eat and are satisfied, when you build fine houses and settle down, and when your herds and flocks grow large and your silver and gold increase and all you have is multiplied, then your heart will become proud and you will forget the Lord your God, who brought you out of Egypt, out of the land of slavery.
—Deuteronomy 8:6-14 (NIV)

You may say to yourself, "My power and the strength of my hands have produced this wealth for me." But remember the Lord your God, for it is He who gives you the ability to produce wealth, and so confirms His covenant, which He swore to your ancestors, as it is today.

If you ever forget the Lord your God and follow other gods and worship and bow down to them, I testify against you today that you will surely be destroyed. Like the nations the Lord destroyed before you, so you will be destroyed for not obeying the Lord your God.
—Deuteronomy 8:17-20 (NIV)

In order for our country to survive we must do things God's way. The world's system and the world's "wisdom" have no answer for the place we find ourselves in 2021.

Let's take a closer look at the often read and quoted passage from 2 Chronicles. Some of the words just jump off the page:

"If My people, who are called by My name, will humble themselves and pray and seek My face and turn from their wicked ways, then I will hear from heaven, and I will forgive their sin and will heal their land."
—*2 Chronicles 7:14 (NIV)*

The first word, "If," always strikes me, that conditional word that all else is dependent upon. Until that word is translated in a personal way to "when," we haven't really heard or acted on this Scripture. Another key part of this passage is the phrase, "My people, who are called by My name." That's us—God's people who bear the name Christian, the ones who have said, "Yes, Lord, send me." We are the people the Lord is waiting on and depending on, the remnant. Have our lives lived up to the name "Christian"? Do we even deserve the name?

It is time to stand up, admit our guilt for the destruction of our country that has happened on our watch, sincerely ask the Lord's forgiveness, plead for another chance, that we might do better, and renounce and turn away personally from every evil practice or tolerance of such. Then we must take up our rightful call to be watchmen on the wall to help others admit their sin and guilt, turn from all wickedness, be healed, and become impact players in our badly fragmented country.

We know the Lord will do His part when we do ours. He is faithful and true and wants the best for each of us, and He is able to turn this country right side up and make it greater than ever before. Again, *"If My people, who are called by My name, will..."* That is the big question. With all the evil manifest in our world and with the future hanging in the balance, it is no time to be conscientious objectors or to stand down. If ever there was a time to stand up for the Lord and His values, surely this is the time.

We must remember that God loves America far more than we do. America is His child that He birthed in 1776. After so many years of general lethargy, do we still have it in us to fight for our present and future generations? I have seen this train wreck coming for a long time. The numbing results of deception, denial, apathy and complacency as observed outside abortion clinics reveal our desperate condition as little else can. These spirits have rendered most Americans unaware and immobile, by our own consent. It is an absolute swing of the pendulum away from where we were as a nation through the 1950s. The downward spiral of the culture at such increasing speed was so obvious, even in the Clinton era of the 1990s, that our prayers at abortion clinics took on two directions or goals: for the unborn and for America. Both were being assaulted and killed by evil, and the general public couldn't or wouldn't see it. "Standing for Life" in this book tells much about this erosion and the avalanche coming, as did the story of Hurricane Floyd.

Believers around the world, the remnant, those called by His name, may well be approaching a Red Sea experience. Our part is definitely not to turn back and join the unbelievers, nor is it to fear the enemy behind or the dangerous sea straight ahead, nor is it to doubt that the sea will be parted into a dry roadway for our safe passage. It is not for us to worry about how the raging water on each side will be held back, or whether it will be, or to wonder whether we will get to the other side safely. No, we are to trust and go straight ahead as we are led by the Lord—straight ahead, not turning to the left or to the right, but proceeding with no doubting, and instead, rejoicing with great peace and trust as we receive the Lord's rescue and deliverance. Conditions may look nearly impossible on this side, but they will look far better after we have crossed through.

> *Do not be anxious about anything, but in every situation, by prayer and petition, with thanksgiving, present your requests to God. And the peace of God, which transcends all understanding, will guard your hearts and your minds in Christ Jesus. Finally, brothers and sisters, whatever is true, whatever is noble, whatever is right, whatever is pure, whatever is lovely, whatever is admirable—if anything is excellent or praiseworthy—think about such things. Whatever you have learned or received or heard from me, or seen in me—put it into practice. And the God of peace will be with you.*
>
> *—Philippians 4:6-9 (NIV)*

Over the years, believers have experienced hard times, dangers, toils and snares; His grace has carried His faithful through all of it. This same grace is more than sufficient to carry us through this trial, too. Let us use our perseverance, endurance and developed character so that we might serve as messengers of light and hope to those we see. They may need some faith-and-works help. We have prayed long and hard for the Lord to change this evil culture; now let us be open and embrace the changes He allows and stay close to Him.

As Americans, each of us has been living in a dimming, deteriorating culture, many of us for the majority of our lives, if not our entire lives. This "culture of death," as Pope John Paul II termed it, overwhelms and destroys everything. As hard as it may be to see its wayward roots ripped out and our country rebuilt according to God's original plan, that may be where we are headed; if so, as believers, we must embrace and support this necessary tearing out, rebuilding and healing.

However this "unprecedented" situation has come to be (and that will become clearer as we walk ahead in faith), the answer does not change. If this worldwide ongoing global disaster turns out to be God's chastisement of this disobedient and self-seeking culture that has run far off the rails, then so be it. It will be ours to accept the punishment we have long deserved, draw nearer to God than ever before, and each do what we can to make amends. We serve the one true and merciful God.

"Fear not! Keep your eyes on Me—and your trust in Me.
I will be with you through it all. I have promised and I will do it!"
—From the word above received in January 2020

No temptation has overtaken you except what is common to mankind. And God is faithful; He will not let you be tempted beyond what you can bear. But when you are tempted, He will also provide a way out so that you can endure it.
—1 Corinthians 10:13 (NIV)

Our Response

As we have often heard, it is not what happens to us that is most important, but rather our response to what happens. Living in fear and living in trust bring forth totally different responses to the same event, and usually different results. We all know that we are responsible for most of the events that happen in our lives, but we are not responsible for those that are beyond our control, those that just happen without notice or apparent reason. Some of these events are inflicted by Satan to harass us, hinder us, or worse; some are allowed by the Lord for our growth and development. The correct response is essential. Spirit-led discernment and acting in accordance with that discernment are key. When difficult challenges come, let us deal with them in such a way that they make us better, not bitter.

> *Consider it pure joy, my brothers and sisters, whenever you face trials of many kinds, because you know that the testing of your faith produces perseverance. Let perseverance finish its work so that you may be mature and complete, not lacking anything.*
>
> *—James 1:2-4 (NIV)*

Some challenges and trials presently on the horizon will surpass any we've experienced before, so let us anticipate and embrace them with our most faith-filled and courageous outlook and spirit.

> *"God, grant me the serenity to accept the things I cannot change, the courage to change the things I can, and the wisdom to know the difference."*
>
> *—Reinhold Niebuhr*

In 2012, I started the journey of compiling this book. As the book nears completion, our life in America hardly resembles what it looked like in 2012. Those who have eyes to see shouldn't be surprised by the devastating changes. Our majestic country, with its history of over two hundred years of valor and high standards, has been sabotaged by an assault of evil never before seen or imagined in our land. No doubt this evil will spawn more evil, lawlessness, destruction, chaos, fear, desperation and hopelessness because the world's systems are breaking down. Although most Americans act unaware, the keys of control in our culture have been given over to evil forces, driven by Satan himself. Most would say, "I have done nothing wrong." To be honest, most should confess, "I have done little or nothing to prevent this devastating wrong." If we truly are unaware, we need to take responsibility and get rightly informed.

America's future depends on goodness, honesty, loyalty, integrity and, most especially, strong faith in the Lord. These are necessary to survive, much less to thrive.

> *He has shown you, O mortal, what is good.*
> *And what does the Lord require of you?*
> *To act justly and to love mercy and to walk humbly with your God.*
> *—Micah 6:8 (NIV)*

Too many Americans have stood by and paid no attention as these godly attributes have been replaced by ungodly ideals and disordered intentions. We didn't actually contend for them and protect America the Beautiful as it was being savaged. Now we have the responsibility to rebuild it God's way. The Scripture again calls out to us, and it is past time for us to heed the word.

> *"If My people, who are called by My name, will humble themselves and pray and seek My face and turn from their wicked ways, then I will hear from heaven, and I will forgive their sin and will heal their land."*
> *—2 Chronicles 7:14 (NIV) [My underlining]*

We must get serious and be totally honest, free ourselves from deception and denial, realize it is our problem to admit and correct, and be about this very hard and possibly very long work of rebuilding what we once considered untouchable by evil. America has been a favored country and has long stood head and shoulders above the rest of the world, both in power and in compassion. America's greatness depended on our goodness and God's favor. Consequently, our friendship with the world's hedonistic ways cost us God's favor. Over time, we took America's strength and status for granted and didn't maintain its standards or defend our great land from evil spirits who came to destroy it. Of course, Christianity and America, which have long been roadblocks to injustice and evil, are Satan's foremost targets for infiltration and destruction.

God cannot tolerate evil and will not share His people with evil spirits.

Or do you think Scripture says without reason that He jealously longs for the spirit He has caused to dwell in us? Come near to God and He will come near to you. Wash your hands, you sinners, and purify your hearts, you doubleminded. Humble yourselves before the Lord, and He will lift you up.

—James 4:5, 8, 10 (NIV)

Is our future hopeless? Is our country beyond fixing? Has God's hand been permanently withdrawn from us? Not at all! Must we wait four years, hoping for better results with the next election? By no means! We don't have that luxury. No one knows how much time we have left. We probably are not in the end times, but we may well be in the latter days. If ever we are going to live our faith to the fullest, the time has arrived. We must remember who we are, why we are, and rebuild the America of its glory years. Our faith will be put to the test, but that is where grace takes over.

Our jobs, our finances, our churches, our entire lives may come under fire, be challenged or even taken from us. If that is the cost, we will deal with it as it comes. Maintaining our unwavering faith and trust in the Lord is the key. Only those who *"endure to the end will be saved"* (Matthew 24:13). We must remember that we are in no way "under the circumstances" unless we put ourselves there. God certainly has not. *"We are more than conquerors"* (Romans 8:31-39); we are more than overcomers.

Throughout history, the Lord has heard and responded to true repentance and to His people turning away from rebellion and wickedness and back to Him—and His hand has brought about restoration.

Because I have sinned against Him,
I will bear the Lord's wrath,
until He pleads my case
and upholds my cause.
He will bring me out into the light;
I will see His righteousness.
Who is a God like You,
who pardons sin and forgives the transgression
of the remnant of His inheritance?
You do not stay angry forever
but delight to show mercy.
You will again have compassion on us;
You will tread our sins underfoot
and hurl all our iniquities into the depths of the sea.
— *Micah 7:9,1819 (NIV)*

Hard times come and hard times go, but with faith and the Lord, hard times can be dealt with. Challenges can prove to be the best character builders, and are sometimes even looked back on as priceless. I can confirm that in my own life. The human spirit is amazingly resilient, and in the power of the Holy Spirit, for those with reverence or fear of God, all things are possible.

This all-encompassing storm that we find ourselves in is not a passing-over-and-gone storm, like a powerful tornado. We are engulfed by this storm, and it's here to take us out if we don't fully stand up to it and cast it out from our culture and our country. Let us be clear: This collision of forces is all about the great battle between good and evil. Satan is positioned to go all out to destroy America as we have known it. Hopelessness is Satan's powerful, crushing force, but we know that hope in the Lord is far more powerful. *"Greater is He who is in you than he who is in the world."* *(1 John 4:4)* As part of the Lord's remnant, we are expected to step up to our call and live as such, every moment, everywhere. What an awesome time in history to get to serve the Lord! The darkness that is coming may far surpass anything we have experienced before—a tsunami of smothering darkness intended to spread despair and hopelessness—but that darkness can never extinguish the Light. Our job is to keep our light burning bright. Always bright, everywhere, and all the time, ever brighter.

How can we do that? By continually working toward dying to self and self-interest, by living out our call to serve the Lord and serve others for the higher good, by being vigilant to cast out all doubt and fear by following the leading of the Holy Spirit and staying Kingdom minded and focused on the goal through everything. If we do all of this, surely our light will shine so brightly that it will lead many people out of the darkness, which will surely grow darker.

> *"You are the light of the world. A town built on a hill cannot be hidden...*
> *In the same way, let your light shine before others, that they may see your*
> *good deeds and glorify your Father in heaven."*
> —*Matthew 5:14, 16 (NIV)*

As the darkness in the world increases, let us multiply the good deeds that please and glorify the Lord. We know that many lights are burning bright, and faith, goodness, kindness and compassion are rising in America like we haven't seen in decades. The medical workers, first responders and volunteers who have cared for the sick and dying have been amazing, and at great personal risk. A number of them have relocated across the country to the hardest hit areas just to serve the sick and dying during the pandemic. Many have given their lives for the life of another. Many have provided much needed financial help to those who have lost everything. We all know that major disasters can bring out the best in humanity. May it be so with this one, Lord—use us as needed.

Prayer of St. Francis
Lord, make me an instrument of your peace: where there is hatred, let me
sow love; where there is injury, pardon; where there is doubt, faith;
where there is despair, hope; where there is dark-
ness, light; where there is sadness, joy;

O divine Master, grant that I may not so much seek to be consoled as
to console; to be understood as to understand; to be loved as to love.
For it is in giving that we receive; it is in pardoning that we are pardoned;
and it is in dying that we are born to eternal life.

There is only one unfailing answer to what is occurring: the triune God, the Father, Jesus and the Holy Spirit. God's ways work. He alone can lead us through safely and with abiding joy; we only need to ask for His help and follow His lead. Our part is to care, share, reach out, show love to the one the Lord puts in our path. He will supply the grace needed. If this rebuild of the Lord's America is to cost us everything here on earth, our eternal reward will be even greater.

> *Therefore if you have been raised with Christ, keep seeking the things*
> *that are above, where Christ is, seated at the right hand of God. <u>Set your</u>*
> *<u>mind on the things that are above</u>, not on the things that are on earth.*
> *—Colossians 3:1-2 (NASB) [My underlining]*

> *Beyond all these things put on love, which is the perfect bond of unity. Let*
> *the peace of Christ rule in your hearts, to which indeed you were called*
> *in one body; and be thankful. Let the word of Christ richly dwell within*
> *you, with all wisdom teaching and admonishing one another with psalms*
> *and hymns and spiritual songs, singing <u>with thankfulness in your hearts</u>*
> *<u>to God</u>. Whatever you do in word or deed, do all in the name of the Lord*
> *Jesus, giving thanks through Him to God the Father.*
> *—Colossians 3:14-17 (NASB 1995) [My underlining]*

If we set our minds on the things above, and keep them there, the increasing clamor of the world will subside and gradually be replaced by love, and *perfect love casts out all fear. (1 John 4:18)* What a trade-off—all our fears for perfect love. The goal and work of a lifetime, but fully worth it, I am sure!

> *If I speak with the tongues of men and of angels, but do not have love,*
> *I have become a noisy gong or a clanging cymbal. If I have the gift of*

prophecy, and know all mysteries and all knowledge; and if I have all faith, so as to remove mountains, but do not have love, I am nothing. And if I give all my possessions to feed the poor, and if I surrender my body to be burned, but do not have love, it profits me nothing.

Love is patient, love is kind and is not jealous; love does not brag and is not arrogant, does not act unbecomingly; it does not seek its own, is not provoked, does not take into account a wrong suffered, does not rejoice in unrighteousness, but rejoices with the truth; bears all things, believes all things, hopes all things, endures all things.
Love never fails; but if there are gifts of prophecy, they will be done away; if there are tongues, they will cease; if there is knowledge, it will be done away. For we know in part and we prophesy in part; but when the perfect comes, the partial will be done away. When I was a child, I used to speak like a child, think like a child, reason like a child; when I became a man, I did away with childish things. For now we see in a mirror dimly, but then face to face; now I know in part, but then I will know fully just as I also have been fully known. But now faith, hope, love, abide these three; but the greatest of these is love.

—*1 Corinthians 13 (NASB 1995)*

Above all else, we must always remember the greatest act of love ever given, Jesus giving His all for each of us on the brutalizing cross, forever, before we even knew Him.

***

For many years, my primary goal has been to finish the journey of life well. As a builder for my entire life, of furniture, of homes, of church furnishings and crosses, I know that to finish well is absolutely essential; otherwise, there are only good intentions and lots of effort. Whenever I've built anything, I have tried to keep the big picture always in mind but really focus on the work at hand, the pieces and parts, and stay present to the moment. Every project that is worth starting deserves to be completed well. When we do our best with each element, the assembled, finished product will meet our expectations and quite possibly even surpass them.

Since the journey of life is the ultimate project, the project of a lifetime, and comprises so many pieces and parts, moments, hours, days and seasons, we do well to live present to the moment, to give each moment our full attention and our best effort, with full trust. Then we will come to see what the Lord's plan has accomplished. If we abandon ourselves fully to the Holy Spirit and follow His lead, the finish may well be the very best leg of our journey.

Being confident of this, that He who began a good work in you will carry it on to completion until the day of Christ Jesus.
—Philippians 1:6 (NIV)

It is extremely important to remember that it was He who began this good work, and it is He who will perfect it. I am still amazed that He cares enough about each of us to begin such a great work: the work of redemption and reclamation in each individual soul.

We can expect the road ahead to get narrow and steep, with challenging footing and unforeseen obstacles. Many travelers will think the journey is too hard to finish and will fall back or drop out. Some may even try to convince those around them to drop out. Others may struggle daily but keep their hearts invested in the ultimate prize. It will be our job to help them along toward Glory.

Brothers and sisters, I do not consider myself yet to have taken hold of it. But one thing I do: Forgetting what is behind and straining toward what is ahead, I press on toward the goal to win the prize for which God has called me heavenward in Christ Jesus.
—Philippians 3:13-14 (NIV)

If we give our all to fully walk in His will and in the Holy Spirit, we can expect His restoration and His glory to go before us.

Do you not know? Have you not heard? The Lord is the everlasting God, the Creator of the ends of the earth. He will not grow tired or weary, and

His understanding no one can fathom. He gives strength to the weary and increases the power of the weak. Even youths grow tired and weary, and young men stumble and fall; but those who hope in the Lord will renew their strength. They will soar on wings like eagles; they will run and not grow weary, they will walk and not be faint.

—Isaiah 40:28-31 (NIV)

As you have traveled through this book, I hope the Spirit has revealed glimpses of Glory to you. It is a brief overview of life as I have come to know and experience it, but there is so much more yet to be discovered. He offers this life now and forever to anyone who invites Him in to dwell. Each life is different, but none is any less important or less special to Him. Let us fully partake of and enjoy what God has for each of us.

I sincerely pray that each of you will finish well, and in no way have that fulfillment and joy kept from you, so that when you meet Him face to face you will hear, *"Well done, My good and faithful servant." (Matthew 25:21)* Since you have taken the journey of reading this book, I feel a connection with you, and I value the opportunity I've had to share with you. I pray you will ask the Lord to draw you ever closer and give you more, just as needed.

If you have not committed your life to the Lord and asked Him to help lead and guide the rest of your journey, or if you are not sure whether you truly have, I invite you, beseech you, to pray this prayer or a prayer from your heart as the Spirit leads. A prayer spoken out loud is best. Wherever you have been or find yourself today, the Lord Jesus loves you just as you are and wants you with Him forever; He does not want you to be left behind. He is waiting for you to invite Him in, and you can trust Him!

Lord Jesus, I am a sinner. I have sinned against You, against others and against myself, in the things I have done and the things I have failed to do. For all these sins, I am truly sorry, and I ask Your forgiveness. Lord, I know there were times when I have avoided You, have run away from You and have even denied You. For each of these times I am deeply sorry. Please forgive me.

Lord, I thank You for going to the cross and dying for my sins that I could be washed clean and made whole. I ask for another opportunity to receive You as my Savior and the Lord of my life and to be with You forever.

I ask You to come in, take over and give me a fresh start. I know I can't do this on my own. Please take all my mistakes, brokenness and failures today and turn them into something worthy, as only You can. From this day forth, I want to live my life for You, just as you gave Your life for me. Please use me, Lord, to help others come to know You.

Thank you, Lord Jesus.

There is always more that we can give to the Lord and receive from Him—this applies to every Spirit-filled believer. He seems to reveal that "more" in stages or degrees as we live in accord with what He has already given us. Let us make sure we give Him the keys to every part of our lives and the green light to use us as He will. We know that, *"To him who has been given much, much is expected." (Luke 12:48)* Let us hold nothing back from the One who gave His all for each of us.

Lord, I thank You for all the ways You have been there for me ever since You took over my life. Your presence and transforming power have given me peace, purpose and blessings beyond anything I could have hoped for; You have given me life itself.

Holy Spirit, I know there is more that You have for me and expect from me. This day, I turn loose any hold I have on my life and anything I have held back from You. I ask for Your will in my life. I want to live fully, totally and completely for You and do it your way, and in your time.

Please empower and refresh me through the Holy Spirit to be "all in" and release spiritual gifts within me to be used at Your disposal, and the grace to live out any call You put on my life. Please send me, Lord, and use me up to contend for and build Your Kingdom here on earth. Thank you, Lord.

Dear friends, although I was very eager to write to you about the salvation we share, I felt compelled to write and urge you to contend for the faith that was once for all entrusted to God's holy people.
—Jude 1:3 (NIV)

"In the last times there will be scoffers who will follow their own ungodly desires." These are the people who divide you, who follow mere natural instincts and do not have the Spirit. But you, dear friends, by building yourselves up in your most holy faith and praying in the Holy Spirit, keep yourselves in God's love as you wait for the mercy of our Lord Jesus Christ to bring you to eternal life. Be merciful to those who doubt; save others by snatching them from the fire; to others show mercy, mixed with fear—hating even the clothing stained by corrupted flesh.

To Him who is able to keep you from stumbling and to present you before His glorious presence without fault and with great joy—to the only God our Savior be glory, majesty, power and authority, through Jesus Christ our Lord, before all ages, now and forevermore! Amen.
—Jude 1:18-25 (NIV)

AMEN AND AMEN! COME QUICKLY, LORD JESUS!

The Word of God (Epilogue)

When all else is said and done, the unalterable Word still stands.

Jesus Christ is the same yesterday, today and forever.
—Hebrews 13:8 (GNT)

'For I know the plans that I have for you,' declares the Lord, 'plans for welfare and not for calamity to give you a future and a hope. Then you will call upon Me and come and pray to Me, and I will listen to you. You will seek Me and find Me when you search for Me with all your heart.'
—Jeremiah 29:11-13 (NASB, 1995)

Now faith is the certainty of things hoped for, a proof of things not seen... And without faith it is impossible to please Him, for the one who comes to God must believe that He exists, and that He proves to be One who rewards those who seek Him.
—Hebrews 11:1, 6 (NASB)

"Whoever will call on the name of the Lord will be saved."

How then will they call on Him in whom they have not believed? How will they believe in Him whom they have not heard? And how will they hear without a preacher? How will they preach unless they are sent? Just as it is written, "How beautiful are the feet of those who bring good news of good things!" However, they did not all heed the good news; for Isaiah says, "Lord, who has believed our report?" So faith comes from hearing, and hearing by the word of Christ.
—Romans 10:13-17 (NASB, 1995)

'Behold, I stand at the door and knock; if anyone hears My voice and opens the door, I will come in to him and will dine with him, and he with Me. He who overcomes, I will grant to him to sit down with Me on My throne, as I also overcame and sat down with My Father on His throne.'
                              —Revelation 3:20-21 (NASB)

There was the true Light which, coming into the world, enlightens every man. He was in the world, and the world was made through Him, and the world did not know Him. He came to His own, and those who were His own did not receive Him. But as many as received Him, to them He gave the right to become children of God, even to those who believe in His name, who were born, not of blood nor of the will of the flesh nor of the will of man, but of God. And the Word became flesh, and dwelt among us, and we saw His glory, glory as of the only begotten from the Father, full of grace and truth.
                              —John 1:9-14 (NASB, 1995)

Jesus answered and said to him, "Truly, truly, I say to you, unless one is born again he cannot see the kingdom of God... unless one is born of water and the Spirit he cannot enter into the kingdom of God. That which is born of the flesh is flesh, and that which is born of the Spirit is spirit. Do not be amazed that I said to you, 'You must be born again.' The wind blows where it wishes and you hear the sound of it, but do not know where it comes from and where it is going; so is everyone who is born of the Spirit."
                              —John 3:3-8 (NASB, 1995)

"I am the vine, you are the branches; he who abides in Me and I in him, he bears much fruit, for apart from Me you can do nothing. If anyone does not abide in Me, he is thrown away as a branch and dries up; and they gather them, and cast them into the fire and they are burned. If you abide in Me, and My words abide in you, ask whatever you wish, and it will be done for you."
                              —John 15:5-7 (NASB, 1995)

"Enter through the narrow gate; for the gate is wide and the way is broad that leads to destruction, and there are many who enter through it. For the gate is small and the way is narrow that leads to life, and there are few who find it."
—Matthew 7:13-14 (NASB, 1995)

Now the deeds of the flesh are evident, which are: immorality, impurity, sensuality, idolatry, sorcery, enmities, strife, jealousy, outbursts of anger, disputes, dissensions, factions, envying, drunkenness, carousing, and things like these, of which I forewarn you, just as I have forewarned you, that those who practice such things will not inherit the kingdom of God.
—Galatians 5:19-21 (NASB, 1995)

So this I say, and affirm together with the Lord, that you walk no longer just as the Gentiles also walk, in the futility of their mind, being darkened in their understanding, excluded from the life of God because of the ignorance that is in them, because of the hardness of their heart...
—Ephesians 4:17-18 (NASB, 1995)

The people went out to see what had happened; and they came to Jesus, and found the man from whom the demons had gone out, sitting down at the feet of Jesus, clothed and in his right mind; and they became frightened. Those who had seen it reported to them how the man who was demon-possessed had been made well. And all the people of the country of the Gerasenes and the surrounding district asked Him to leave them, for they were gripped with great fear; and He got into a boat and returned. But the man from whom the demons had gone out was begging Him that he might accompany Him; but He sent him away, saying, "Return to your house and describe what great things God has done for you." So he went away, proclaiming throughout the whole city what great things Jesus had done for him.
—Luke 8:35-39 (NASB, 1995)

And you were dead in your trespasses and sins, in which you formerly walked according to the course of this world, according to the prince of the power of the air, of the spirit that is now working in the sons of disobedience. Among them we too all formerly lived in the lusts of our flesh, indulging the desires of the flesh and of the mind, and were by nature children of wrath, even as the rest. But God, being rich in mercy, because of His great love with which He loved us, even when we were dead in our transgressions, made us alive together with Christ (by grace you have been saved), and raised us up with Him, and seated us with Him in the heavenly places in Christ Jesus...

—Ephesians 2:1-6 (NASB, 1995)

But a natural man does not accept the things of the Spirit of God, for they are foolishness to him; and he cannot understand them, because they are spiritually appraised. But he who is spiritual appraises all things, yet he himself is appraised by no one. For who has known the mind of the Lord, that he will instruct Him? But we have the mind of Christ.

—1 Corinthians 2:14-16 (NASB, 1995)

...if indeed you have heard Him and have been taught in Him, just as truth is in Jesus, that, in reference to your former manner of life, you lay aside the old self, which is being corrupted in accordance with the lusts of deceit, and that you be renewed in the spirit of your mind, and put on the new self, which in the likeness of God has been created in righteousness and holiness of the truth.

—Ephesians 4:20-24 (NASB, 1995)

Therefore if you have been raised up with Christ, keep seeking the things above, where Christ is, seated at the right hand of God. Set your mind on the things above, not on the things that are on earth. For you have died and your life is hidden with Christ in God. When Christ, who is our life, is revealed, then you also will be revealed with Him in glory.

—Colossians 3:1-4 (NASB, 1995)

Then He said to Thomas, "Reach here with your finger, and see My hands; and reach here your hand and put it into My side; and do not be unbelieving, but believing." Thomas answered and said to Him, "My Lord and my God!" Jesus said to him, "Because you have seen Me, have you believed? Blessed are they who did not see, and yet believed."

—John 20:27-29 (NASB, 1995)

"Believe Me that I am in the Father and the Father is in Me; otherwise believe because of the works themselves. Truly, truly, I say to you, he who believes in Me, the works that I do, he will do also; and greater works than these he will do; because I go to the Father. Whatever you ask in My name, that will I do, so that the Father may be glorified in the Son. If you ask Me anything in My name, I will do it. "If you love Me, you will keep My commandments. I will ask the Father, and He will give you another Helper, that He may be with you forever; that is the Spirit of truth, whom the world cannot receive, because it does not see Him or know Him, but you know Him because He abides with you and will be in you."

—John 14:11-17 (NASB, 1995)

But He said to them, "It is not for you to know periods of time or appointed times which the Father has set by His own authority; but you will receive power when the Holy Spirit has come upon you; and you shall be My witnesses both in Jerusalem and in all Judea, and Samaria, and as far as the remotest part of the earth." And after He had said these things, He was lifted up while they were watching, and a cloud took Him up, out of their sight. And as they were gazing intently into the sky while He was going, then behold, two men in white clothing stood beside them, and they said, "Men of Galilee, why do you stand looking into the sky? This Jesus, who has been taken up from you into heaven, will come in the same way as you have watched Him go into heaven."

—Acts 1:7-11 (NASB)

When the day of Pentecost came, they were all together in one place. Suddenly a sound like the blowing of a violent wind came from heaven and filled the whole house where they were sitting. They saw what seemed to be tongues of fire that separated and came to rest on each of them. All of them were filled with the Holy Spirit and began to speak in other tongues as the Spirit enabled them.

—Acts 2:1-4 (NIV)

But the fruit of the Spirit is love, joy, peace, patience, kindness, goodness, faithfulness, gentleness, self-control; against such things there is no law. Now those who belong to Christ Jesus have crucified the flesh with its passions and desires. If we live by the Spirit, let us also walk by the Spirit.

—Galatians 5:22-25 (NASB, 1995)

Put on the full armor of God, so that you will be able to stand firm against the schemes of the devil. For our struggle is not against flesh and blood, but against the rulers, against the powers, against the world forces of this darkness, against the spiritual forces of wickedness in the heavenly places. Therefore, take up the full armor of God, so that you will be able to resist in the evil day, and having done everything, to stand firm. Stand firm therefore, having girded your loins with truth, and having put on the breastplate of righteousness, and having shod your feet with the preparation of the gospel of peace; in addition to all, taking up the shield of faith with which you will be able to extinguish all the flaming arrows of the evil one. And take the helmet of salvation, and the sword of the Spirit, which is the word of God.

—Ephesians 6:11-17 (NASB, 1995)

For in Scripture it says: "See, I lay a stone in Zion, a chosen and precious cornerstone, and the one who trusts in him will never be put to shame." Now to you who believe, this stone is precious. But to those who do not believe, "The stone the builders rejected has become the cornerstone," and, "A stone that causes people to stumble and a rock that makes them fall." They stumble because they disobey the message—which is also what they were destined for. But you are a chosen people, a royal priesthood, a holy nation, God's special possession, that you may declare the praises of Him who called you out of darkness into His wonderful light. Once you

*were not a people, but now you are the people of God; once you had not
received mercy, but now you have received mercy.*

—*1 Peter 2:6-10 (NIV)*

*Therefore, since we have so great a cloud of witnesses surrounding us, let
us also lay aside every encumbrance and the sin which so easily entangles
us, and let us run with endurance the race that is set before us, fixing
our eyes on Jesus, the author and perfecter of faith, who for the joy set
before Him endured the cross, despising the shame, and has sat down at
the right hand of the throne of God. For consider Him who has endured
such hostility by sinners against Himself, so that you will not grow weary
and lose heart.*

—*Hebrews 12:1-3 (NASB, 1995)*

*"Blessed are you when people insult you and persecute you, and falsely
say all kinds of evil against you because of Me. Rejoice and be glad, for
your reward in heaven is great; for in the same way they persecuted the
prophets who were before you."*

—*Matthew 5:11-12 (NASB, 1995)*

*They said to you, "In the last times there will be scoffers who will follow
their own ungodly desires." These are the people who divide you, who
follow mere natural instincts and do not have the Spirit. But you, dear
friends, by building yourselves up in your most holy faith and praying in
the Holy Spirit, keep yourselves in God's love as you wait for the mercy of
our Lord Jesus Christ to bring you to eternal life. Be merciful to those who
doubt; save others by snatching them from the fire; to others show mercy,
mixed with fear—hating even the clothing stained by corrupted flesh.*

—*Jude 1:1823 (NIV)*

*For all who are being led by the Spirit of God, these are sons of God. For
you have not received a spirit of slavery leading to fear again, but you have
received a spirit of adoption as sons by which we cry out, "Abba, Father!"
The Spirit Himself testifies with our spirit that we are children of God,*

and if children, heirs also, heirs of God and fellow heirs with Christ, if indeed we suffer with Him so that we may also be glorified with Him. For I consider that the sufferings of this present time are not worthy to be compared with the glory that is to be revealed to us.
—Romans 8:14-18 (NASB, 1995)

I have been crucified with Christ; and it is no longer I who live, but Christ lives in me; and the life which I now live in the flesh I live by faith in the Son of God, who loved me and gave Himself up for me.
—Galatians 2:20 (NASB, 1995)

"But immediately after the tribulation of those days the sun will be darkened, and the moon will not give its light, and the stars will fall from the sky, and the powers of the heavens will be shaken. And then the sign of the Son of Man will appear in the sky, and then all the tribes of the earth will mourn, and they will see the Son of Man coming on the clouds of the sky with power and great glory. And He will send forth His angels with a great trumpet and they will gather together His elect from the four winds, from one end of the sky to the other."
—Matthew 24:29-31 (NASB, 1995)

For the Lord Himself will descend from heaven with a shout, with the voice of the archangel and with the trumpet of God, and the dead in Christ will rise first. Then we who are alive and remain will be caught up together with them in the clouds to meet the Lord in the air, and so we shall always be with the Lord.
—1 Thessalonians 4:16-17 (NASB, 1995)

And I saw heaven opened, and behold, a white horse, and He who sat on it is called Faithful and True, and in righteousness He judges and wages war. His eyes are a flame of fire, and on His head are many diadems; and He has a name written on Him which no one knows except Himself. He is clothed with a robe dipped in blood, and His name is called The Word of God.
—Revelation 19:11-13 (NASB, 1995)

And I heard a loud voice from the throne, saying, "Behold, the tabernacle of God is among men, and He will dwell among them, and they shall be His people, and God Himself will be among them, and He will wipe away every tear from their eyes; and there will no longer be any death; there will no longer be any mourning, or crying, or pain; the first things have passed away."

And He who sits on the throne said, "Behold, I am making all things new." And He said, "Write, for these words are faithful and true." Then He said to me, "It is done. I am the Alpha and the Omega, the beginning and the end. I will give to the one who thirsts from the spring of the water of life without cost. He who overcomes will inherit these things, and I will be his God and he will be My son."

—Revelation 21:3-7 (NASB, 1995)

"Look, I am coming soon! My reward is with Me, and I will give to each person according to what they have done. I am the Alpha and the Omega, the First and the Last, the Beginning and the End. Blessed are those who wash their robes, that they may have the right to the tree of life and may go through the gates into the city."

He who testifies to these things says, "Yes, I am coming soon." Amen. Come, Lord Jesus.

—Revelation 22:12-14, 20-21 (NIV)

I am very blessed along with my wife, my family, and many close friends to live a life in the Holy Spirit filled with God's favor, blessings and protection, along with signs, wonders and miracles and His blessed assurance. We have great expectations from the Lord- and see them fulfilled. This is just a glimpse of the life the Lord has for us, which has already surpassed all my hopes.

I am also quite mindful that this is not true for most people who haven't turned their life over to the Lord for His will and direction. Those whose goal is position and favor in the world are courting disaster- it is only a matter of time. All of this is clearly foretold in God's unalterable Word.

There is an earthshaking collision of good and evil coming, one like we have never seen in America. The stage is set, it is inevitable. No one who is thinking right wants to put themselves or their family on the wrong side in this collision, there will be no exemptions or exceptions. Strong faith and trust will be essential.

If you find yourself resisting, kicking against, or saying no to the things of God, I beseech you to turn to God quickly. repent, be reconciled, and be put on the right path by the Lord. Jesus gave His life for each one of us, He loves us no matter where we are, and He wants each of us to live the great life He has planned for us- He alone is our doorway to GLORY.

Journey to Glory-Contending for the Faith unpacks
this epic journey one page at a time.

Do not love the world or anything in the world. If anyone loves the world, love for the Father is not in them. For everything in the world— the lust of the flesh, the lust of the eyes, and the pride of life—comes not from the Father but from the world. The world and its desires pass away, but whoever does the will of God lives forever. I John 2:15-17 NIV

Gary and his wife Nancy have been members of Alleluia Covenant Community since 1984 and have headed up pro-life activities for the last twenty-five years. They have been married since 1958 and have four married children, fourteen grandchildren, and an increasing number of great grands. Gary has been a master woodworker/ artisan for over six decades. He was a designer/general contractor of luxury homes for seven years, and has devoted the past forty years to their business Images of the Cross, designing and building liturgical church furnishings for scores of churches, and crosses around the world.

Gary published his first book detailing an extraordinary life in the Spirit, Swept Up by the Spirit-Journey of Transformation in 2012. This is his second book which picks up after his first and propels us toward GLORY.

"When Gary speaks, people listen. His words have a way of making the reader feel they are at the scene. His new book, Journey to Glory: Contending for the Faith, teaches, entertains, touches hearts, and may transform lives for Christ Jesus. Some readers may find the stories unbelievable. However, we have known Gary for over thirty years, and he speaks the truth. He is bold enough to speak truth even if others do not like what he is saying, because he serves Jesus Christ. Why are his stories so powerful? You will have to read the book to find out."

—Patrick Mongan, MD, deacon in the Catholic Church, and Ellen Mongan, inspirational writer and speaker

"The written word, more than any other blessing, facilitates the sharing of the gifts of the Spirit with consistent quality and without boundaries of time or distance. That truth is what has brought God's children to His inspired word throughout the ages. In much the same way, you will see that this book is a remarkable gift—a revelation of how the Spirit of God has worked through Gary Garner for forty years. From the introduction to its conclusion, you will find comfort in seeing how a person of unwavering faith successfully navigates a world that increasingly separates itself from its loving Creator.

"The stories that Gary shares from his walk in faith (and that of other modern disciples) are instructive to anyone who seriously desires to use God's gifts to glorify Him on earth. Although most people who seek relationship with God will not likely have to face down Satan and his lapdogs, the experiences Gary shares will cause you to discover your own spiritual gifts and motivate you to be the disciple God expects you to be. You will see, as I did, that those who persevere in the faith are showered with humble patience, kindness, and love that inspire believers while confusing the enemy, as did Christ himself."

—Daniel Craig, Superior Court Judge

"Not only is Gary a gifted artisan of church furnishings of wood that serve as beacons which call believers to the holiness of the Triune God, he has the gift of oration and preaching through story and narrative. The stories he shares in this book bring the Scriptures to life in the present. As one reads and digests his revelations, one must come to the conclusion that the Creator, Redeemer and Sanctifier is speaking loudly today through this woodworker's voice.

—Pastor Michael Freed, Ascension Lutheran Church

"I can enthusiastically encourage you to read this book for 3 reasons.

"The first reason is Gary himself. He has been a stalwart warrior in the prolife movement without ever yielding to negativity or hopelessness. He also is one of the best examples I know of someone being willing to reach out personally to the lost, the lonely and the poor.

"The second reason is that Gary is a consummate storyteller. His stories are not always Pollyanna victory stories, but they are full of love and compassion. And his stories teach Kingdom principles as well as methods of what to do and what to be careful of.

"The third reason is that this book fits into a larger story being written by the Holy Spirit. Most of the world has moved from a Christendom age where the cultural somewhat supported the Gospel story to an age where, like the early apostles, we must reach out to individuals who have been taught by a culture that is either indifferent or hostile to the Gospel. Pope Francis in restructuring (CHARIS) the charismatic renewal in the Catholic Church said to focus on three areas. 1. Spread the baptism in the Holy Spirit to every Christian. 2. Work to establish Christian unity so that the world might believe 3. Reach out to the poor and the lost especially those on the margins. Gary's book focuses on all three. Read the book but especially DO THE STUFF."

— Chuck Hornsby
Member, Contributor and Speaker for
National Service Team of CHARIS